GIVING THE DEVIL HIS DUE

Giving the Devil His Due

SATAN AND CINEMA

Jeffrey Andrew Weinstock and Regina M. Hansen,
Editors

FORDHAM UNIVERSITY PRESS   NEW YORK 2021

Fordham University Press has no responsibility for the persistence or
accuracy of URLs for external or third-party Internet websites referred
to in this publication and does not guarantee that any content on such
websites is, or will remain, accurate or appropriate.

Fordham University Press also publishes its books in a variety of electronic
formats. Some content that appears in print may not be available in
electronic books.

Visit us online at www.fordhampress.com.

Library of Congress Cataloging-in-Publication Data available online at
https://catalog.loc.gov.

Printed in the United States of America

23 22 21   5 4 3 2 1
First edition

Contents

GIVING THE DEVIL HIS DUE

Introduction

Giving the Devil His Due

Regina M. Hansen and Jeffrey Andrew Weinstock

In 1646, Jesuit Father Athanasius Kircher made the mistake of conjuring the devil. Experimenting with mirrors and light, he projected images onto his German monastery wall and even onto clouds of smoke to entertain his fellow monks. He went too far, however, when his magic lantern novelties included images of devils and demons. "In danger of being exorcised or tortured," as Terry Lindvall puts it,[1] Kircher put quill to paper and explained himself in his 1646 *Magnus Ars Umbra et Lucis*—the great art of shadow and light—a work presenting his magic lantern as an educational device to be used to "emulate the wonders of . . . nature and glorify their 'wondrousness.'"[2] Kircher, as Mannoni explains, "did not want to pass himself off as a sorcerer."[3]

Others, however, didn't share his scruples. While Kircher disavowed being a practitioner of the dark arts, many who followed in his wake embraced and capitalized on the occult associations with projected images. According to Murray Leeder, because the magic lantern needed darkness, it was sometimes referred to as the "Lantern of Fear" and "naturally tended to grotesque and ghostly images."[4] In the eighteenth century, Leipzig shop owner Johann Schröpfer used the lantern to hold séances and present himself as a necromancer,[5] and Étienne-Gaspard Robert then followed suit in the 1870s, staging "gloomy Phantasmagorical spectacles in the crypt of an abandoned Capuchin convent" in Paris that included cat- and cattle-headed demons and devils riding demon horses.[6]

Present at the birth of what Charles Musser refers to as "screen practice,"[7] the devil was again there at the birth of cinema proper in the last decade of the nineteenth century. Just about 250 years after Athanasius Kircher alarmed his fellow monks by projecting devils and demons on the monastery wall,

1

cinema and special effects pioneer Georges Méliès also conjured the devil. In his 1896 *Le manoir du diable* (*The House of the Devil*)—shown in the United States as *The Haunted Castle*—a captured cavalier in a medieval castle has to fend off a mischievous devil and his minions. Because of its images and themes—including a devil, a bat, and a skeleton—*Le manior du diable* is considered by some to be the first horror movie and, as Russ Hunter addresses in this volume, Méliès often returned to this same well, drawing up the devil in many of his late nineteenth- and early twentieth-century productions.[8] Lucifer's appeal to early filmmakers is obvious: the trickster devil afforded Méliès the opportunity to try out all kinds of special effects, causing skeletons to appear out of thin air, a young woman to transform suddenly into a crone, furniture to move unexpectedly, and people to disappear in the blink of an eye.

The appeal of Satan in cinema, however, goes beyond the opportunity for filmmakers to wow audiences with clever and spectacular effects. As the essays in this collection attest, the devil embodies culturally specific anxieties and desires as well, reflecting conceptions of good and evil, right and wrong, sin and salvation. All supernatural creatures in literary and cinematic narrative, of course, are "cultural bodies," to borrow from Jeffrey Jerome Cohen's famous formulation concerning monsters.[9] They are embodiments of "a certain cultural moment—of a time, a feeling, and a place."[10] But what sets the devil apart from other supernatural creatures that find their origins in folklore, literature, and film is the centrality of the religious dimension. Unlike, say, immortal vampires cut from the cloth of Bela Lugosi's Dracula or shambling zombies imported from Haiti by way of early twentieth-century cinema, many people around the world in the twenty-first century—even highly educated ones— *believe* in Satan as an active force in the world who participates in a larger cosmic battle between good and evil. The devil is not just one monster among many; nor is he the "prince of darkness" merely because he has repeatedly flickered across cinema screens in darkened rooms since the origins of the medium. For many, he is instead a force active in their lives. Films featuring the devil, therefore, are not just flights of fancy but narratives—usually reinforcing, although occasionally revising or calling into question entirely, a familiar belief system.

This collection of scholarly essays on representations of Satan in cinema targets a gap in cinema scholarship—given how frequently the devil has appeared in film since the medium's late nineteenth-century origins and, indeed, how closely Satan has been associated with the cinematic apparatus going all the way back to Kircher, it is curious how little attention has been paid to representations of the devil in film. We are, in this sense, attempting, at long last, to "give the devil his due." The thirteen essays in this collection are organized more or less chronologically according to the films they address (some essays address more than one film, so there is an occasional overlap in time period), and we have sought to attend to the most well-known cinematic representations of the devil.[11] While the essays do not adopt a uniform approach to their subject matter—some engage in a closer reading while others focus more fully on historical contextualization—the project as a whole largely falls under the rubric of what Richard Maltby has characterized as "new cinema history"—an approach that, among other things, "examines cinema as a site of social and cultural exchange."[12] The collection is therefore less immediately invested in horror studies per se than in broader considerations of the relationship between film and culture as filtered through religion and fantasy. We hope, therefore, to find an audience not just among those with specific interests in the Gothic and horror films but also among those who focus on film history, religious studies, and cultural studies more generally. The ubiquity of representations of the devil in film from the origins of the medium to the present suggests that the figure is one of perpetual interest. We feel that it is time to take a closer look at just what the devil has to say.

The Cinematic Satan's Origins

Bearing in mind the multiplicity of names under which Satan has appeared in scripture and literature—and the fact that, as William H. Wandless tells us, "to speak of *the* Devil rather than *a* devil requires circumspection"[13]—it is nevertheless possible to trace the origins of the Satanic figures most prominent in modern film narratives. Although Satan is usually associated with the serpent in the Garden of Eden, tempting Adam to sin, that creature does not actually have a name. Satan first appears by name in the Book of Job, as the *ha-satan*, or "adversary," who wagers that prolonged suffering will turn the pious Job against God. The Satan of the Gospels expands this adversarial role into one closer to that of the serpent, a creature whose goal is to corrupt innocence and tempt humans to sin. In Matthew 4:1, Satan tempts Christ in the desert, and in 1 Peter 5:8 the reader is warned: "Be sober, be vigilant; because your adversary the devil, as a roaring lion, walketh about, seeking whom he may devour."[14] Although the Bible does not fully describe Satan, the association with ferocious animality can be seen in the Book of Revelation (12:9) which depicts a "huge dragon, the ancient serpent, who is called the devil and Satan, who deceived the whole world."[15] The current, anthropomorphized depiction of Satan developed over time. While the classic image, with horns and cloven hooves, is borrowed from images of the Greco-Roman goat God Pan, Dante Alighieri describes the devil as a winged monster with three faces devouring the souls of the damned. This portrayal of Satan as ravenous beast was also common in paintings of the era, such as Giotto's *Last Judgment* (1306).

For their part, early and medieval Christian theologians cared less about what Satan looked like than about his nature—his role as the author of sin. In the *Summa Theologica* (1485), Thomas Aquinas writes: "The devil is the occasional and indirect cause of all our sins, in so far as he induced the first man to sin, by reason of whose sin human nature is so infected, that we are all prone to sin: even as the burning of wood might be imputed to the man who dried the wood so as to make it easily inflammable."[16] Aquinas also lays out the Christian interpretation of Satan as a fallen angel by linking it to a particular verse from the Book of Isaiah: "How art thou fallen from heaven, O Lucifer, son of the morning!"[17] Directed at the King of Babylon, this verse is nevertheless recalled by Jesus in the Gospel of Luke: "I saw Satan fall like lightning from heaven" (Luke 10:18).[18] The Fall of Satan and his angels is more fully described in the Book of Revelation's narrative of a "war in Heaven" (12:7) in which the good angels, led by the Archangel Michael, defeat Satan and his followers.[19]

Lucifer, or light-bringer, is only one translation of Isaiah 14:12; the modern translation is more often "Daystar" or "Morningstar." Still, Lucifer is one of the many names used for the devil in Dante's *Inferno* (1320), and the name became more commonly associated with Satan because of John Milton's *Paradise Lost* (1667). In his epic poem, Milton created such a complex and magnetic devil that William Blake was (tempted) to conclude in his *The Marriage of Heaven and Hell* (ca. 1790–93) that Milton was "of the devil's party without knowing it." Milton's sympathetic representation of Lucifer/Satan began centuries of such characterizations. These include Charles Baudelaire's poem "Litanies of Satan" (1857), which casts Satan as the injured party in the heavenly drama and rejects religion, as well as charming characters such as Lucifer Morningstar from Neil Gaiman's *Sandman* comics and Professor Woland, the disguised Satan in Mikhail Bulgakov's *The Master and Margarita* (1967), an inspiration for the Rolling Stones' "Sympathy for the Devil."

At the same time, in many texts, Satan's charm and appearance of reasonableness are presented as the most important tools he uses to tempt people to sin. The idea of Satan as tempter appears in both Christopher Marlowe's *Doctor Faustus* (ca. 1592) and Johann Wolfgang von Goethe's *Faust* (1829), in which the devil (here going by the name of Mephistopheles) is charming and sophisticated. The trope of the "Faustian" or devil's bargain appears again in Stephen Vincent Benét's "The Devil and Daniel Webster" (1936) in which the

soul of the protagonist Jabez Stone is redeemed through the eponymous lawyer's ability to argue. The devil's bargain is used to comic effect in both the
Broadway play (1955) and eventual film (1958) *Damn Yankees* and the country
song "The Devil Went Down to Georgia," which applies the trope to a narrative of a fiddle contest between the devil and a young man named Johnny.
The association of Satan with music also surfaces in the story of Robert Johnson, a real blues musician around whom the legend swirls that he sold his soul
to the devil to attain his musical skill.

Cinema, Religion, and Satan

Histories of cinema and religion often emphasize that religion and film were
intertwined from cinema's beginnings. Jolyon Mitchell and S. Brent Plate
introduce the Routledge *Religion and Film Reader*, for example, by explaining
that "Films appropriated religious subject matter from the start, and religious
groups used films as promotional tools as soon as they could find the means
to do so."[20] Terry Lindvall's essay on silent films in the *Routledge Companion
to Religion and Film* argues that early silent films often included religious
themes as a strategy to attract an audience. "Many early Christians," adds John
Lyden, "did not initially perceive the cinema as a threat to Christian values (as
it was often understood later), but rather as an opportunity to convey Christian
stories and values to a wider audience in an immediate and effective way."[21]

Film theorist André Bazin has argued that "the cinema has always been
interested in God,"[22] and it is certainly the case that Jesus was present early in
the history of cinema—Adele Reinhartz notes that the first-known example of
a Jesus movie is the 1898 production *The Passion Play at Oberammergau*,
directed by Henry Vincent.[23] However, the devil—who generally gets second
billing—was there first. This, of course, makes a certain amount of sense. After
all, the devil is the Prince of Lies and—as early cinema pioneers such as
Méliès gleefully explored and the history of cinema has since elaborated—
film is the art of illusion. From smoke and mirrors and magic lanterns in the
seventeenth century to IMAX in the twenty-first, the projected image has
been presented as a kind of conjuration that weaves a spell over the viewer,
enticing them into a world that S. Brent Plate in *Religion and Film: Cinema
and the Re-Creation of the World* calls a "re-creation" of the known world: "a
world of fantasy, a world of ideology, a world we may long to live in or a world
we wish to avoid at all costs."[24] While this phantasmatic recreation of the
world in cinema has often been addressed in relation to spectrality,[25] the less-
explored connection between cinema and the devil might be even more
apropos because the devil is a trickster and what is cinema if not, at heart, a

trick—and one that relies on a kind of bargain made with the viewer? Cinema undeniably has provided a congenial home for Satan, allowing him (and, on rare occasions, her) a wide playground to entice screen characters with idle hands or wicked desires, as well as viewers who have flocked to sit in darkened rooms and be entertained by tales of the devil and his ways.

Writ large, Satan's role in cinema—together with that of his minions—has generally been a conservative one (at least on the surface). Satan, as the embodiment of evil, tempts and seduces with tabooed pleasures, seeking to lure the morally flawed or weak in character to surrender their souls in exchange for worldly success, forbidden knowledge, or carnal delights. Satan as antagonist thus conventionally represents in film, as he does in literature and religion more broadly, a value system viewers understand they are supposed to reject. One must cherish and protect one's eternal soul above all else such films assert, which entails rejecting the devil and the ephemeral materialistic pleasures he dangles to entice the unwary off the path of righteousness—and for those who have wandered, a return to conventional religious faith is the antidote to devilish desire and the key to salvation. When science and violence come up short, the cross remains the besieged's last best hope in defeating Satan—sometimes this is literal, as when the cavalier in Méliès's 1896 *Le manoir du diable* wards off the devil with a large cross he takes down from the wall; sometimes this is figurative as when John Constantine (Keanu Reeves) in Francis Lawrence's 2005 *Constantine* (armed with a "holy shotgun" in the shape of a cross) avoids Peter Stormare's Lucifer dragging him down to hell by making his last request a benevolent one (even as he flips Lucifer the bird as he starts to ascend to heaven!)

Such films, while reinforcing specific values for the individual such as honesty and selflessness, also often function as broader forms of conservative cultural critique, highlighting the pernicious consequences of the waning of conventional religious faith, institutional decay, and "progressive values." As W. Scott Poole explains, for example, in *Satan in America: The Devil We Know*, in the 1960s "conservative evangelicals, traditionalist Catholics, and many Pentecostals believed they were in a literal struggle for the soul of America,"[26] and this struggle played out in box office hits, including Roman Polanski's *Rosemary's Baby* (1968), William Friedkin's *The Exorcist* (1973), and Richard Donner's *The Omen* (1976). In these films and others like them, the world is ripe for devilish predation and the Antichrist's arrival because conventional religious faith has diminished, and with it "traditional values." Taylor Hackford's *The Devil's Advocate* (1997) offers a similar form of cultural critique through a 1990s lens with its focus on Kevin Lomax (Keanu Reeves), a lawyer who has never lost a case, even though he knows those he defends are often guilty—the film in fact opens with Kevin securing a not guilty verdict for a child molester he knows is culpable. That it is not just Kevin who is corrupt but the entire American legal system is made clear by the fact that the devil within the film, playfully going by the name John Milton (performed with gusto by Al Pacino), is head of a major New York City law firm. The devil in such films thus becomes an avatar for a culture of corruption—decay associated with the abandonment of traditional religious belief structures.

The appeal of these messages for religious believers about the power of the devil and the necessity of religious faith to combat him is easy to see. Such films echo and reinforce the understanding that the devil is real and in a war against God and Christianity. However, what enticements such a story holds for those who don't subscribe to that narrative—those who aren't Christian, don't believe in the devil—is less obvious. Some of the appeal can, of course, be chalked up to the magic of the cinema and the power of narrative. After all, movie-going audiences enjoy fantasy worlds of all types in cinema that they recognize aren't real. As magic lanternists and early filmmakers appreciated, there is something intrinsically alluring in the production and manipulation of image and, later, sound. Likely going all the way back to the casting of shadows by firelight on walls, human beings have found delight in "special effects"—and stagecraft can become even more enticing when combined with an engaging story. One need not believe in the literal existence of the devil any more than one must in extraterrestrials or hobbits to enjoy narratives and films involving them.

The allure of image and story can explain much, particularly when the story being told affirms one's beliefs and worldview. Where the devil is concerned—and the supernatural more generally—however, there may be more to it than this. In *The Secret Life of Puppets*, Victoria Nelson argues that science fiction and fantasy in popular literature and film—particularly narratives involving "the demonic"—have filled in the hole left by the waning of traditional religious belief. For millennia, according to Nelson, human beings believed directly in the existence of a transcendent realm, "another, invisible world besides this one."[27] But the "post-Reformation, post-Enlightenment prohibition on the supernatural and exclusion of a transcendent, nonmaterialist level of reality from the allowable universe has created the ontological equivalent of a perversion caused by repression."[28] Craving confirmation of the transcendent, but, according to Nelson, barred or discouraged from naïve belief by the modern episteme of scientific materialism, religious belief has been sublimated into works of popular culture: "Because the religious impulse is profoundly unacceptable to the dominant Western intellectual culture, it has been obliged to sneak in this back door, where our guard is down. Thus, our true contemporary secular pantheon of unacknowledged deities resides in mass entertainments, and it is a demonology, ranging from the 'serial killers' in various embodied and disembodied forms to vampires and werewolves and a stereotypical Devil."[29] For Nelson, fantasy and horror films affirming Satan's existence participate in feeding the repressed desire for a transcendent realm. Deep down inside, we want to believe that there is more to the universe than what our senses permit us to know. Stanley Donen's *Bedazzled* (1967), Alan Parker's *Angel Heart* (1987), or Robert Eggers's *The Witch* (2015) are thus religion sneaking in the back door.

Nelson's claims here are provocative and not unproblematic. For one thing, her assertion of a kind of collective unconscious desire for what we might call a "religious sensibility" is impossible to prove; for another, as Poole points out, plenty of people across the twentieth century and even today, both inside and outside of academia, subscribe—many devoutly—to conventional religious faiths. Religious belief may not be as prohibited or unacceptable as she assumes. But one need not give credence to the premise of a deep-seated unconscious desire for the transcendent to recognize the appeal of what we might call a "re-enchanted world." Sailing the same sea as Nelson, but adopting a somewhat different tack, is Michael Saler who, in his *As If: Modern Enchantment and the Literary Prehistory of Virtual Reality*, shares Nelson's assertion that "imaginary worlds and fictional characters" have today "replaced the sacred groves and tutelary deities of the premodern world."[30] Fantasy, for Saler, is a means to restore wonder to an "allegedly dis-enchanted world."[31] What marks this modern form of enchantment, however, is what Saler refers to as the "as if" attitude—a "self-conscious strategy of embracing illusions while acknowledging their artificial status."[32] Something like the idea of willing suspension of disbelief, the "as if" attitude is a playful orientation adopted by readers, viewers, and gamers who embrace the enchantments of the recreated worlds of speculative media without consciously or unconsciously believing in the existence of a transcendent invisible world. The desire for the devil from this perspective then is the desire for a world different from the one we know: perhaps a world of magic, ritual, and magical creatures, or perhaps a simplified moral universe in which the distinction between good and evil is readily apparent, lacking the ambiguities and complicating circumstances of the "real world." Fantasy and horror narratives involving the devil thus appeal to us because they ask us to imagine a world governed by different principles.

Specific legends and stories about Satan's existence have persisted throughout history, from relatively harmless tales of the devil playing cards or showing up at country dances—born of Celtic, French-Canadian, and Appalachian folklore—to the more destructive narratives that led to incidents like the Salem witch trial hysteria of 1692 and 1693. Urban myths regarding Satanist practices have come and gone in the United States and were especially prominent during the 1970s and 1980s (see Romano). In recent years, the imagery of Satan and Satanism has been appropriated by the Satanic Temple, an organization that espouses no belief in Satan but is recognized as a tax exempt church by the US government. The Satanic Temple's stated mission is "to encourage benevolence and empathy among all people, reject tyrannical authority, advocate practical common sense and justice, and be directed by the human conscience to undertake noble pursuits guided by the individual will."[33] Jesuit commentator James Martin suggests that members of the Temple are "playing with fire" and writes, "In my life as a Jesuit priest, and especially as a spiritual director, I have seen people struggling with real-life evil. In the *Spiritual Exercises*, his classic manual on prayer, St. Ignatius Loyola, the founder of the Jesuits, calls this force either the 'evil spirit' or 'the enemy of human nature.' Sophisticated readers may smile at this, but this is a real force, as real as the force that draws one to God."[34] That a famously liberal Christian like Martin is made uncomfortable by the Satanic Temple's activities is evidence of a persistent modern belief in Satan, or at least in evil as a personified force.

At this point however, it must be recognized that any consideration of the cinematic devil as simply avatar of evil to be rejected is far too reductive. Yes, as Poole asserts, Satan has "encoded humanity's most profound anxieties about violence, horror, and the inexplicable nature of suffering in a universe allegedly ruled by a loving God"[35]—and it is easy to abdicate our responsibility for failures by blaming Satan. But sometimes those anxieties encoded in Satan have to do not with the righteous being tempted toward sin but rather with the veracity of the established narrative and the hypocrisy of those professing to do the Lord's work. Put differently, sometimes the devil, rather than reassuring the faithful, calls into question the faith itself by highlighting the sins of the righteous.

That evil is a matter of perspective is highlighted in films involving Satan that focus on the patriarchal control of women. While, as Poole points out, the cinematic tradition involving Satan has often participated in a broader misogynistic trend focusing on women as both easily seduced and as willing participants in seduction,[36] more recent films involving Satan have also foregrounded the kinds of violence and exclusion to which women are subject in orthodox religious belief systems and Western culture more generally. Darryl Jones has argued, for example, that *Rosemary's Baby* "is a film about men controlling women's bodies."[37] In George Miller's *The Witches of Eastwick* (1987), adapted from John Updike's 1984 novel of the same name, Jack Nicholson's Satan prompts three women dissatisfied with their lives to discover their power, sexuality, and autonomy. And notably in Robert Eggers's *The Witch* (2016), Satan's offer to Thomasin (Anya Taylor-Joy) to "live deliciously" is presented as a form of liberation from the stultifying constraints of New England Puritanism. In films such as these, Satan's "evil" inheres in opposing a patriarchal order that uses religion as a bludgeon against women to keep them docile and subservient.

Perhaps more profoundly, Satan's presence in cinema can highlight God's absence. In *The Devil's Advocate*, the devil describes God to Kevin Lomax as a sadist who has endowed humanity with desires for the express purpose of forbidding their satisfaction and as an "absentee landlord" who watches humanity's struggles without intervening. While Pacino's Satan is more explicit in raising questions about God's benevolence than most, films featuring the devil can often "work against the grain" by making God seem distant or absent entirely, while giving us a devil who is dynamic and appealing. This is apparent just from considering the long list of actors who have played Satan, including Al Pacino, Jack Nicholson, Robert De Niro, Viggo Mortensen, Gary Oldman, Peter Fonda, Jeff Goldblum, Elizabeth Hurley, and Christopher Lee! William Blake famously said of Milton's *Paradise Lost* in *The Marriage of Heaven and Hell* that Milton was "of the devil's party without knowing it," and one could reasonably arrive at a similar conclusion regarding not just Pacino's John Milton but many other films that contrast a charismatic and freewheeling Satan against either a representative of God, such as an angel or priest, or the protagonist's conscience. Indeed, the success of many contemporary films featuring Satan may depend on a kind of ironic spectatorial double consciousness in which the conventional conclusion rejecting the devil and his seductions is merely a kind of alibi allowing us to relish the devil's enticements. From this perspective, the tidy conclusion reasserting conventional morality is just one more of the devil's tricks.

Giving the Devil His Due

This volume, curiously the first of its kind given both the ubiquity and popularity of films featuring Satan, seeks to "give the devil his due" by exploring the history and significance of representations of Satan on screen. Starting with film's beginnings in the 1890s and early 1900s, the contributions move us through the twentieth century and into the twenty-first, examining what cinematic representations tell us about the art of filmmaking, the desires of the film-going public, the cultural moments the films reflect, and the reciprocal influence they exerted. The first essays explore appearances by Satan in early film, which were quite commonplace as Russ Hunter argues in "The Sign of the Cross: Georges Méliès and Early Satanic Cinema." Hunter focuses on the work of Georges Méliès before 1906 and argues that Méliès's characterizations of the devil—and those of other early filmmakers—served a symbolically antagonistic function (one might say bringing Satan back to its roots) and helped in "demonstrating that cinema was a particularly effective medium with which to explore the macabre." Barry C. and Eloise R. Knowlton bring this volume's examination of the filmic Satan in "Murnau's *Faust* and the Weimar Moment" into the interwar period and place the film in the context of both Goethe's *Faust* and Christian theology. The Knowltons argue that, as Murnau's Faust was eventually forgiven for succumbing to the devil's temptations, Germans of that era were meant to see in Faust a symbol of their own essential goodness and redeemability. "Disney's Devils" also covers the period of the 1920s through the 1940s. Here, J. P. Telotte examines the ways in which representations of the devil and devilish characters in Disney animation reveal a "modernist spirit" that challenges the idea of Walt Disney and the Disney Corporation as purveyors of essentially conservative narratives. Then, in "What's the Deal with the Devil? The Comedic Devil in Four Films," Katherine A. Fowkes surveys the figure of the comedic Satan in the context of the trickster tradition.

The resurgence of cinematic Satan in the 1960s and 1970s is analyzed in the volume's next two essays. In "His Father's Eyes: *Rosemary's Baby*," David Sterritt suggests that the success of Roman Polanski's film, propelled by Satan's dominance and eventual triumph within the narrative, is especially telling since he barely appears on screen and may be explained by human intellectual fascination with evil. Satan's ultimate ascendancy is also explored in R. Barton Palmer's "From the Eternal Sea He Rises, Creating Armies on Either Shore: The Antichristology of the *Omen* Franchise." Palmer examines the *Omen* films in the context of evangelical Christian understanding of the end times and suggests that the films see Satan's triumph as inevitable, thus undermining Christian eschatology.

Carl H. Sederholm's "The Weird Devil: Lovecraftian Horror in John Carpenter's *Prince of Darkness*" brings the volume into the 1980s. Sederholm examines how Carpenter eschews traditional representations and understandings of Satan to focus instead on the figure's unknowability and ultimately on the human inability to fully comprehend reality. Murray Leeder's "Narration and Damnation in *Angel Heart*" revisits Méliès's Satanic figures to argue that "narrative manipulation" is itself a Satanic tendency. Turning to written narrative, in "The Devil's in the Details: Devilish Desire and Roman Polanski's

The Ninth Gate," Jeffrey Andrew Weinstock examines the link between an attraction to ancient books of "arcane lore" and the human longing for the transcendental, arguing that the attraction of Satanic narratives lies, at least in part, in the desire for evidence of a world beyond the physical.

The last four essays break with the loosely chronological format of the rest of the volume to compare films across eras and genres. In "Agency or Allowance: The Satanic Complications of Female Autonomy in *The Witches of Eastwick* and *The Witch*," Simon Bacon asserts that the "female liberation" achieved in the two films is complicated by the fact that such liberation is offered by Satan, an "excessively masculine, if often transgressive figure." The next two essays place the filmic figure of Satan within the context of scriptural and theological writings. Catherine O'Brien's "'Roaming the Earth': The Presence of Satan in *The Last Temptation of Christ* and *The Passion of the Christ*" examines two cinematic interpretations of the Christian Gospels and argues that, though different in tone and political leanings, both films ultimately embrace the idea of Satan's defeat born of Christ's sacrifice. Regina Hansen's "Lucifer, Gabriel, and the Angelic Will in *The Prophecy* and *Constantine*" also emphasizes narrative assurances of Satan's defeat but attributes that defeat to human reason and free will, exposing the films' challenges to religious orthodoxy. Finally, in "Advocating for Satan: The Parousia-Inspired Horror Genre," David Hauka's analysis moves beyond theological understandings of the devil, introducing the notion of "America's Satan."

Guiding the contributions to this volume is the overarching idea that cinematic representations of Satan reflect not just the hypnotic powers of cinema to explore and depict the fantastic but also the shifting social anxieties and desires as concerns human morality and, indeed, place in the universe. In Méliès's 1896 *Le manoir du diable*, the captured cavalier fends off the devil with a cross, presumably saving his life and soul—and, in the process, reasserts a conventional morality tale in which faith in God saves one from evil. In David Eggers's 2016 *The Witch*, the cavalier's means of salvation becomes a bludgeon for the main character, Thomasin (Anya Taylor-Joy), who turns her back on the harsh Christianity of her Puritan community and embraces the devil as a form of liberation. In both, the existence of the devil confirms the existence of a transcendental realm beyond the material—and whether we take the devil's part or not, there is perhaps comfort to be found in the idea of persistence beyond death. The point is that, when we conjure up Satan with a puff of smoke on-screen, he doesn't appear out of nothing but rather emerges from a roiling cloud of cultural forces asserting and contesting ideas of good and evil, right and wrong. Attentive consideration of the cinematic Satan has much to tell us about those forces and shifting ideas.

Notes

1. Terry Lindvall, "Silent Cinema and Religion: An Overview (1895–1930)," in *The Routledge Companion to Religion and Film*, ed. John Lyden (New York: Routledge, 2009), 13.

2. Thomas L. Hankins and Robert J. Silverman, *Instruments and the Imagination* (Princeton, NJ: Princeton University Press, 1995), 5.

3. Laurent Mannoni, *The Great Art of Light and Shadow: The Archaeology of Cinema* (Exeter, UK: University of Exeter Press, 2000), 23.

4. Murray Leeder, *Modern Supernatural and the Beginnings of Cinema* (New York: Palgrave, 2017), 50.

5. Leeder, 50.

6. Leeder, 50.

7. Leeder, 47.

8. See Murray Leeder, *Horror Film: A Critical Introduction* (New York: Bloomsbury, 2018), 6.

9. Jeffrey Jerome Cohen, "Monster Culture (Seven Theses), in *Monster Theory: Reading Culture*, ed. Jeffrey Jerome Cohen (Minneapolis: University of Minnesota Press, 1998), 4.

10. Cohen, 4.

11. While one might expect Satan to play a significant role in North America's vast—and vastly profitable—Christian film industry, this is actually not quite the case. Most Evangelical films are presented as romances or "problem pictures" in which faith in Christ helps a suffering protagonist resolve a problem or overcome an obstacle such as in 2014's *Heaven Is Real* (Randall Wallace) or 2019's *Breakthrough* (Roxann Dawson). The emphasis in such films is not on Satan as much as on surmounting a crisis of faith. Satan does play a part, either directly or indirectly, in the *Left Behind* film series in which believers are transported directly to heaven, leaving the nondevout to grapple with the horrors of the end-times, as well as in other films produced by the Canadian company Cloud Ten Pictures, which is run by Evangelical Christians Peter and Paul LaLonde. Satan also appears in the LaLonde brothers' eschatologically themed features *Apocalypse: Caught in the Eye of the Storm* (1998), *Revelation* (1999), *Tribulation* (2000), and *Judgment* (2001), whereas Satan and the occult are subjects of the Cloud Ten produced documentary *The Games Children Play* (1990). A study of Satan in the Christian film industry calls for separate research and would need to include social and historical scholarship that goes beyond the purview of the present volume, which focuses exclusively on mainstream film.

12. Richard Maltby, "New Cinema Histories," in *Explorations in New Cinema History: Approaches and Case Studies*, ed. Richard Maltby, Daniel Biltereyst, and Philippe Meers (Hoboken, NJ: Wiley-Blackwell, 2011), xii.

13. William H. Wandless, "Devil, The," in *The Ashgate Encyclopedia of Literary and Cinematic Monsters*, ed. Jeffrey Andrew Weinstock (Burlington, VT: Ashgate Publishing, 2014), 156.

14. *The Bible: Authorized King James Version* (Oxford: Oxford University Press, 2008).

15. *New American Bible*, rev. ed. (Washington, DC: United States Conference of Catholic Bishops, 2011).

16. Thomas Aquinas, *Summa Theologica*, rev. 2nd ed., trans. Fathers of the Dominican Province (Canton, OH: Pinnacle Press, 2017), I:63, 5.

17. *Bible: Authorized King James Version.*

18. *Bible: Authorized King James Version.*

19. *Bible: Authorized King James Version.*

20. Jolyon Mitchell and S. Brent Plate, *The Religion and Film Reader* (New York: Routledge, 2007), 2.

21. John Lyden, introduction to *The Routledge Companion to Religion and Film*, ed. John Lyden (New York: Routledge, 2009), 2.

22. André Bazin, "Cinema and Theology," in *Bazin at Work: Major Essays and Reviews from the Forties and Fifties*, ed. Bert Cardullo (London: Routledge, 1997), 61.

23. Adele Reinhartz, "Jesus and Christ-Figures," in *The Routledge Companion to Religion and Film*, ed. John Lyden (London: Routledge, 2009), 421.

24. S. Brent Plate, *Religion and Film: Cinema and the Re-Creation of the World* (New York: Columbia University Press, 2017), 3.

25. See Murray Leeder, *Cinematic Ghosts: Haunting and Spectrality from Silent Cinema to the Digital Era* (New York: Bloomsbury, 2015).

26. W. Scott Poole, *Satan in America: The Devil We Know* (Lanham, MD: Rowman and Littlefield Publishers, 2009), 161.

27. Victoria Nelson, *The Secret Life of Puppets* (Cambridge, MA: Harvard University Press, 2001), vii.

28. Nelson, 19.

29. Nelson, 18.

30. Michael Saler, *As If: Modern Enchantment and the Literary Prehistory of Virtual Reality* (Oxford: Oxford University Press, 2012), 3.

31. Saler, 6.

32. Saler, 13.

33. The Satanic Temple (website), accessed October 16, 2020, https://theSatanictemple.com.

34. James Martin, "Satanic Group Playing with Fire," America: The Jesuit Review, July 27, 2015, accessed October 16, 2020, http://www.americamagazine.org.

35. Poole, *Satan in America*, xiii.

36. Poole, 132–133.

37. Darryl Jones, *Horror: A Thematic History in Fiction and Film* (London: Arnold, 2002), 185.

The Sign of the Cross

Georges Méliès and Early Satanic Cinema

Russ Hunter

In a 2014 exhibition at Stanford's Cantor Art Center, forty pieces of work from over five hundred years of artistic representation of Satan were put on display.[1] *Sympathy for the Devil: Satan, Sin, and the Underworld* was a three-month-long exploration of the ways in which artists have visualized and utilized the image of the devil and of Hell. The exhibition outlined the ways in which depictions of Satan, his minions, and Hell had altered over time to reflect changing artistic understandings of his religious and cultural significance. The representation of Satan through art, although necessarily varied in nature, has been a crucial tool for reinforcing Christian teachings about the dangers of the temptation offered by Lucifer. But religious art—and specifically images of the devil—have an address beyond the spiritual. They can also serve a wider cultural function. Satan, the idea of an overarching malignant spiritual force, has also been used by artists, as well as writers and filmmakers, as an important narrative agent. The devil therefore can act as both a specifically religious symbol with a set of spiritual meanings and as the archetypical antagonist in a variety of cultural forms. Images of Christ may have a much longer artistic history, but as the exhibition's curator Bernard Barryte noted: "people are more fascinated with evil than with good."[2]

From the start, cinema demonstrated its own fascination with evil by employing the figure of Satan in numerous films. Cinema's adoption of the devil generally differed from the religious imperatives of much earlier artistic traditions, instead of using Satan in ways that integrated with the needs of the new medium. This essay explores the dynamics behind the use of Satan in early cinema (1896–1915) in reference to the work of Georges Méliès. Specifically, it focuses upon his cinema before 1906, a period that has undergone a

15

number of reassessments by film historians, and where there has been a shift from "models that privilege the development of narrative as the principle axis of film history" to models that recognize that early cinema was "often structured by displays of visual spectacle."[3] I want to suggest that the use of Satan by Méliès, among others, during this early period of cinema was important for demonstrating its possibilities in dealing with macabre themes and images. In this way, cinematic depictions of the devil (and importantly Hell and the minions with which Satan is associated) provided a cinematic reference point for later filmmakers to use, adapt, or diverge from, and thus influenced the much later development of horror as a distinct genre. I do not suggest that early directors such as Méliès "invented" the genre (indeed, we might view some of his works as "proto-horror" films); rather, I will argue that his contributions to demonstrating that cinema was a particularly effective medium with which to explore the macabre—and how it might begin to do so—were integral in both facilitating and providing visual reference points for the bit-by-bit development of the horror as a fully-fledged cinematic genre. The presence of Satan in films such as *Le manoir du diable / The Haunted Castle* (1896), *Le diable au couvent / The Devil in a Convent* (1899), *Le diable géant ou le miracle de la madonne / The Devil and the Statue* (1901), *Le puits fantastique / The Enchanted Well* (1903), and *Les quat'cents farce du diable / The Merry Frolics of Satan* (1906) helped to cement cinema's position as a medium that was well-suited to exploration of not only the macabre, but also Manichean narratives (even if rather playfully employed by Méliès himself).

As historian Robert Muchembled notes in *A History of the Devil: From the Middle Ages to the Present*, Satan has always had both religious and cultural significance in that his representational form at any given time sheds light upon how societies deal with "the imaginary." This he sees as manifesting itself as a "mass phenomenon produced by the many cultural channels that irrigate a society," creating "explanatory systems and [motivating] both individual actions and group behavior."[4] For Muchembled, both the individual and the social systems around them are "junctions of meaning . . . where the experiences of past centuries are accumulated and passed on."[5] Thus, mobilizing and realizing the idea of "Satan" came loaded with a long history of meanings and associations. For cinema, particularly during its nascent period before 1906, the presence of Satan on-screen functioned in a variety of ways. Given the desire for filmmakers, most notably George Méliès, to use cinema as a way of providing entertainment as an extension to that offered by the stage (and sometimes even including it on the stage) and subsequently exploring the potential of the medium itself, Satan provided an instantly recognizable symbol of evil, a clear and unambiguous visual, narrative, and moral reference point.

This was crucial as it meant that within the bounds of short one-reel scenes it was possible to rapidly establish the conceit of any given scenario. The devil in this way could act as an effective shorthand to rapidly suggest certain character traits and as an immediately recognizable narrative type.

But the devil was important for reasons that went beyond his impact upon the storytelling potential of cinema. The presence of demonic forces, most usually the devil or malevolent forces controlled by him, also meant that within the bounds of any given scene filmmakers were, in effect, licensed to use a variety of spectacular effects and tricks. But the tricks evident in such films were not generated purely because of the creation of cinema. In many cases, they drew upon a much longer tradition of stage magic and effects, being influenced by several factors (both from France and abroad). Méliès's purchase of the Théâtre Robert-Houdin in 1888 saw him hone his craft as a magician and utilize the kinds of physical effects that he would later integrate into—and expand upon—in the cinema. While these often relied upon the clever use of mirrors and the employment of masking devices, such as puffs of smoke or (hidden) pulleys, the new medium offered an expanded and more seamless magical "toolkit." In general cinematic terms, Méliès's main contribution was vast and centered on the "organization of his fictional compositions around modern concepts of filmmaking, such as scenario, costume, makeup, background set, editing cuts, and, of course, actors."[6] However, within this, the cross-fertilization of stage magic with the possibilities offered by working on film meant that Méliès's pioneering work in relation to cinematic special effects should not be underplayed. While his contributions here are numerous (and have been well documented), his development of and experiments with multiple exposures and jump cuts were crucial in allowing for the effective and uncanny presentation of Satan within his work (and that of others).

Theatrically, his stage work drew heavily upon his time spent in London and, notably, the melodramatic féerie play tradition, which stressed—among other things—the fantastic leavened with morally inflected narratives where good usually triumphed over evil. The féerie had endured in popularity since the period after the French Revolution and was noted for "extravagant visual effects with sudden transformations, disappearances, instantaneous voyages in time or space and the like," with Alan Williams noting that, "severed heads and disembodied bodies were common, as were appearances by the devil himself."[7] As he has argued, cinema could effectively multiply the number of magical devices possible in the theater and that the "controlled, chamber theatre of illusion spawned in film a chaotic nightmare world," moving beyond the physical limitations of a theatrical space.[8] The stress upon malign forces (of varying kinds) in the féeries and their influence upon both his stage and screen work, as Williams recognizes, is testament to Méliès's recognition that "wicked, disruptive elements were more interesting than the forces of sweetness and light. . . . It is not a coincidence that one of his favorite roles was the devil."[9] In short, the devil was the most interesting, poignant, and fruitful character Méliès could bring to the silver screen. As Wyman wryly notes, the "Devil made for the perfect magician."[10]

In the latter half of 1896, Méliès used his experiments with both jump cuts and double-exposures on the *The Haunted Castle*, a three-minute film set in the gothic surrounds of a haunted castle. This was the beginning of Méliès's exploration of using Satan as his central cinematic antagonist. Such films were not unusual during the early period of cinema's development, and *The Haunted Castle* was merely one of the numerous films Méliès would make that explored the medium using the devil. As Nikolas Schreck has contended, the extent to which the diverse and regular representation of Satan in particular was a feature of early cinema demonstrates its embedded nature within early Western filmic representations. In the two decades following the invention and popularization of cinema, European filmmakers increasingly began to explore supernatural, mythical, and quasi-religious themes and imagery within which the devil (naturally) played a central role.[11]

The Haunted Castle takes place in a single location. The film begins with what looks to be some inner chamber or courtyard of a gothic castle, as we see a bat flying around the center of the frame before a jump-cut transform into a dark-cloaked figure with a pointed beard, angular boots, and skullcap with two long horn-like feathers protruding from the top of it. The figure, immediately recognizable as Mephistopheles, causes a cauldron to appear before summoning an imp and making a female figure appear out of it. Two elegantly dressed gentlemen stroll into the shot apparently quite unaware of the devilish forces they are about to encounter. An imp appears out of thin air (another jump-cut) and prods them with a pitchfork before disappearing, leaving them both confused. One man runs away, leaving the other to face whatever remains. A series of objects appear and disappear (including a bench and a skeleton), before a bat materializes and the man attacks it with his sword, at which point it once again transforms into Mephistopheles. He conjures an imp, ghosts (who cause the man to faint), then a woman who turns into a witch, and then four witches. The man's friend returns but is scared off by them (in fact, he appears to jump off the edge of the castle). Mephistopheles finally confronts him, but the man grabs a large nearby crucifix and causes the devil to flee.

Mephistopheles was the guise in which Satan would repeatedly appear in Méliès's work. A traditional antagonist in German folklore as part of the legend of Faust, he is usually positioned as a servant of the devil whose task is to collect souls by tricking their owners into bargaining them away. But Mephistopheles's use by a variety of writers as a de facto manifestation of the devil has seen him become a folk-devil and an embodiment of the earthly temptations offered by Satan. This has had the effect of making him a cipher for Satan himself; indeed, across art, literature, and film, Mephistopheles has come to symbolize the devil. This looseness of usage meant that "the name is a purely modern invention of uncertain origins [making] it an elegant symbol of the modern Devil with his many novel and diverse forms."[12] For Méliès, appearing in the form of Mephistopheles had a practical appeal. While he had been pictured with wings in some illustrations, contemporary depictions of Mephistopheles were much more humanoid in form. To create him for the screen therefore required minimal makeup, and costumes that Méliès would already have had as part of his stage show could be easily used.

As Schreck has noted, there was a tradition of fin de siècle stage magicians attempting to draw an association between their own skill and some form of Satanic possession. This tactic was employed regularly, the idea being that if "credulous audiences imagined that the wonders were the result of the magician's Satanic alliance, then so much the better."[13] Schreck observes that Méliès "affected a deliberately Satanic appearance, sporting a barbed goatee" and typically dressed in the red-lined cape that was normally associated with the devil in both the theater and the opera.[14] Posters for the Théâtre Robert-Houdin, often showed a variety of supernatural and occult images, including those of animated skeletons, specters, and wizards. It is unsurprising therefore that the image of the devil that he chose to employ in his cinematic work was congruent with this image. Thus, in films such as *The Haunted Castle*, *The Devil in a Convent*, *The Devil and the Statue*, and *The Enchanted Well*, Satan consistently appears in the form of Mephistopheles with a variation of dark cloak, pointed shoes, and feather-horned hat. Given its proximity to Méliès's successful career as a stage magician (which in part ran alongside his filmmaking), the film demonstrates a congruity between the cinema and some of the techniques and tricks employed at his stage shows. Patrons of the theater were well accustomed to seeing objects (including people) apparently disappear as part of magic routines. When combined with the suggestion that the onstage magicians might be part of some other-worldly influence, cinema—with all the editing trickery it could offer—could deepen this association.

For Henri Langlois (a film pioneer in his own quite different way), *The Haunted Castle* was "conceivable only in the cinema and due to the cinema."[15] In effect, Langlois argues that the medium specificity of cinema meant that only it could fully realize the effects displayed within the film. While it is possible to recognize the theatrical nature of *The Haunted Castle*, it was only in cinema that, for instance, a bat could apparently instantly transform into Satan, or an imp could be conjured out of (apparently) thin air. As such, Lynda Nead has argued, "The magic in Méliès films changed from the straightforward filming of tricks, performed by a magician on the stage, to the creation of major special effects, involving multiple exposure, stop-motion and other devices, which were difficult or impossible to achieve in the theater in front of a live audience."[16]

Michael Bird in *Religion in Film* suggests that *The Haunted Castle* was symptomatic of a certain kind of Méliès film because the director "created extravagant and surrealistic sets substituting stage illusion for everyday events, and who augmented perception with fantastic adventures of the imagination," meaning such works were "excursions into inaccessible fantasy worlds."[17] The latter point is worth interrogating as *The Haunted Castle* plays with visual tropes that had been long established in other mediums. Its castle setting and the presence of supernatural elements are suggestive of the influence of Gothic literature and art, which has led some to view this not only as the first horror film but the first *Gothic* horror.[18] Moreover, in providing a cinematic version of the devil, Méliès was merely employing a very familiar kind of representation of Satan.

Given its release in 1896, *The Haunted Castle* falls under the auspices of Gunning's ideas around the cinema of attractions. The film has increasingly been recognized as the "first" horror film and, released in the latter half of 1896, would, therefore, place the horror genre among the very first in cinematic history.[19] That said, we might more fruitfully view the film, as well as Méliès's other macabre-inflected work, as proto-horror—a set of images that, bit by bit, contributed to the broader visual and thematic reference points of a genre. As such, the film is important precisely because it acts as a transition point for the visual representation of Satan to include cinema. In so doing, it also demonstrated the visual possibilities for cinema as a medium in approaching macabre subject matter more generally. As James Morgart has noted, "Despite being only three minutes in length, the film establishes precedents for many of the visual motifs that have become synonymous with Gothic horror films ever since, including the visual depictions of witches, ghosts and bats."[20] Although it is possible to view early attempts at horror cinema (however problematic the application of that term might be) as rather tame by contemporary standards, they are important in that they "assist in tracking the evolution of the application and innovation of Gothic horror aesthetics."[21] Effectively, they provided the technical, aesthetic, and cultural building blocks that meant horror as a genre had a cinematic reference point as it developed. While this did not make the development of "horror cinema" as a generic category inevitable, it is clear that early cinema engaged with ideas and motifs that we can now see would later develop into tropes of horror cinema.

The Devil and the Statue is also representative of the ways in which the use of Satan allowed for the spectacle of cinema to be underlined via the display of special effects and tricks drawn from both stage magic and the crossbreeding with cinema as facilitated by Méliès. The film shows a clear connection to what Tom Ruffles has viewed as "part of the stage-magic tradition" that began with his illusion work from 1888 onward at the Théâtre Robert-Houdin and continued, albeit intermittently, with his film work.[22] Made in 1901, the film lasts a little over two minutes and, as was typical of its director's work in this period, limits the action to one location. It concerns a woman in an elegant baroque room being wooed by a suitor, who is singing to her from outside of her window. Almost unnoticed in the far right-hand corner of the frame, a statue of the Virgin Mary looks on (in reality an actor standing stock-still). When the young man leaves, the woman paces around the room in rapture before blowing a kiss to where he stood before. At this moment, we see a puff of smoke as a jump-cut makes the devil appear out of thin air (played by Méliès, made-up to look like Mephistopheles). With another jump-cut he makes bars appear across the previously open window and dances as if to mock her imprisonment. As he does so, he slowly and menacingly increases in size until the statue of the Virgin Mary comes to life, shrinks him, and then banishes him. She then removes the bars from the window as the two lovers are happily reunited.[23]

In this way, cinema effectively acted as a continuum in the development of images and techniques employed to represent Satan, a process Muchembled argues has metamorphosed with each new historical epoch and its associated social and cultural developments. Therefore, cinematic representations of the devil resonate with audiences because "they make an implicit connection with a stock of images and ideas drawn from a range of chronological periods."[24] For early cinema audiences during a period when religious observance, church attendance, and the general centrality of religion to daily life were much stronger, the cinema offered a new dynamic for representations of a variety of religious matters. The cinematic fantastic was thus able to function as a "literary and cultural way of treating the supernatural."[25]

As the *Sympathy for the Devil* art exhibition demonstrates, cinema was, of course, not unique in providing a visual representation of Satan. As Muchembled notes, the "devil has been part of the fabric of European life since the Middle Ages and has accompanied all its major changes."[26] The birth of cinema was no different in this respect, providing another medium through which the culturally created figure of the devil could circulate and be explored. Within visual culture, depictions of the devil had appeared in art since at least the fourteenth century. But representations of the devil were always dynamic since, over time, his shifting socioreligious function led to gradual changes in the ways in which he was realized. For early artists, such as Albrecht Dürer and Hieronymous Bosch, there were few visual reference points that could be drawn upon to create an image of the devil. The vagueness of his depiction (and that of Hell) in the Bible meant that they tended to piece together "imagery from older traditions that had already decided what demons looked like,"[27] and, prior to the sixteenth century, artists "borrowed features from the Arcadian god Pan and from Celtic, Egyptian and Near Eastern deities" while during the Renaissance they "found inspiration in accounts by Homer, Dante and Virgil." Drawing upon representations of demons from several pre-Christian religions, early visualizations of Satan often stressed his bestial, animalistic qualities. In effect, there was no definitive source from which to derive images of the devil until artists could begin to use each other's works as reference points. By the twentieth century, the devil was depicted in a much more obviously human form, with paintings such as Jerome Witkins's *The Devil as a Tailor* (1978–79) representing a move away from the more animalistic, bestial Satan of earlier periods and presenting him as distinctly humanoid (and indeed as "one of us").[28] The devil's presence in Western art is just part of what can be viewed as Europe, by the invention of cinema, having been bequeathed "an extraordinary diabolic heritage."[29]

As one of early cinema's key pioneers, Méliès has long been recognized as "the first to exploit cinematic devices systematically" by using them in a way that meant they "were to play an enormous role in the future" of cinema.[30] A hugely innovative early adopter of cinema, Méliès's contributions in developing and establishing some of the basic grammar of film and his dynamic use of cinematic stagecraft have resulted in his being recognized as "an *auteur* in every sense."[31] To the modern eye his work now looks rather naïve and static. So, although he is "universally acknowledged to be an early film pioneer," Méliès's work has frequently been characterized as "simplistic, both narratively and technically."[32] As Elizabeth Ezra has noted, increasing evidence of early cinema's modernity has meant that characterizations by its critics such as Noël Burch as "primitive" now look outmoded. And while Tom Gunning's positioning of the period before 1906 as one of a "cinema of attractions" has reframed it in relation to its desire to present "the spectacular," this school of thought has also suggested that such films lack clear narratives. However, in her book *Georges Méliès*, Ezra challenges this norm, arguing that the French director's work was not devoid of narrative structure and that "his films lend themselves to narrative analysis."[33] Such narratives may be short, straightforward, or lacking in nuance, but that does not mean that they cannot be examined. In *The Enchanted Well*, for instance, an old crone begs for alms in a medieval village well but is unceremoniously shooed away by one of the villagers. Affronted, she sneaks back and places a curse upon the well. After the villager who had earlier thrown her out the village comes to use the well, several creatures issue forth from it, until eventually the devil himself appears. He is quickly attacked by the village inhabitants before turning into a bat and flying off. It is a short film of just over four minutes in length and yet there is a clear, simple narrative of sorts within it, even though it is concise and not extensively developed.

This is important as it influences how we view the role of Satan in early cinema. If we accept that films during the cinema of attractions are all about spectacle and lack narratives, then Satan can be seen to function solely as an instantly recognizable visual symbol but, importantly, one whose presence allows for the inclusion of the kind of effects that Méliès developed and championed. But it need not be that this is viewed as a zero-sum game. If we accept his films before 1906 as part of the cinema of attractions, that does not mean they cannot also contain simple narratives. In this way, the devil's function within such films changes, and he becomes a familiar symbol who can lend narrative clarity to films based around the idea of spectacle. Indeed, even if filmmakers like Méliès were not particularly fascinated in filmmaking for its storytelling potential and were more interested in trick films or cinema as a series of displays, a sense of narrative—no matter how loose—is still possible.[34]

The appearance of the devil is part of a long sociocultural process related to the embedded nature of Christian imagery in Western culture. As such, when cinema developed as a medium, religious images were a ready-made frame of reference for audiences. In effect, the cinema represented an extension of more than five hundred years of visual culture depicting Satan. Just as *Sympathy for the Devil: Satan, Sin, and the Underworld* demonstrated the ways in which artistic representations of Satan changed over time, reflecting differing socioreligious dynamics, so have cinema's representations. Méliès was not unique in depicting Satan on-screen. Famously, Segundo de Chomón would depict a dancing Lucifer in *The Red Spectre* (1907), where he is portrayed as a curious mix between Mephistopheles and a skeleton. Indeed, the development of longer film form and of feature films after 1906 meant it was possible to weave Satan into longer, more complex narratives. Méliès would again return to the figure of Mephistopheles in *Les quat'cents farces di diable / The Merry Frolics of Satan* (1906). Lasting a touch over seventeen minutes, the narrative was based around the Faust legend, with the Englishman William Crackford signing his soul away to the devil and eventually having to pay his debt by roasting on a spit for all eternity. Satan would also feature in notable later films, such as *L'inferno / Inferno* (Francesco Bertolini, Adolfo Padovan, and Giuseppe de Liguoro, 1911), Stellan Rye and Paul Wegener's *Der Student von Prag / The Student of Prague Haxan* (Benjamin Christensen, 1922), and *Eine deutsche Volkssage / Faust* (F. W. Murnau, 1926). Although the devil himself would, for a time, fade in terms of his usage on-screen, as the 1920s shifted to the 1930s and Universal developed its popular series of monster movies, his influence was significant (although perhaps fittingly rather diffuse).

The use of Satan made sense in early cinema for filmmakers for several reasons then. In both the Catholic France of Méliès and the West more generally, Satan was a clearly recognizable reference point. As such his frequent appearance on film in early cinema is unsurprising. He could be used in a variety of ways. Thus, when cinema began to develop as a medium, it was natural that among the subject matter explored would be those that had particular cultural significance as societal frames of reference. In early cinema, Satan was not necessarily mobilized in ways that he traditionally had been as either a spiritual symbol or as a means to structure an artistic or literary narrative. He would be used in this way by early film practitioners too, but the desire for early filmmakers, such as Méliès, to experiment with film form in order to provide increasingly spectacular cinematic forms of entertainment meant that Satan also provided a supernatural rationale for the employment of a number of tricks. Moreover, in mobilizing the devil, cinema practitioners had, of course, to use the kinds of macabre, ghoulish imagery that had long been associated with him. This meant that from at least 1896 onward—that is, from its beginnings—cinema would begin to explore the macabre. The path toward these images becoming realized as the horror genre would take time, but it was a path whose flagstone was laid by Georges Méliès.

Notes

1. The exhibition was organized by the Cantor Arts Center at Stanford University and ran from August 20 to December 1, 2014, accessed June 11, 2021, https://arts .stanford.edu/event/sympathy-for-the-devil-satan-sin-and-the-underworld/.

2. Carey Dunne, "The Changing Face of Satan, from 1500 to Today," *Fast Company*, August 18, 2014, accessed October 17, 2020, https://www.fastcompany.com/3034309/the-changing-face-of-satan-artistic-depictions-of-the-devil-1500-to-today.

3. Matthew Solomon, introduction to *Fantastic Voyages of the Cinematic Imagination: Georges Méliès's Trip to the Moon*, ed. Solomon Stone (New York: State University of New York Press, 2011), 14.

4. Robert Muchembled, *A History of the Devil: From the Middle Ages to the Present* (Cambridge: Polity, 2003), 2.

5. Muchembled, 4.

6. Rémi Fournier Lanzoni, *French Cinema: From Its Beginnings to the Present* (London: Continuum, 2005), 34.

7. Alan Williams, *Republic of Images: A History of French Filmmaking* (Cambridge, MA: Harvard University Press, 2000), 37.

8. Williams, 37.

9. Williams, 37.

10. Kelly J. Wyman, "Satan in the Movies," in *The Continuum Companion to Religion and Film*, ed. William L. Blizek (London: Continuum, 2009), 301.

11. See Nikolas Schreck, *The Satanic Screen: An Illustrated History of the Devil in Cinema 1896–1999* (London: Creation Books, 2001).

12. Jeffrey Burton Russell, *Mephistopheles: The Devil in the Modern World* (Ithaca, NY: Cornell University Press, 1990), 61.

13. Schreck, *Satanic Screen*, 13.

14. Schreck, 14.

15. Quoted in Siegfried Kracauer, *Theory of Film: The Redemption of Physical Reality* (Princeton, NJ: Princeton University Press, 1997), 33.

16. Lynda Nead, *The Haunted Gallery: Painting, Photography, Film, c. 1900* (New Haven, CT: Yale University Press, 2007), 97.

17. Michael Bird, "Film as Hierophany," in *Religion in Film*, ed. John R. May and Michael Bird (Knoxville: University of Tennessee Press, 1982), 11.

18. See James Morgart, *A History of the Devil: From the Middle Ages to the Present* (Cambridge: Polity, 2013).

19. Patricia Allmer, Emily Brick, and David Huxley, introduction to *European Nightmares: Horror Cinema in Europe Since 1945*, ed. Patricia Allmer, Emily Brick, and David Huxley (London: Wallflower Press, 2012), 1.

20. Morgart, *History of the Devil*, 377. We need to be cautious, however, in using the term *horror cinema* too freely. It has become increasingly commonplace for those writing about films produced prior to the 1930s to refer to "horror films." The horror genre itself, however, is typically not viewed as developing, as an industrial film category at least, until sometime in the mid-1930s. For the most part, the kinds of films under discussion here—the kinds that numerous authors have assigned the generic label of "horror" to—were marketed and discussed very generally as fantastic films and have tended to be viewed by film historians as "trick films." While genre

definitions are often highly subjective and notoriously elastic, horror has increasingly been mobilized in problematic ways. For instance, Bruce F. Kawin, in *Horror and the Horror Film* (London: Anthem, 2012), claims *"The Haunted Castle* was Méliès's fifth horror film, with *A Terrible Night, The Vanishing Lady, The Devil's Manor,* and *A Nightmare* all being made a year earlier in 1896" (210 n2). It is debatable as to whether any of the four films Kawin lists as coming before *The Haunted Castle* could be identified as horror films in any case. *The Devil's Manor* is, in fact, an alternative title for *The Haunted Castle* (and so is a repetition) and only *A Nightmare* can have any claim to being a horror film of sorts.

21. Morgart, 376.

22. Tom Ruffles, *Ghost Images: Cinema of the Afterlife* (Jefferson, NC: McFarland, 2004), 36.

23. The illusion of the Devil increasing and decreasing in size was created by filming him separately and slowly moving the camera toward (and away from him) before superimposing it on the image of a baroque room. The film's original French title, *Le diable géant ou le miracle de la madonne* (literally "the big devil or the Virgin Mary's miracle") is significant here in setting up the notion a battle between the forces of good and evil. But, as was typical of George Méliès, this was not a straightforward morality tale. The Virgin Mary reunites the lovers and there is, as with much of his work, a tongue-in-cheek quality to the brief narrative.

24. Muchembled, *History of the Devil,* 7.

25. Muchembled, 7.

26. Muchembled, 1.

27. Duanne, "Changing Face of Satan."

28. In Watkins's painting, Satan is represented as a slightly corpulent and spectacled, bald tailor. He is surrounded by various items of his work and can be seen stitching a concentration camp outfit. The message that the Devil was and has been among us could not be starker.

29. Muchembled, *History of the Devil,* 7.

30. Kracauer, *Theory of Film,* 33.

31. Elizabeth Ezra, *George Méliès: The Birth of an Auteur* (Manchester: Manchester University Press, 2000), 151.

32. Ezra, 2.

33. Ezra, 150.

34. Tom Gunning, *D. W. Griffith and the Origins of America Narrative Film: The Biograph Years* (Chicago: University of Illinois Press, 1994), 41.

Murnau's *Faust* and the Weimar Moment

Barry C. Knowlton and Eloise R. Knowlton

Power is an attractive idea, all the more attractive to those who are disempowered. So, it is no surprise that the idea of a man being offered supernatural power would be taken up in a Germany humbled by its defeat in the Great War and condemned as its sole aggressor. This essay explores F. W. Murnau's *Faust* (1926), setting it against its source text (Goethe's *Faust*), grounding theology, and its mid-Weimar moment. In depicting Faust as a good man saved by divine forgiveness, the film obviates postwar guilt by depicting, for a Germany suffering international condemnation, forgiveness and salvation.

Making movies about the divine and the diabolical is not easy. How can the otherworldly or the underworldly be shown without trivialization or reduction? Some religious traditions avoid the issue by interdicting visual representations of God altogether. Others negotiate it by means of metaphor: sunlight pouring through clouds, a sudden wind. Christianity believes that God became Man and dwelt among us: that God was visible. But when it comes to depictions of the Father, or of his fallen angel, Satan, any depiction risks comic reduction, with God becoming the cutout head of Karl Marx as in *Monty Python and the Holy Grail*, or Satan looking almost as cartoonish, complete with horns, hoofs, and pitchfork. Like the big rubber fish in *Jaws*, the more visible, the more risible. However, we will begin by taking Satan seriously. Who is Satan?

Satan

In Christian theology, Satan is understood to be a fallen angel, created by God and in rebellion against him through the free will granted him by his creator.

Satan can pervert or corrupt what God has made; he can never make or order anything of his own. Goethe's Mephistopheles introduces himself to Faust as "The spirit which eternally denies!"[1] Frustration and consuming envy fuel his malevolence against God's creation, an enmity that can seem puzzlingly unmotivated, as with the Satan-figure Iago in *Othello*, who has no clear reason for his evildoings. And yet, as Peter-Andre Alt explains, "Evil's very deficiency, which has been conceptualized as *privatio boni* ('lack of good') ever since Augustine's *On the City of God*, is the element of a comprehensive order of *creation* governed by the law of good."[2]

Christian tradition, then, understands Satan's power as derivative, secondary, reactionary, marginalized, lesser. As a subversive force, it must remain hidden as much as possible, and can act only indirectly in a kind of guerilla warfare. Milton's Satan expresses this idea when he declares, "To do aught good never will be our task, / But ever to do ill our sole delight, / As being contrary to his high will / Whom we resist."[3] Satan is least powerful when he is clearly seen and clearly known as Satan.[4] It follows, then, that Satan is not only the Prince of Darkness—it's hard to see in the dark—but prince of the sneaky and the subversive, the divided and the double, the world and the underworld. Artifice, imitation, mirroring, disguise, trickery, deceit, all forms of falseness and duplicity (doubleness): These are his tools of perversion and seduction. These are also the tools of the motion picture arts. This suggests not for the first time that there is something foundationally dangerous about cinema and its power to sway us.

The Faust story is about making a deal with Satan. There are two ways in which we might understand such a deal. An individual like Faust might, for his own reasons, make a deal with the devil that goes above and beyond humanity's liability to damnation. Such a deal would be ironclad and irrevocable: Once Faust signs his name, his soul is lost. This sort of Faustian figure might be a tragic hero—the sort of Faust Christopher Marlowe depicts. The other way to understand a "deal with the devil" is to see it as an allegory of humanity's fallen state. Adam and Eve can be seen to have struck such a deal, and everyone else ever since has had to deal with the consequences. In this understanding of the story, Faust as a fallen man is Everyman. There is already a doubleness at the foundation of the tale.

It is fitting that Satan, the great imitator, would imitate God's deals, more properly called "covenants." The Old Testament can be read as a catalog of deals and deal-making. Before the Fall, humanity lived in accord with God's order without need of contract or covenant. Since then, Judaism seeks and Christianity claims to have found means to redeem the fallen world and bring God and humanity back to unity. From the start we can see that deals and contracts, even with God, bespeak a world in which Satan has made his way into the garden. The Old Testament form of covenant was legalistic and covered only the people of Israel. Christianity is a "New Covenant," but one that dispenses with the old legalism: It applies to everyone. The Fall is still in effect, but now there is a prospect of salvation.

The Book of Job, most apposite to the Faust story, perhaps best depicts the Old Testamentary relationship between God and Satan. Job describes a surprisingly casual exchange, but it is clear with whom authority lies when God gives Satan permission to test Job: "Behold, all that he hath is in thy power; only upon himself put not forth thine hand" (Job 2:12).[5] Job's life is never in danger: At stake is his fidelity to God, and he is clearly a test case. Job does not curse God, and so passes the test, having all his wealth returned to him by God, who has won the bet. We see this kind of testing in many biblical narratives (Noah, Abraham, Moses, and even Jesus). In the Murnau film, the bargain makes Faust the marker for all of "the earth." His fate will be the fate of humanity at large, which serves to bring the story home to us. The film's Mephisto thinks that the earth is his; the Archangel Michael insists that it is not, because "Man belongs to God!" But the main thing to understand is that, in order to engage with—and let's just say it, to *enjoy*—any and all stories about Satan (especially the cinematic ones), we have to willingly forget God's prior claim. The devil has us from the start.

The Faust Story and the Weimar Moment

The Faust story has been through many iterations and articulations, and while it is not our intention to exhaust them here, a brief review is helpful, before we focus on what Murnau did with the story. The tale emerges from German oral tradition into written form in the late sixteenth century. An anonymous chapbook, based on the purportedly true story of a Doctor John Faustus, appeared in German (1587), then in an English translation (1592). Titled *The Historie of the damnable life, and deserued death of Doctor John Faustus*, it is a Protestant cautionary tale in a time of Reformation, and concludes with this edifying moral: "And thus ended the whole history of Doctor Faustus his conjuration and other acts that he did in his life, out of the which example every Christian may learn. But chiefly the stiff-necked and high-minded may thereby learn to fear God, and to be careful of their vocation, and to be at defiance with all devilish works, as God hath most precisely forbidden, to the end we should not invite the devil as a guest nor give him place as that Wicked Faustus hath done."[6]

But English-speaking audiences receive the story chiefly through Christopher Marlowe's play *Doctor Faustus* (1604); and German-speakers encounter it through Goethe in his enormous, two-part Romantic drama, published in its final form in 1831, and the basis for the movie's screenplay. Marlowe and Goethe have very different takes on the tale, with Marlowe emphasizing Faust's badness and sending him emphatically to eternal damnation, and Goethe granting him more noble intentions and finding a means by which he is saved in the end. That the English tale condemns and the German tale forgives claims a moral difference that will resonate well with Germany when the story is taken up by F. W. Murnau in the middle years of Weimar.

In the final days of World War I, Germany saw its leaders, like Faust, strike a bad bargain. To avoid occupation, Germany signed the Versailles Treaty, accepting painfully punitive reparations and—even more agonizing to the German sensibility—sole responsibility for starting the war, a stinging rebuke for a people who had accepted it as a defensive war. Abandoned by their Kaiser and thrown into a totally unprecedented democratic turmoil, Germans saw their military disbanded, their industries co-opted, and their middle class dispossessed by hyperinflation. It is only in hindsight, and with eyes fixed firmly on the modernist aesthetic accomplishments of the time, that Weimar can be mythologized as a golden age of freedom between two periods of violence and repression. For ordinary Germans, it was a time of poverty, privation, civil unrest, violence, shame, and insecurity. If they went to the movies—and they did, in great numbers, because it was cheap escapism—they saw movies made by their recent enemies: Most of the movies in the early 1920s were made in Hollywood. They depicted not what Germans were or what they wanted to think they were, but what Americans thought they were: evil. Gerald Mast and Bruce Kawin describe the moment as follows:

> In the final year of World War I, the German government wondered whether preferring bullets to pictures had been a tactical error. Whatever the results of the battles at the front, the German nation and the German character were losing terribly on the screens of the world.
> In a number of very popular films made in America during and after the war, the enemy was portrayed as a villainous, vicious Hun; the evil, sinister, outwardly polished and inwardly corrupt Erich von Stroheim was the perfect stereotype of this newest movie bad guy.[7]

Reclaiming Germany in the eyes of the Germans was the chief motivation for the establishment in December 1917 of Universum Film A.G., known as Ufa, a state-owned consolidated studio with premises outside Berlin.[8] As empire gave way to fragile republic, Ufa was bought by the Deutsche Bank and its initially propagandistic aims were subordinated to commercial ones. Germany began to produce films—distinctive, exciting, technically innovative films—on a scale rivaling Hollywood, and with far greater aesthetic daring. Some, starting with *The Cabinet of Dr. Caligari,* were what we now think of as German Expressionism; others were simply movies made in the traditional mold. But they were made in Germany, by Germans. Power rests with the storyteller, and with Ufa in the twenties, Germany regained control of its own narrative.

F. W. Murnau had served in the war and returned to Germany from internment in Switzerland to apply his prewar theater expertise to the business of making movies. The industry in those years was still very much dependent on the theater for its stories and its talent, both in front of and behind the camera. Feature films had yet fully to establish themselves as legitimate cultural expression, the nickelodeon era was still recent, and any infringement on the rights of the family and the clergy to determine what children saw was still suspect. Censorship, not in effect at the outset of the Republic, was reimposed in May 1920. Feature films, although often supplemented with musical or orchestral accompaniment, were themselves silent until *The Jazz Singer* in 1927. Telling the story without sound can now be seen as an important formative stage for film as an art: The pictures had to do the work. Murnau, steeped from childhood in drama and puppetry—his brother built him a stage and he wrote and directed plays as a child—already understood something of the craft's fundamentals. In 1925, he wrested the script of *Faust* away from another director, assembled a cast, and began production.

Faust is the story of a good man, a scholar, seduced by the devil into agreeing to sell his soul for youth and pleasure. After an unspecified period of sinful indulgence, a moody and yet unsatisfied Faust returns to his hometown and falls in love with Gretchen, a pure young girl on her way to Easter mass. The devil cannot distract Faust from this love and so uses it to undo him. A magical gold necklace erodes Gretchen's moral sensibility; she and Faust court and couple. Gretchen's mother catches them in the act and dies from the shock. Mephisto ensures that the girl's brother is alerted, and a confrontation and swordfight follow in which the brother is killed by Mephisto. Faust is made to believe he struck the fatal blow, and he flees. Gretchen, left disgraced and pregnant, is condemned first to the pillory, then to ostracism. Her child is born but dies of exposure when—on a melodramatically depicted, bitterly cold Christmas Eve—none of the townspeople takes her and the child in. She is charged with its murder and sentenced to die at the stake. In the final climactic scene, Faust somehow hears her anguished cry from atop the pyre and flies to her. As the flames rise around her, Faust, turned back into an old man by Mephisto, joins her. She recognizes him as her lover, her beatific face signifies she loves him still, and the movie ends with a bright light from above enfolding them both as their souls rise to heaven, saved.

Watching *Faust*

What would an audience on October 14, 1926, taking its seat for *Faust's* first showing, have made of this? First and foremost, the film's Germanness would have been apparent from the opening credits, which are in the Gothic black letter—the type of the Gutenberg Bible. This typeface persisted in Germany and only in Germany, astonishingly, until the twentieth century. The Nazis embraced it despite its unreadability and used it officially until 1941 because they saw it as properly and authentically German. The rest of Europe had long been using typographies derived from Roman letter, or newly designed, as with types developed by "degenerate" modernists. By 1926, Gothic black letter signified not only the Gutenberg Bible and all things biblical but something distinctly—and soon to be militantly—German.[9]

Faust's source text intensifies the identification. *Faust* isn't based on just any German legend, but on the one chosen by the national poet, Goethe. Though this is never identified in the film itself or its credits, audience members would immediately have recognized the story as that of Goethe, arguably the most lauded of all German poets. Omitting to cite his source certainly wasn't any form of subterfuge on Murnau's part: The title is identical to that of Goethe's work. (Murnau, fresh from losing a copyright suit to Bram Stoker's widow for making *Nosferatu* without permission, would be tender on questions of attribution.) Rather, the omission suggests there was no need to acknowledge the source: Everyone would already know. A properly German story, received through Goethe, would signify to audiences in 1926 that this is no mere entertainment, but a serious work of national art.

The seriousness derives not only from the work's source, but from its topic. *Faust* is first and foremost a religious movie, not something audiences would have expected to appear on the screen. Melodramatic morality was familiar enough, but serious treatments of religious topics drawn from serious literature were not. Fritz Lang's *Nibelungen*, released the previous year, was perhaps the first grandly ambitious treatment of a German classic, but it skirts the question of religion. *Faust* may have opened a door to more such movies; its screenwriter Hans Kyser's *Luther* would be released in Berlin in February 1928.

The audience's expectation for technical innovation and expert editing would have been high, given Murnau's recent achievements and the general quality of Ufa's offerings. The opening sequences of the Archangel Michael, the infernal Mephisto, the plague and the pact, even though visible today as highly artificial, are still impressive, perhaps especially so to viewers who might imagine that real special effects only began with CGI. There is magic in this movie, and it is firmly associated with the magic *of* movies, where the filmmaker can give the devil power to appear and disappear, conjure plague and fire, change an old man into a young one, and fly through the night sky high over the earth. The film's special effects, far more artificial than those of Murnau's previous film, *The Last Laugh*, are one of the strongest elements of the film and play a central role in the story.

If, then, this is a German film, made by and for Germans, depicting Germanness, what do we see? The legend emerges from a time before writing, but writing, books, scholarship, and learning—those peaceful, creative pursuits—are at the center of the tale, reminding Germany of its cultured, rather than its militant, past. Faust is associated with books and bookishness, humanist scholarship, and, shading into the dark side of these accomplishments, with alchemy and magic. His precise profession or area of expertise is problematic to a contemporary mind. Is he a theologian, a philosopher, a chemist, a physicist, a sorcerer, a necromancer, a wise man, a mad scientist? Goethe's Faust studies philosophy, law, medicine, and theology (in that order), and then, because none of these pursuits has satisfied him, he turns to magic. Murnau's Faust lectures on theology, dabbles in alchemy, and concocts a medicine he hopes will cure the plague. Faust's learning, in whatever academic discipline, is clearly literate and erudite, with a sense that book learning conveys mysterious and perhaps sinister powers. (This suspicion is the stamp of an oral culture long gone in Germany of the 1920s.) Given this, the audience might expect to see Faust do some magic, or at least demonstrate some kind of power, either natural or supernatural. But in Murnau's *Faust*, all the magic resides with the devil through the director.

Our first view of Faust establishes his piety and fundamental goodness, which is, after all, what is at stake. Faust stands for Germany, and as such must be taken as fundamentally good. Michael directs Mephisto to "Look below!" and so we look too, and see Faust teaching his students the theological premise that grounds the story: God made us and gave us free will: "All things in heaven and on earth are wonderful! But the greatest wonder is man's freedom to choose between good and evil!" This highly artificial—that is, formal—shot seems to be influenced by Vermeer or Rembrandt: We know Murnau's work is at moments highly allusive to painting. Certainly, the chiaroscuro contrast of black and white is marked.

We see both white and black smoke or mist, and then the figure of Faust, old and bearded, in a black cloak but with his head in the light. He is holding open a large book, the pages of which are illuminated by the light. A large

Faust teaching in Murnau's *Faust*: "But the greatest wonder is man's freedom to choose between good and evil!"

model of a globe, brightly lit from within, sits below, behind, and to his right. It is surrounded by rings that could represent either the rings of a planet like Saturn or the orbits of planets that revolve around the sun. Though it is brightly lit, it is not the source of the light that illuminates Faust.

Faust is surrounded by his students—we see only their faces, some distinctly, others obscurely, all listening intently. Faust seems to be standing with his back to them, but is looking up and to his right, as if toward his students; and then down and to his left toward the book, presumably but not certainly the Bible, in the center of the frame. On the right side of the frame, we can only just discern a shadowy figure, apparently helping Faust hold up the book. An angel? Or is the devil already on site? The backlit close-up of Faust that follows conveys his saintliness, in order to intensify the drama of his fall. The deadly sin of pride, specifically intellectual pride, associated with Faust in Marlowe and other treatments—Satan's sin was pride, after all—is not in evidence here. We are presented with a humble and pious pedagogue.

This is our first view of Faust, and Michael asks, "Dost thou know Faust?" Mephisto knows him for a knave, on account of his dabbling in alchemy. As if to confirm Mephistopheles's assertion, we then see Faust engaged in his alchemical experiments. He is working with a large globe-like apparatus like the one featured in the scene of teaching. Lights flash within the globe, and smoke billows around it as he works. Then the smoke overcomes him—he raises his arms to cover his face—and we are to understand that his experiment has failed.

It is at this point that Mephisto proposes the wager. "I will wrest Faust's soul away from God!" Michael accepts: "If thou canst destroy what is divine in Faust: the earth is thine!" Once the bet is made, Mephisto introduces the plague, visible as a thick fog, into Faust's city. The label tells us that "To find the cure for the Plague, Faust spent day and night in prayer with God." The result of the prayer is a bottle of medicine. Just then a young girl comes to the door of Faust's study, pleading with him to save her mother, who is ill. He goes with her and administers the medicine, but the woman dies. The plague rages on and Faust loses all hope of a cure. He returns to his study and begins to burn the books that now represent his powerless scholarship.

The question of who initiates contact with the devil is problematic in the Murnau film. Faust despairs when he is unable to save those stricken by the plague, and despair is usually a prelude to Satan's arrival, since it means total loss of hope of redemption. In burning his books, Faust—as if accidentally—comes across one that tells him how to summon the devil. He indeed follows those directives at the crossroads (always a symbol of choice) and Mephisto appears on cue. But Faust has already been singled out as marker in a bet, and the audience knows that the plague that set him on this path was conjured by Mephisto with him in mind. Who, then, has called whom?

However Faust and Mephisto come to strike their deal, it initially gives Faust the ability to cure those stricken by the plague. He cures an old man who is brought to him and receives the adulation of the crowd. A young woman is then brought to him, but she is holding a crucifix, and Faust is unable to come near her. The crowd concludes rightly that he is in league with Satan and begins to stone him. He retreats to his study and is about to kill himself when Mephisto persuades him instead to embrace youth and pursue pleasure.

Faust the film is structured like the Bible, in two distinct parts. The first part is something of an "Old Testament," caught up in questions of legality and law, ritual and ceremony, covenants between Man and the Supernatural. Through Goethe it strongly invokes Job, at one point nearly quoting it. It centers on Faust, his temptation and downfall, and takes place in an unspecified time of year, lost in history. Old Faust is dressed in flowing robes, long white hair and beard suggesting a rabbi or a prophet. Books, all but unseen in the later parts of the film, are piled everywhere in Old Faust's rooms, and the sign of his despair is his burning them, in a scene difficult not to (anachronistically) associate with book burnings under the Nazis. Old Mephisto appears wearing a skullcap reminiscent of a yarmulke and wears locks on either side of his face, signs of Jewishness that suggest a degree of anti-Semitism. Faust summons Mephisto, then attempts to evade him. But wherever he goes Mephisto inexorably appears and doffs his skullcap in mock greeting, thereby establishing his character and calling attention to the Jewish-marked costume choice. Later, after transforming Faust from an old into a young man, he transforms himself into a youth clad in a shiny cloak and feathered hat. As a note to the Norton Critical Edition of *Faust* explains, "Mephistopheles wears the conventional theatrical costume of a Spanish cavalier."[10] Whatever the devil is, he clearly isn't German.

In fact, there are few markers of Germanness in these initial scenes, and once Faust has made his pact, he immediately leaves Germany for foreign places. His sin will happen elsewhere, implying that Germany and Germans remain pure. Mephisto spirits him away to Parma where his sexual satisfaction awaits. "Take me to her!" Faust cries after seeing the nearly naked image of the Duchess Mephisto has conjured. The Duchess of Parma scenes depict a faraway Oriental luxury, and clearly bespeak a space that isn't the homeland. We do not see much of the sinful indulgence we are to understand Faust has indulged in. Another treatment of the tale might have plumbed those depths exhaustively. Mephisto literally draws a curtain (his cloak) over Faust's enjoyment of the Duchess, and, after that, we don't see him until he is sitting, alone and unsatisfied, on a very Romantic, David Caspar Friedrich–inspired mountaintop. Pleasure exhausted, Faust is still unhappy, and his thoughts turn to home. This moment marks the hinge of the film between the Old Testamentary first half, concerned with books, writing, contracts, deals and dealmaking, to a New Testamentary second half, emphatically Christian and specifically Catholic, concerned with love and the possibility of forgiveness and salvation.

The action returns to a visibly German place and to a clearly Christian world: Faust returns on Easter morning, and the town is on its way to Easter mass. "It is as if life had stood still: All is as it once was!" says Faust, highlighting his own change. We won't see many books from now on (there is a single prayer book in Gretchen's room) but we will see churches, statues of the Madonna and Child, and crosses. This becomes even more clearly a New Testamentary space in the later scenes at Christmas, when Gretchen and her child are shunned by the townspeople, there is no room for them in the inn, and she is clearly depicted as a Mater Dolorosa in transparent Renaissance fashion.

Faust arrives back in the town he had hoped to save from plague, and this return seems to reawaken something, perhaps a moral sensibility, in him. He sees Gretchen on her way to Easter mass: Resurrection defines their first moment and their last. His attraction to her is clearly displeasing to Mephisto,

Gretchen as Mater Dolorosa in Murnau's *Faust*.

who attempts to dissuade Faust, saying, "An innocent little girl, running to a priest . . . she is not for you!" and in true Satanic fashion attempts distraction, "I know more obliging wenches for you here!" A newly resolute Faust replies, "I want only her. Do as I command!" suggesting that there is something more than carnal desire motivating him. The "only" suggests a turn away from empty pleasure to a different kind of love. The Duchess of Parma was "the most beautiful woman in Italy"; Gretchen appeals in her beauty, yes, but also in her German purity and Christian piety. Mephisto, playing along with Faust's desire for Gretchen, plants the gold necklace in Gretchen's room. This necklace is not, or is not *only*, a pretty thing: Wearing it appears to erode the will. Gretchen herself, after all, is not only pretty, pious, and pure; she, too, is human. She senses something is wrong with the bauble. She first resists, then yields. She conceals it from her mother—a first deceit—who urges her to "Tell the mother of God, if you cannot tell me!" Perhaps sensing that she will meet with approval there, she visits her Aunt Marthe and shows it to her. Aunt Marthe brews and sells love potions, suggesting she is familiar with magic and may already be acquainted with the devil.

At this point, the film cuts back and forth between parallel courtships: Mephisto and Aunt Marthe in the kitchen in comic mode, and Faust and Gretchen in the garden in tragic mode. After some pastoral frolicking, Faust "marries" Gretchen by putting a ring on her finger and vowing, "I am yours forever!" Is this a real marriage? Obviously not in a legal sense—we have put legalities behind—but in a theological one? The marriage takes place in a garden, just as marriage began in the garden as part of God's plan for an unfallen world. The serpent was somewhere but did not intervene. One of the lesser-known Catholic doctrines about the sacrament of marriage is that the parties administer it to one another: The bride and bridegroom "mutually confer" the sacrament. Consent is essential: Both must be making a free choice. The priest doesn't "marry" the man and woman in the same way he says mass or forgives sins. With those sacraments, he *does* something to bring down the power of the Holy Spirit. In a Catholic marriage, the priest merely witnesses the marriage for the Church. Any marriage thus sacramental, the Church holds, is indissoluble, which is why Catholics cannot divorce. Divorce dissolves a marriage; annulment says there was none to begin with. The idea is that if marriage is a sacrament, then something happened that made things different forever: an event, rather than a legal contract. Contracts are deals and can be undone. Sacraments are events and cannot be undone.

Marriage for Catholics, then, is sacramental and permanent, part of the order God established with Adam and Eve, which is why Mephisto finds it offensive. It is no accident that he chooses the Duchess of Parma as a proper instrument of seduction for the magically young Faust and intervenes precisely on her wedding night. She is the most beautiful woman in the world, yes, but she has also just been married. By killing her bridegroom and granting his conjugal rights to Faust instead, Mephisto simultaneously accomplishes Faust's undoing and prevents the Duchess's marriage's consummation, changing good sex into bad sex. Devilish, indeed.

Are Gretchen and Faust married in the eyes of the church, which would presumably be in the eyes of God? It is interesting that the marriage ritual they complete happens when Mephisto is elsewhere, distracted with Marthe. His vigilance has slipped, and that's suggestive. Sex might happen with him nearby, as with the Duchess where it is literally under his cloak, but a marriage certainly would not. In the *History of the damned life*, Faust announces that he wants not to enjoy the sexual favors of any woman, but to marry one of them; and although throughout much is made of Mephistopheles's obligation

Sacraments cannot be undone: Faust and Gretchen married in Murnau's *Faust*.

to do whatever Faust demands, here he puts his hoof down, and declares that if Faust does not put the idea out of his mind, he will tear him to pieces—"For wedlock is an institution ordained of God."[11] To read this scene as sacramental marriage would help us understand why Gretchen, such a good girl, would bring Faust so willingly into her bed. (Catholic marriages require sexual consummation to be considered fully valid.) It would explain the Jane Eyre moment when the forsaken Gretchen cries out for Faust, and he somehow hears her: Theirs is a bond transcending space and time, far exceeding a merely legal agreement. It would explain the final scene with Gretchen on the pyre when, even in her madness, she mystically sees through Faust's appearance as an old man. It would help explain why her love is still present and powerful, even after he has abandoned her and their now-dead child—a response that most definitely needs some explaining. And it would explain the final moment of their joining, when the flames engulf them, and they die together. In some cuts they are seen to rise to heaven; in others a powerful light from above more elliptically signifies their resurrection. Either way, seeing Faust and Gretchen as sacramentally married shows how we might get around the devil, despite his efforts and pretensions, and go to Heaven when we die, which, after all, is what God wants—this is his prior claim. Redemption is possible, both for those who have made a deal that entails guilt and for those who are only as guilty as anyone else who has been through as much. The devil has us from the very beginning, but God has us in the end.

The final shots of the movie neatly return to and resolve the initial exposition. The camera pans upward and stops when it comes to the sun, the light of which spins and pulsates for several seconds. The scene fades to black, and we see Mephisto back in his infernal costume of horns and wings, holding the contract Faust signed. Michael appears and charges, "Here is no place for thee!" We see Michael in the left foreground, with his sword raised and Mephisto in the right background, much lower down. Mephisto raises the contract, and shouts, "I claim my wager!" Michael looks down at him, then looks up, and says, "One Word breaks thy pact!" That word, appearing out of bright light, first growing, then fading, is "Liebe." The one word that undoes all of Satan's works is "Love." It is what is divine in Faust, and it has not been destroyed. The word grows then fades and we see a dominant Michael, white wings and sword raised in the background, and a suddenly submissive Mephisto, black in the foreground, with his arms raised as if to fend off a blow. Michael brings down his sword, and Mephisto sinks out of sight, vanquished. No matter what evil has been done, despite loss and pain, abandonment and madness, salvation is still at hand in a Christian Germany. The harshness of the Treaty of Versailles, the shame of international exile, the burden of reparations—all this can be put behind and wiped away in the powerful light of divine forgiveness.

Notes

1. Johann Wolfgang von Goethe, *Faust*, trans. Walter Arndt, ed. Cyrus Hamlin, 2nd ed. (New York: Norton, 2001), 1338.

2. Peter-Andre Alt, "Mephisto's Principles: On the Construction of Evil in Goethe's *Faust* I," *Modern Language Review* 106, no. 1 (2011): 154.

3. John Milton, *Paradise Lost*, in *The Portable Milton*, ed. Douglas Bush (New York: Viking, 1964), 1.159–162.

4. C. S. Lewis's *Screwtape Letters* (1942) takes us fully into an intimate exchange between Satan and one of his minions, and the intent there is to fully reveal and so to overturn evil's standard strategy of deceit and manipulation. See C. S. Lewis, *The Screwtape Letters* (New York: HarperOne, 2015).

5. *King James Bible Online*, accessed October 17, 2020, https://www.kingjames bibleonline.org/Job-1-12/.

6. Christopher Marlowe, *Doctor Faustus*, ed. Sylvan Barnet (New York: Signet, 2010), 157.

7. Gerald Mast and Bruce Kawin, *A Short History of the Movies* (Boston, MA: Allyn and Bacon, 1996), 150.

8. An English translation of "the birth certificate of Ufa," a letter from General Erich Ludendorff to the Royal Ministry of War written July 4, 1917, appears in Anton Kaes, Nicholas Baer, and Michael Cowan, eds., *The Promise of Cinema: German Film Theory 1907–1933* (Oakland: University of California Press, 2016), 275–277. Ludendorff later collaborated with Adolph Hitler in the 1923 Putsch.

9. For a brief review of the history of German Black Letter, see "The Blackletter Typeface: A Long and Colored History," *Sitepoint*, November 7, 2009, accessed October 17, 2020, https://www.sitepoint.com/ the-blackletter-typeface-a-long-and-colored-history/.

10. Goethe, *Faust*, 42.

11. Goethe, 113.

Disney's Devils

J. P. Telotte

While often described as cute and conservative and linked to a rising tide of realistic representation in animation, early Disney cartoon efforts trouble such broad assessments. Mickey Mouse and Silly Symphony cartoons of the late-modernist era (1920s to 1940) are particularly rife with disturbing images—of dancing skeletons (*Skeleton Dance*, 1929), revivified mummies (*Egyptian Melodies*, 1931), ghosts (*The Haunted House*, 1929), mad scientists (*The Mad Doctor*, 1933), murderous gorillas (*The Gorilla Mystery*, 1930), even Satan—and they often set these figures in a world of dizzying change or nightmarish possibilities. However, as the Disney cartoons became more popular and the company more successful in the later 1930s, there was a distinct move to tame these characters and render both them and their environments more like our own. For Walt Disney, this move was largely about trying to develop the art of animation, as if making his cartoons more in the real world's image somehow rendered them better or simply more satisfying. However, for many of his critics it was something more—evidence of what Esther Leslie terms an "accomplished sell-out of the quintessence of cartoons: their modernistic dissolution of conventional reality," in effect, their temptation and fall at the hands of a figure that Marc Eliot, in his sensationalistic biography of Disney, likened to the devil, terming him "Hollywood's Dark Prince."[1]

For others, most animated films of the 1920s to 1940s are characterized by a negotiation between these attitudes, between a modernist subversion or questioning of the real and an effort at carefully reproducing it. Thus, Paul Wells suggests that we might more accurately describe animation of this late-modernist period as symptomatic of a "conservative modernism," a compromise approach that is "based on the naturalization of impossible events" and of the generally exaggerated images that typify cartooning.[2] I want to examine this element of compromise, particularly in its "naturalizing" developments, through early Disney's handling of one of the most disturbing and unnatural of characters: the devil. In the studio's treatment of this touchstone figure, we can see Disney himself not in the simple styling Eliot offers, as a kind of devilish figure, nor as someone striving to "better" his studio's animation by making it look more like a live-action film, but as a studio head whose productions in this period were constantly shadowed by a modernist sensibility like that which Leslie and others champion—a sensibility that shows its persistence in this rather un-Disney-like character.

Of course, one of the devil's or Satan's primary characteristics is his own subversive nature, his status as a kind of ultimate threat to the human status quo, in some ways like the modernist spirit, always ready to overturn things. As archetypal psychologist James Hillman offers, the image of Satan, as well as his kingdom of Hell or Hades, has traditionally been perceived as "overwhelming" and not open to compromises of any sort, not only because of the inevitable connections with ultimate categories like death and dissolution, but also because he represents a kind of "violation, dragging one out of life"— or perhaps what Leslie terms "conventional reality"—while also dragging the life out of one. When this figure appears, as Hillman says, it is as if "the bottom falls out" of reality itself.[3] The result is to suggest at least in part, much as Leslie offers about early animation, "a universe of transformation, overturning and provisionality"—that is, a realm predicated on overturning or subverting our own, on evoking a kind of unstable or what we have at times termed a *be-deviled* world.[4]

And indeed, for many that effect—if not the imagery itself—as exemplified in some early animation is a positive thing, quite in keeping with the form's own provisional character and its ability to visualize or bring to life a world that is far more complex, more dimensional, and more challenging than conventional notions of the real usually allow. This effect is central to the claim many have made for early animation's attraction and even *value*. For example, in discussing cartoons of this early period, Stefan Kanfer explains that they were not simply "bright, brittle entertainments without much substance or importance," as many would have them, but rather part of the "serious business" of humor.[5] And their subversive, even devilish power is just indicative of how much animation at its core, that is as a form that usurps a divine ability to endow with life, to breathe in spirit—*anima*—is a product of the modernist moment, consistently providing us with, as Donald Crafton offers, the fundamental "imagery of modernism"—albeit an imagery that is, in fact, often a site of contention, drawing the narrative in one direction or another, by turns brightly entertaining, even familiar, and also seriously subversive.[6]

Of course, modernism was never simply one effect or central characteristic. As Bruno Latour has chronicled, it "comes in as many versions as there are thinkers or journalists"—or even film critics and historians.[7] Thus, Anthony Vidler offers a more fundamental way of thinking about modernism, as well as graphic arts like animation, suggesting that at its base was "the unsettling of representation itself," as the "real" and the "certain" were infected by "abstraction,"[8] became, as others such as Latour have suggested, "impure" or uncertain. The decidedly modern imagery of a Marcel Duchamp, for instance, as in *Nude Descending a Staircase, No.* 2 (1912), is not simply a retreat from or "subverting" of the real; rather it is an attempt to imbue an ordinary depiction of action with a sense of time and duration—giving its representation a wholly new and dynamic character and thus allowing its multiple images to *represent differently* and for different vantages—in such a way that we might never see even the most basic *depicted* motion in the same way again. While no early animation quite compares to Duchamp's avant-garde imagery, there is often, as Wells argues, a sense that a work "oscillates between" positions, resulting in texts "in which assimilation and de-familiarisation are simultaneous effects."[9] That same oscillation, though, could also bulk beyond individual texts, characterize a body of works produced by a studio like Disney, for example, and thus pose a challenge to any effort at globally—or simply—characterizing its products. This sense of a kind of *shiftiness* between the real and the abstract, or between representation and what we might term its *discontents*, is part of the story of Disney's devils. For in the studio's unlikely embrace of a figure that was itself always tied to the real world, but also conventionally represented as an undermining or troubling spirit, its animation gained a resonance, reminding us of our world's own often disturbing complexity.

As an initial example, we might consider the early Silly Symphony cartoon *Hell's Bells* (1929), the fourth entry in this series and a close cousin to the first and similarly eerie effort, *Skeleton Dance* (1929). Like that previous film—and as the titles of both quickly suggest—*Hell's Bells* finds its main attraction in a strange combination of musical and macabre elements, as it depicts various creatures typically associated with the underworld—spiders, bats, dragons, Cerberus the three-headed dog, and multiple small devils—all of them cavorting to music and entertaining a stylized Satan as he sits on a rocky throne. They are, of course, also meant to entertain *us*, despite their ghastly looks and actions. Thus, as with *Skeleton Dance*, much of the film is shot as if staged, rather conventionally, in a hellish proscenium arch, the actions directed to us as much as to Satan. The small devils here play musical instruments made of

Performing for Satan in Disney's *Hell's Bells*.

bones and pitchforks, dance wildly in the rubber-hose fashion of early animation, milk flames from a dragon that they then offer to the spectator, in this
instance Satan who greedily drinks the offering down. Despite its unsettling
imagery, the film finds an appeal in its very rhythms, as well as its ability to
discover an unlikely, even entertaining, musical character in the devilish
events we witness, in effect to render even such bizarre activities as—sort
of—normal.

Yet, while the music was paramount in *Skeleton Dance*, *Hell's Bells* gradually, even devilishly, shifts the balance to the macabre—that is, away from
musical performance and to a kind of narrative that apparently characterizes
Satan and his misrule. The key characteristic of that narrative is its own oscillation between presenting a "naturalized"—that is, simply comic—image of
Satan and his actions, much as Wells might suggest, and an unsettling, more
subversive vision of this *underworld* and its ruler, even dropping "the bottom"
out of this realm. While not entirely comic, the various scenes described above
generally work within a familiar register, its musical gags, exaggerated actions,
and scenes of comic entertainment drawing upon a kind of conventionalized

representation of Satan and his realm with Satan differing little, except in size, from the small devils who entertain him. He is horned, has sharp fangs and a pointed tail, is fur-covered, and has rubber hose–type arms and legs; there is, simply, little of human seeming here and much exaggeration of form. Through the first half of the film the dark hijinks of Satan and his attendants are no more disturbing or unusual than the sort of figures and actions encountered in some other early Disney cartoons or—perhaps more to the point—in a variety of works from other studios in this period, such as Max Fleischer's KoKo the Clown films *KoKo Sees Spooks* (1925) and *KoKo's Haunted House* (1928), his forthrightly imitative Betty Boop film *Red Hot Mama* (1934), wherein Betty actually serenades the devil with a song entitled "Hell's Bells," Walter Lantz's Oswald the Rabbit efforts *Hell's Heels* and *Spooks* (both 1930), the Van Beuren Tom and Jerry film *Wot a Night* (1931), or Ub Iwerks's Willy Whopper cartoon *Hell's Fire* (1934). In effect, *Hell's Bells* in part operates within a conventionalized cartoon pattern of the era, one that allowed for a comically exaggerated presentation of evil figures, for the sort of naturalization Wells describes, and for the sort of taming of those disturbing spirits that Leslie laments.

However, the actions here are framed or interrupted by a series of events that eventually casts them in a more unsettling light, one that undermines such conventional representation. In a common visual gimmick of early animation—seen, for example, in Winsor McCay's *Bug Vaudeville* (1921)—a large spider swings toward the foreground, its mouth opening wide and blacking out the image, as if it had swallowed the camera, only to then, in the following shot, be itself consumed by flames from a central pit; a serpent snatches and swallows a passing bat, whose wings then sprout through the serpent's sides and, to the serpent's obvious dismay at this unexpected transformation, fly off with it. Satan grabs one of the small devils that had fed him and then feeds it to Cerberus, each of whose three heads responds appreciatively to the snack; and then Satan himself, tripped up by another small devil trying to escape being turned into a snack, is grabbed and gobbled up by flames, personified as tormenting and grasping hands—a bit like Satan's own and arising from a pit even deeper than his throne. Thus, the various scenes of infernal entertainment repeatedly give way to sites/sights of feeding and destruction, in this vision of "overturning and provisionality" wherein even the prince of this realm is fed to the flames or "overturned."

While Leonard Maltin characterizes *Skeleton Dance* as "a mood piece," *Hell's Bells*, perhaps in trying to top its predecessor, is clearly something more.[10] It offers not just a string of gags or the presentation of a somber show, but a series of actions demonstrating a world—or spirit—at odds with itself, as dance and play become the flip side of devilish torment and destruction. It is, very simply, a dark film with its darkness coming not so much from the infernal antics depicted as from the manner in which the film advances familiarly, but then slides away from a conservative modernism and its "naturalization" of the impossible, and with "representation" repeatedly subverted—as when the bat-swallowing serpent turns into a bat-serpent or Satan's servant becomes an appetizer for Cerberus. Here the playful show, framing Satan and his varied minions in what Wells would term "a magical and comical" context, gives way to a frightening round of consumptions, an Ouroboros-like pattern in an entirely provisional world, and a final vision that is, fittingly, just one of all-consuming flames.[11]

A slightly later Silly Symphony effort, *The Goddess of Spring* (1934), however, would bring a marked change in presentation of both Satan and his world. Based on the Greek myth of Pluto and Persephone, the cartoon is one of the most elaborate and expensive of all the Silly Symphonies. While films of the previous year such as *Three Little Pigs* and *Old King Cole* cost $16,000 and $21,000 respectively, *The Goddess of Spring* was far more expensive at $37,600—a budget that was quite visible on-screen thanks to this film's use of Technicolor rather than black and white, extensive effects animation, and

Combining devilish imagery with Greek myth: The Devil in Disney's *Goddess of Spring*.

especially its effort at animating human-looking characters—a more difficult and time-consuming task, but also symptomatic of that felt tension between what I have termed representation and its discontents, especially in treating the devil who is here as fully humanized as the eponymous "Goddess."[12] Moreover, at nine minutes and forty seconds, *The Goddess of Spring* is the longest of all the Silly Symphony cartoons, a circumstance that may have resulted from its complex mixture, as the narrative tries to bind together its devilish imagery with Greek myth and with a different sort of subversive thrust—a parodic treatment of this material.

Paving the way for—if also ultimately troubling—that parodic element is the decidedly realistic shift in presentation noted above. Thus, the proscenium arch vision of *Hell's Bells* gives way to a more naturalistic three-dimensional vision of both the surface and the underworld—one that looks toward Disney's development of multiplane effects for a slightly later Silly Symphony like *The Old Mill* (1937) as well as subsequent features. The central characters are Pluto—who in legend simply presides over the underworld but is here dressed in conventional Satanic costume and assisted, as in *Hell's Bells*, by an army of small black devils—and Persephone. Both are carefully drawn, human-looking figures, no longer of the rubber-hose variety. In fact, animator Les Clark notes that, because of the difficulty the artists were having with a new studio initiative at crafting life-like rather than exaggerated or simply stylized human figures—an effort forecasting the studio's early preparations for *Snow White and the Seven Dwarfs* (1937)—he brought in a real girl, his sister Marceil, to serve as a model for Persephone and help him perfect certain poses.[13] And in contrast to the "naked" and furry devils of *Hell's Bells*, the characters' costuming here is elaborate, multicolored, and conventional. But this humanizing element and the grounding of Pluto, Persephone, and Hades in a more naturalistic representational scheme was at least initially tied to a different subversive strategy, to providing the narrative with a base for its simultaneous parodic exaggerations of tone, manner, and genre.

As cartoon historian Michael Barrier notes, when an outline for this short was first circulated around the Disney studio in early 1934, "it included a request for 'any gags burlesquing grand opera,'" and the traces of that original subversion of what many might term "high art" are readily apparent.[14] They show especially in the way the central characters of Satan/Pluto and Persephone, despite their naturalized physical appearance, still assume highly melodramatic poses, sing all of their lines in what Barrier terms "a pseudo-operatic style,"[15] repeating in the exaggerated fashion of grand opera various key lines, in the choral work of the smaller devils, and especially in Pluto's suddenly and incongruously evoking the familiar figure of Cab Calloway, as he and his devil minions drop their operatic styling for a jazzy rendition of "Hi De Hades" and dance around while lit by hellish fires that cast exaggerated silhouettes, as if suggesting a musical number from the famed Cotton Club of the era.[16] These lingering effects all suggest an effort to shift emphasis from the narrative's potentially troubling infernal subject matter that had been so obviously foregrounded in *Hell's Bells*, to its manner of presentation, in effect, to find another avenue of subversion, although in this case by shifting focus to something less disturbing, satirizing the highly conventionalized representations of grand opera.

However, that difficult turn falls short here, as the conservative modernist vision tilts decidedly—if artificially—away from a modernist impulse. That effect derives in large part from an element outside of the world of animation that was, perhaps indicating some trouble with the film's original thrust, grafted onto the narrative. For along with a directive from Walt Disney to craft more "believable" human figures,[17] and in this case even rendering the devil like a character in an opera, the film also followed a relatively recent vogue in the Silly Symphony cartoons (seen, for example, in such contemporary efforts as *Babes in the Woods* [1932], *The Pied Piper* [1933], and *Lullaby Land* [1933]) to use a voice-over narrator, here one who sings—but not in the exaggerated, aria-blasting style of Pluto and Persephone—a framing commentary for the story, one that sounds, in contrast, almost like a lullaby. That narrative device shifts emphasis away from musical parody to a fairy-tale form, as it recounts how everything visualized here took place "long, long ago" when "there was joy and laughter everywhere" and "the world grew more lovely each day." The narration gives further reason to this happy state by introducing "the goddess of eternal spring," Persephone, surrounded by swaying flowers, singing birds, dancing elves, and animate trees—a scene resembling not so much *Skeleton Dance* or *Hell's Bells* but rather *Flowers and Trees* (1932)—the first Technicolor Silly Symphony cartoon, first winner of an Academy Award for animated short, and a film that represented the first distinct push in that more realistic, illusion-of-life direction Leslie criticizes. That idyllic vision is violently subverted when the skies suddenly darken and thunder claps; "the bottom" literally drops out of the meadow where Persephone and her company are dancing as smoke and fire surge forth and Pluto appears, physically undermining this happy image while operatically singing of his "burning" desire for her. Yet after providing a vision of the underworld that recalls *Hell's Bells*, the cartoon's disruptive vision of desire dissolves as Pluto grants Persephone permission to return to the surface world for half of every year. On that note of resignation, the story effectively returns to the narrator's control, as he provides a coda for the film, explaining that "now you know the reason why there's a winter season instead of eternal spring."

That lightly intoned "explanation" not only retreats from the film's parodic tone and subversive possibilities; it frames them, as if subversion and change were never really a concern. Moreover, it literally gives untroubling reason to the seasons by casting the devil—that is, Pluto who is here depicted conventionally as Satan—as little more than another fairy-tale convention, naturalized as, in fact, an embodiment of the cycles of nature. And even though we understand that Pluto and his dark intentions to recall Persephone to the underworld for half the year still hold sway, the film leaves us with what the narrator terms "a new day of happiness"—a *temporary* vision of joy, celebration, and balance that suggests the sort of forced compromise that often characterizes the conservative modernist vision and that *Hell's Bells* had managed to elude.

While the devil would feature in no more Silly Symphony cartoons (since the series ended in 1939), he would make a dramatic reappearance in a feature film at the end of this period that was a kind of compendium of Silly Symphony episodes. The "Night on Bald Mountain" sequence from *Fantasia* (1940), described by one contemporary reviewer as a "provocative" film, "visualized with a weird and terrifying assortment of skeletons, ghouls, and imps swirling around the monstrous devil," offers another and, as that commentary suggests, more affecting and impressive interpretation of the devil—in both tone and implication.[18] Based on the Mussorgsky musical composition of that title, the sequence introduces Satan, here named Chernabog after a Slavic version of the devil (or black god who was opposed to the Slavic Belobog, the white god), as an almost literally naturalized figure. He appears not emerging from some deep and fiery pit, nor as some sudden subversion of an idyllic natural world, but as part of the surface world—a sudden transformation of a dark mountaintop, as if rock come alive; he then calls his worshippers to come forth from the earth, a nearby village, and their graves. It is, as this film's narrator, Deems Taylor, offers, an attempt to provide "a picture of the struggle between the profane and the sacred" throughout history. However, that narrative commentary would not easily hold sway, for 1940 audiences certainly could not help but see in this depiction something more: suggestions of that other "struggle" between Nazi Germany and its neighbors then being played out in European landscapes like the one envisioned here. So, while Chernabog begins as a naturalized figure, even an archetypal one, he easily slips out of the narrative's confining impulse and into a pointedly metaphoric representation of the period's inescapable real-world concerns, while reminding us of just how slippery—or multiple—all representation can be.

That struggle, moreover, is depicted not simply in the sort of *approximate* realism that marks *The Goddess of Spring*. Rather, like much of *Fantasia*—and we might especially note the film's opening sequence which translates both musical instruments and their sounds into abstract patterns in space—"Night on Bald Mountain" is itself a highly stylized narrative, one that, despite its readily recognizable pattern of conflict, both earthly and spiritual, further pulls the narrative in a modernist direction, while troubling conventional representation. As noted above, the sequence opens on a note of stark and disturbing transformation, as the peak of "Bald Mountain" slowly changes into the devil's upper torso, as if he were there all along, a kind of unseen evil that is part of the earth and part of human life, simply waiting for darkness to reveal himself and exercise his powers. With his horns, bull-like face, massive bat wings, and muscular, human-looking upper torso, he seems a nightmarish amalgam, unlike any previous Disney depictions of the devil. In summoning his worshippers, Chernabog morphs into a series of shadowy tentacles, reaching down into an expressionistically styled village whose houses, churches, half-ruined structures, and grave markers angle, twist, and turn, as if suggesting the tortured souls he is calling forth. And in the sequence's longest scene, after Chernabog gathers some of these figures and casts them into fires burning inside the mountain, he takes up a handful of the flames and transforms that formless matter, first into dancing maidens, then into beasts, and finally into multiform goblins and small devils. In all of these actions, Chernabog seems to preside over—and clearly embodies—a world of change and transformation, an unpredictable chaos of "overturning and provisionality," not unlike the vision of earthquakes, dinosaur combat, and volcanic eruptions depicted in *Fantasia's* equally famous "Rite of Spring" sequence.

While that image of the devil here is, on one level, fairly realistically conceived—in terms of the obvious, even human musculature, of heft, and even of an emotional sense, as he clearly takes pleasure in his infernal creations, as well as in his ability to destroy them—it is more a distorted realism at work. For despite those superficial effects, Chernabog is pointedly a product of caricature and exaggeration. To assist the studio's artists in capturing human-like movements, Disney brought in various actors and filmed them going through the actions and adopting the poses of many of *Fantasia's* characters. However, the live-action reference provided to chief animator Bill Tytla, who had been tasked with animating the most dramatic of these figures, Chernabog, was not just an actor but rather a figure tightly bound to a world of caricature and

Drawing on Slavic myth: Chernabog in Disney's *Fantasia*.

overstatement, famed horror film star Bela Lugosi, who, following his success in *Dracula* (1931), had figured in a long line of fantasy, horror, and mystery films—and whom Disney had already broadly caricatured in 1933's *Mickey's Gala Premiere*. In keeping with that convention-bound character, Lugosi was, as biographer Arthur Lennig offers, "photographed . . . with swirling cape and outstretched hypnotic hands so that animators could reproduce his gestures" in all of their exaggerated, if easily recognizable, form.[19] The plan, it seems, was to present this devil not just with some realistic characteristics but in a very familiar context, his subversive potential tied to but also effectively tamed by common movie conventions, thus fitting him within a conservative-modernist mold.

And yet what Lugosi brought to the depiction of Chernabog cannot be so simply accounted for. While Lugosi himself has described his efforts as the sort of exaggerated "histrionics" for which he was so well known,[20] Tytla would claim that he found those affected poses and actions inconsistent with his own emerging vision of the figure, and that, instead, he turned to sequence director Wilfred Jackson as a more useful, genuinely affecting, and even more "human" visual model.[21] However, the resulting animated character is multiform,

modeled dramatically, marked by burning eyes, dark shadows, and unnatural lighting. In effect, Chernabog seems to have been born out of several very
different conceptions of the character, certainly one partly human in shape
but another of exaggerated gestures and even some of those residual movie
conventions. While not at all parodic in nature as in *The Goddess of Spring*—
and as it might have seemed if simply styled after Lugosi—this devil is multiply conceived, an image of both *unsettling* and *unsettled* nature, and ultimately
a rather subversive vision of the world and of human nature.

More a combination of human and demon, of the real and the conventional than any earlier Disney conceptions, Chernabog might be seen as
underscoring the rather devilish difficulties the studio was beginning to have
in presenting this sort of unsettling figure, especially at a time when war fears
were starting to settle on the country and to color audience perceptions. While
quite literally naturalized—as a transformation of the mountain—Chernabog
finally has nothing of the comic or even the parodic about him, his powers are
violently even cruelly manifested, and his shifting shape is disturbing. His
seeming control over nature, assault on the sleeping village, and tormenting
of dead souls all point to the sort of "dissolution of conventional reality"
linked to the modernist spirit, although without the potential for positive
change also often associated with that spirit. While escaping, both stylisti-
cally and thematically, the compromising confines of a conservative modernist vision, this devil simply suggests a violent potential for change, stripped of
reason or purpose.

Perhaps the difficulty of dealing with this figure shows just as clearly in the
way that *Fantasia* concludes—by grafting a separate musical sequence onto
"Night on Bald Mountain" in what seems an effort to allay its powerfully disturbing vision. The sequence ends with the distant sounds of a church bell
ringing and then a hint of dawn's light, sending the skeletons, ghosts, and
spirits of every sort retreating back to the expressionistically styled village, the
earth, and the graves from which Chernabog had summoned them, and with
the devil then turning away as well, back to his rocky lair/mountain disguise.
A dissolve then leads into the film's concluding sequence, a processional of
people carrying lights, or more accurately, *embodied* as lights, across a bridge
and through a highly stylized yet three-dimensional forest, another strange
combination of realistic and fantastic impulses.[22] That movement eventuates
in a vision of the sunrise, of natural light returning to the world, accompanied
by the strains of Schubert's "Ave Maria." This final sequence seems almost
forcibly attached to "Night on Bald Mountain," as if the power of the previous vision needed some external counter, an alternative possibility for
change in contrast to the frightening transformations wrought by Chernabog,

a suggestion of hope, even the eventual triumph of good and light, in that struggle with a powerful evil. And certainly, it strikes a note of hope amidst the world's new conflict. Yet the image of Chernabog remained one of the most memorable and often commented upon of those in the film—a power that we might see underscored by Disney's recent announcement of plans to capitalize on what a commentator allows is one of the studio's "darkest characters" by producing a live-action movie based on "Night on Bald Mountain."[23]

Of course, Disney has a long-standing reputation for producing such memorable villains, as evidenced by its many witches, wicked stepmothers, cursed pirates, etc. But these figures have all been fairly easily contained within the sort of fairy-tale framework that has become a hallmark of later studio efforts. And in more recent years and the few instances in which it has returned to this figure, Disney has even found a way to frame its devils in a purely comic context, as evidenced by films like *The Devil and Max Devlin* (1981) and the classically sourced villain Hades of *Hercules* (1997), as well as the game world of *Kingdom Hearts* (2002) wherein Chernabog has found yet another role. But in an earlier era, and before Disney had become bound to such formulaic presentations, the shadow of modernism lingered over Disney animation, allowing it to explore and exploit the highly resonant figure of Satan, one that still evoked some of the exciting provisionality associated with the new art of animation, while at least partially resisting a general industry tendency toward a conservative modernism.

In the quite literally subverted world of Depression- or early war-era America, the Disney films of this period had in Satan or his various menacing stand-ins such as Pluto, Chernabog, and various smaller devils, made-to-order representation for an obviously, on many levels, bedeviled world, one that the modernist impulse suggests needed to be seen in all of its failings and uncertainties. If Disney works such as *Hell's Bells*, *The Goddess of Spring*, and *Fantasia's* "Night on Bald Mountain" sequence suggest to some critics the studio's all-too-careful stance, its "sellout" of animation's challenging stylistic-cum-political possibilities, to others they simply indicate that Disney's films were, like most animated efforts of the period, largely compromises, naturalizations, as Wells offers, of a subversive spirit that ran through all such works in the early years of American animation. However, both views are finally rather essentialist ones, efforts at making the body of Disney animation fit within an account that views it in a conservative, naturalistic, and unchallenging light, as entertainments without much real bite.

But Disney's devils, I would suggest, can help us see a range of effects that also trouble any simple account. While a film like *The Goddess of Spring* most nearly fits within that conservative modernist mold Wells offers, even managing to contain—or blunt—the narrative's original parodic thrust, both *Hell's Bells* and *Fantasia*'s "Night on Bald Mountain," at opposite ends of a troubled decade, push beyond such categories. Both offer visions of a contingent world, suggest normally unseen forces at work, and even toy with the nature of representation—especially as Chernabog molds and remolds human spirits into, by turns, attractive and grotesquely misshapen forms for his own amusement—which was also, after a fashion, precisely what the Disney animators did to craft their Chernabog. And while *Hell's Bells* leaves viewers with an unsettling sense of instability, as when a serpent becomes a bat, and eaters, including Satan himself, become the eaten, "Night on Bald Mountain" finds that same instability in the natural world, embodied in the mountain-devil Chernabog. These films—and their devils—point to a level on which a particular Disney text not only might oscillate between subversive and conservative principles but also suggests a larger pattern of oscillation between works, as different stylistic and thematic elements surface in Disney animation during this late modernist period. Disney's devils simply point up the range of possibilities that remained at work in its animation, certainly well into the war years, as the chaotic world envisioned in a film like *The Three Caballeros* (1945) might suggest. The modernist spirit that drove early animation, that informed both style and characters at Disney and elsewhere, that even led Walter Benjamin to praise Mickey Mouse cartoons as works that "disavow experience more radically than [films] ever before" (20), lingered at the Disney studio, even today bedeviling our efforts at creating a simple conservative account of its output.

Notes

1. Esther Leslie, *Hollywood Flatlands: Animation, Critical Theory and the Avant-Garde* (London: Verso, 2002), 149.

2. Paul Wells, *Animation and America* (New Brunswick, NJ: Rutgers University Press, 2002), 28.

3. James Hillman, *The Dream and the Underworld* (New York: Harper and Row, 1979), 49.

4. Leslie, *Hollywood Flatlands*, 49.

5. Stefan Kanfer, *Serious Business: The Art and Commerce of Animation in America, From Betty Boop to "Toy Story"* (New York: Da Capo Press, 1997), 15.

6. Donald Crafton, *Before Mickey: The Animated Film, 1898–1928* (Chicago: University of Chicago Press, 1993), 4.

7. Bruno Latour, *We Have Never Been Modern*, trans. Catherine Porter (Cambridge, MA: Harvard University Press, 1993), 2.

8. Anthony Vidler, *Warped Space: Art, Architecture, and Anxiety in Modern Culture* (Cambridge, MA: MIT Press, 2000), 3.

9. Wells, *Animation and America*, 27.

10. Leonard Martin, *Of Mice and Magic: A History of Animated Cartoons*, rev. ed. (New York: Plume, 1987), 35.

11. Wells, *Animation and America*, 28.

12. I take these budget figures from Michael Barrier's authoritative history of the Hollywood cartoon. He notes that while other Disney cartoons of 1934 had effectively doubled the typical working budget of those done in 1933, *The Goddess of Spring* was still a third higher in cost than others done in 1934. See Michael Barrier, *Hollywood Cartoons: American Animation in Its Golden Age* (Oxford: Oxford University Press, 1999), 106 and 123.

13. Frank Thomas and Ollie Johnston, *Disney Animation: The Illusion of Life* (New York: Abbeville, 1981), 109.

14. Barrier, *Hollywood Cartoons*, 124.

15. Barrier, 124.

16. We might note that the Fleischer studio had already made this association multiple times, inserting both live performances and rotoscoped images of Calloway into a number of cartoons in which Betty Boop visits the underworld: *Minnie the Moocher* (1932), *Snow White* (1933), and *The Old Man of the Mountain* (1933). In the sort of cross-studio imitation that most commentaries have overlooked, *The Goddess of Spring* seems to have been consciously evoking these recent efforts by Disney's primary competitor.

17. Thomas and Johnston, two of Disney's famed "nine old men," describe this directive in their *Disney Animation: The Illusion of Life*. They, as well as the animators involved in *The Goddess of Spring*, believed that "Walt was thinking ahead to *Snow White*" and the problems of human animation that film would pose. See Thomas and Johnston, *Disney Animation*, 109.

18. Bosley Crowther, *"Fantasia,"* *New York Times*, November 14, 1940, accessed February 3, 2016, https://www.nytimes.com/1940/11/14/archives/the-screen-in-review -walt-disneys-fantasia-an-exciting-new.html.

19. Arthur Lennig, *The Immortal Count: The Life and Films of Bela Lugosi* (Lexington: University Press of Kentucky, 2010), 307.

20. William M. Kaffenberger and Gary D. Rhodes, *Bela Lugosi in Person* (Albany, GA: BearManor Media, 2015), 198.

21. Thomas and Johnston, *Disney Animation*, 139.

22. While the Disney multiplane camera was used extensively on *Fantasia*— one cameraman noting that he "worked almost a year . . . 12 hours a day" shooting multiplane scenes for the film (Thomas and Johnston, 310)—this concluding scene is one of those in which its depth effects are most apparent and pointedly tied to the narrative. In this case a horizontal multiplane camera was employed to suggest human movement as mankind seemingly emerges from darkness and

confusion into light and clarity. For an explanation of this special horizontal camera's use in *Fantasia*, see Thomas and Johnston, *Disney Animation*, 264–265.

23. Kirsten Acuna, "Disney's Giving One of Its Darkest Characters—A Demon Gargoyle from 'Fantasia'—Its Own Movie," *Business Insider*, June 3, 2015, accessed February 5, 2016, https://www.businessinsider.com.au/disney-chernabog-live-action -movie-2015-6.

What's the Deal with the Devil?

The Comedic Devil in Four Films

Katherine A. Fowkes

While most people think of Satan as scary, several movies have used Satan as a vehicle for humor. As comedies, these movies provide a generic framework that defuses the diabolical in favor of a lighthearted approach to life's miseries and travails. In comedies like *Bedazzled* (Stanley Donen, 1967; Harold Ramis, 2000), *Oh, God! You Devil!* (Paul Bogart, 1984), and the comedy/musical *Damn Yankees* (George Abbott and Stanley Donen, 1958), the devil is both a tempter of the weak and a trickster character, who serves as the personification of everything evil or unpleasant. All four movies employ the notion of a contract between the devil and a clueless human who fails to read the fine print or else is tricked by clever loopholes (yes, as always, the devil is in the details). While *Damn Yankees* taps into a uniquely American fanaticism for baseball, the other movies highlight the scourges of modern-day life, suggesting that the devil is to blame for everything from war and pollution to more trivial annoyances like parking tickets and junk food. Linking all of the films is the insistence that one must be true to oneself. The devil trades in facades; authenticity is key to exorcizing his influence.

Emphasized in the comic movie, Satan is the very trickiness of the character, a fact that links some of the truly evil aspects of the devil to a more benign character of myth and folklore, namely that of the trickster. Variations of the trickster abound across time and cultures, but in most cases the trickster preys upon human (or animal) weaknesses with humorous results. The outcome is generally benign, and the portrayal is more of a cheeky conman rather than a force of unbridled evil and fear. Lewis Hyde establishes a link between the devil and tricksters but also points out this key difference when he writes, "The Devil is an agent of evil, but the trickster is *amoral*, not *immoral*."[1] Thus, while in these films, the devil *is* an agent of evil, the comedic approach and the generic assurance of a happy ending make his or her character closer to that of the trickster whose typically marginalized status requires an under-handed approach rather than an outright power grab. While the devil may be powerful, she or he has fallen from God's grace (hence "cast" out and margin-alized) and so in each of these movies supernatural power is ultimately insuf-ficient to thwart goodness, love, or God himself. And as with many tricksters, in these movies, the devil is himself eventually tricked or outwitted, echoing a strand of the trickster tradition in which the character's mischievousness ultimately backfires.

All of the films can be seen as comic variations of the ubiquitous Faust myth, made perhaps most famous originally by Christopher Marlowe's play, *Doctor Faustus* (1594), which, according to Bronwyn Johnston, was one of the most "popular and influential plays of its time and spawned a series of devil dramas."[2] Other famous "spawns of Satan" include Johann Wolfgang von Goethe's two-part play, *Faust* (early 1800s), and Thomas Mann's *Doctor Faustus* (1947), in which a man makes a pact with the devil in order to find not just success, but also love. The two *Bedazzled* films likewise feature male charac-ters whose empty lives are only made worse by unrequited romantic/sexual obsessions with a female character. When the devil offers the protagonists seven wishes in exchange for their souls, each agrees, believing that he will succeed in winning the object of his affections. In *Oh, God! You Devil!* (henceforth *OGYD*), the main character, Bobby Shelton (Ted Wass) signs a contract guaranteeing him that in exchange for his soul, his languishing musi-cal career will finally take off in a spectacular way. And in *Damn Yankees*, an aging baseball fan, Joe Boyd (Robert Shafer), hopes for his team to finally beat those damn Yankees and win the Pennant. Joe gets in "league" with the devil (Ray Walston), making a deal that entails him taking the physical form of a whiz-kid baseball player, thereby making him the hero if the Senators win. Unfortunately, the devil has plans to disappoint Joe and all the rest of the Sen-ators' fans by ruining at the last minute what looks to be a sure win. Why? Because he's the devil and (as in all of these films), it's the devil's "job" to sow unhappiness.

Perhaps the most famous example of the Faust story is Goethe's version. As with Goethe's character Faust, the original *Bedazzled* features Stanley Moon (Dudley Moore) as a bored, frustrated, and suicidal character. His job as a fry-cook at a Wimpy Bar in London positions him to have a daily view of a statu-esque young waitress, Margaret Spencer (Eleanor Bron), whom Stanley clearly "moons for," as she utters such poetic gems as "Wimpy Burgers twice, one MR, one well, heavy on the onions." Thus, the humor begins, as the movie routinely pairs cosmic motifs with the utterly mundane. (Goethe's *Faust* features the character of Margarete—clearly a reference here, as in both cases the women represent impossible or doomed love.) Margaret is barely aware of Stanley's existence, and Stanley cannot even muster the courage to have a conversation with her. Stanley soon decides his life is not worth living. In these movies, the characters verbally ask for help in some way, either through a prayer or words that indicate that the character would "do anything" to get what they want. While Stanley unwittingly alerts the devil by praying to God in church, it is Stanley's botched suicide attempt that cues the devil to make his entrance: "Good Evening," says Mr. George Spiggott, aka the devil. "I couldn't help noticing that you were making an unsuccessful suicide bid." Of course, as Mr. Spiggott points out to Stanley, "You realize that suicide's a criminal offense. In less enlightened times they'd have hung you for it." Yes, a bit ironic. A further irony is that suicide is itself often considered an unpardonable sin in Christian and other religious traditions.[3] Thus, if Stanley had succeeded, he would have been effectively damned to Hell without the "help" of the devil's wishes.

In many versions of *Faust*, the main character acts out of overreaching ambition and hubris. But in these films, the main characters' dreams and desires are seen as reasonable. Their inability to realize their desire is due to circumstances or quite mundane human weakness. In each case, the protagonists are portrayed sympathetically, and all are redeemed in the end. For example, in the original *Bedazzled*, Stanley appears to be a sweetheart, but he's too shy and inarticulate to woo Margaret, as is Elliot (Brendan Fraser) in the remake, where his pitiful attempts to attract Alison fail miserably. Elliot is also incredibly annoying, trying too hard to be funny and hip and in denial that he has no friends.[4] In *OGYD*, Bobby just wants to get a break so he can make a living and fulfill his dreams of being a professional musician. And he doesn't even realize he's making a deal with the devil (George Burns), so he is not "guilty" when he makes the poor decision to sign a contract with Satan. Finally, in *Damn Yankees*, Joe is portrayed as a wistful, disappointed sports fan whose poor decision is mitigated, at least somewhat, by the idea that his glory will extend to all the other loyal Senators fans and help an underdog team experience a feel-good triumph, the hallmark of so many other sports-themed movies.

The portrayal of Satan as a supernatural character who preys on human weakness became increasingly popular in the fifth century as the Christian church struggled to develop new converts and remove any taint of misfortune from God's ambit.[5] In doing so, they promoted a "vision of the Devil as a figure stalking humankind looking for each and every sign of a chink in the armor."[6] Likewise, despite the protagonists' benign motives, all of the movies show the devil monitoring earth for characters with a weakness to exploit. Both *OGYD* and the remake of *Bedazzled* portray this process quite literally on monitors or as movie or computer screens, as if the world were one giant reality show. *OGYD* shows the devil searching for possible victims on a screen in his car, while the remake of *Bedazzled* opens with a kind of *Koyaanisqatsi*-style, fast-paced montage of people and cars moving around their environments.[7] Periodic freeze-frames of people are accompanied by computer-like read-outs of hidden character traits such as "couch potato" or "horny"—all as if detected from a vantage point on high. The sped-up camera work makes a point about fast-paced modern life as well as suggesting that we are but mosquitoes who live and die in a short time frame compared to the devil's eternity. In addition, it once again suggests that the devil finds his victims specifically by searching for character flaws, frequently portrayed as a kind of hypocrisy, with a freeze-frame of a cowboy at a rodeo accompanied by the moniker "vegetarian" or a person labeled "environmentalist" caught in the act of littering. When Elliot racks up a ridiculously large number of weaknesses ("desperate," "lonely," "doormat," etc.), the devil knows she has a sucker to exploit.[8] (Note that this is one of the few movies featuring a female devil, played by Elizabeth Hurley.)

All four movies feature the protagonists in alternate universes that represent their wish or wishes. In *Damn Yankees* and *OGYD*, the characters experience a single alternate scenario to correspond with their one wish. But both versions of *Bedazzled* use the characters' seven wishes to create alternate universes in which the actors can showcase their acting talents to play different characters in what essentially amounts to "skits" about insufficiently specific wishes. (Note that Moore and Cooke were known for their sketch comedy, influencing the likes of Monty Python and others.) For example, besides playing Stanley as a sincere nebbish, Dudley Moore gets to variously play a pretentious aesthete, a rich art lover, a loving husband and father, a rock star, and a nun. (Yes, a nun.) And he even voices an animated fly on the wall of the morgue where the police are expecting to find Stanley's body after reading his suicide note.

In each "skit," the devil creates a scenario where Stanley's wish is fulfilled to the letter, but not the spirit of the law. For example, in one scenario he fails to get into Margaret's pants during a hot date, despite impressing her with his wished-for superior intellect and newfound ability to be articulate. He flings himself at her, mistakenly believing her to be a free spirit who appreciates spontaneous sex. But when she screams rape, he realizes he must revise his next wish to be more specific. The next time, he therefore attempts to ensure his complete license to bed Margaret by specifying that he will be married to her, and that he will be rich and successful to boot. Of course, having a marriage license doesn't ensure reciprocated lust. Thus, upon magically arriving at this wish-scenario, Stanley finds that he is, indeed, married to Margaret and lives in a beautiful mansion surrounded by lush grounds. Unfortunately, Margaret and some young fellow—aptly named "Randy"—completely ignore Stanley and are practically in full "snog" at every moment, their hands running constantly up and down each other's bodies. Stanley tries in vain to get Margaret's attention by trotting out newly purchased expensive art works and luxurious furs, but Margaret only has eyes (and body) for her illicit Adonis.

What to do? The devil knows full well that none of Stanley's wishes will pan out and so instructs him to "blow a raspberry" whenever he wants to return to his former state. A similar situation occurs in the remake, where Elliot has the wisdom to specify that he's not only to be rich but actually married to Alison. As in the original, Elliot learns that not only is Alison having a steamy affair with her English tutor, but that she actually despises Elliot. Furthermore, Elliot's vast wealth derives from the fact that he is now a Columbian drug lord who has pissed off his heavily armed Russian clients who are suddenly trying to kill him. As in the original, Elliot is given a method of "escape" (kind of like a "safe" word, or perhaps it's the Satan Clause). All he has to do is type "666" into a pager in order to be returned to "normal" and try again to devise a wish with no loopholes.

Except for *Damn Yankees*, the films feature an oft-used trope of Satan as a fallen angel in a cosmic struggle or wager with God. In *Bedazzled*, the devil is trying to gain more souls than God in order to win his bet that he can thoroughly screw up the world, despite God's power. *OGYD* makes an explicit connection between this cosmic bet and ordinary gambling. The movie begins with a character praying to God to save his sick young son (Bobby as a child). As the boy lies feverishly sweating in bed, his father sings him a song from *Guys and Dolls*, "I've got the horse right here, His name is Paul Revere. . . . Can do, Can do." The movie ends with George Burns cast as both God and the devil in a Las Vegas casino, playing a game of poker in which the fate of Bobby's soul is at stake. It seems that Bobby had persuaded the devil to agree to only a trial period in his contract thus creating a gray area in which the forces of dark and light can once more become part of a wager. If the devil wins the hand, he gets to keep Bobby's soul and all the others he has already won. If God wins the hand, he gets Bobby's soul back, plus the protection of any other potential souls—even those who intentionally ask for the devil's help (unlike Bobby). The devil finds God's bet too rich and so folds his hand, thus forfeiting Bobby's soul. He then learns that God was actually bluffing. Oh God, you trickster! Although Bobby has just committed suicide in his hotel room through an overdose of pills, God saves him, bringing him back from a ghostly existence to explain that when Bobby's father had prayed, God had promised to look after Bobby throughout his life. (Note that by casting Burns in both roles, the film makes the point that God and the devil are often seen as two sides of the same cosmic coin.)

In all of these films, as in Goethe's *Faust*, the characters are saved from damnation by the films' conclusion. In the original *Bedazzled*, the devil ends up with more than enough souls to win his bet, and so returns Stanley's in a magnanimous gesture, hoping to recover God's favor and be returned to his rightful place beside God in heaven. Unfortunately, he then has the audacity to gloat: "I've done a good deed. I gave that little twit his soul back. Wasn't that generous? Made me feel marvelous!" Even though the devil has technically won the bet, he is denied reentry to heaven because his gesture was done for the wrong reasons—for his own gratification. Thus, Stanley returns to normal and instead of being damned to Hell is now merely damned to work in the same old Wimpy Bar. In the remake, Elliot is released from his contract after the devil unsuccessfully tries to scare him by sending him to Hell (or the illusion of Hell) for refusing to make his final wish. Elliott is thus pressured into making a wish, but this time instead of trying to win Alison's love, he instead wishes for her to have a happy life, with or without him. Here, turn-about is fair play, and this selfless gesture is the loophole in his contract that allows Elliot to recoup his soul and return to his normal life. (As the devil explains, nobody ever reads the fine print!) In *Damn Yankees*, Joe has negotiated an escape clause that will let him return to normal if he exercises it by a certain date and time. Right before the final game, the devil is drugged to sleep by Lola (Gwen Verdon) who has come to love Joe despite her assignment to distract him with sex (to facilitate the devil's betrayal of Joe's wish). Upon awakening from his drugged stupor, the devil fears he may be too late, but just in the "old nick" of time, the devil arrives at the final game and turns the young Joe back into the old Joe, guessing that old Joe's body will not be up to the task. But, in fact, the old Joe manages to catch the fly ball that wins the game, and amid the commotion of the Senators' triumph, Joe succeeds in escaping unseen to return to his wife (Shannon Bolin), while the young Joe (or his body) simply disappears from whence he or it came. Yet, again, the devil's penchant for contracts backfires and the film concludes with him trying in vain to once again distract Joe from his life with Meg. (Note that the name Meg is another variation of Faust's Marguerite.)

While most obvious in the *Bedazzled* movies, all of the films conclude with a variation of the message that one should be true to oneself. Stanley may be stuck in a Wimpy Bar and ignored by Margaret, but he decides this "authentic" existence is preferable to deals with the devil. In the remake, this idea also returns us to the theme of the film's opening, where instead of seeming to be one thing—but really being another—as in the many hypocrites introduced as potential Satan-bait, Elliot now seems comfortable in his own skin. Gone are his many lame attempts to be cool, and the annoying aspects of his character fall away to reveal a genuinely nice and appealing guy. Although the devil has cheated him out of being with Alison, at the end of the film Elliott meets a young woman who physically resembles her (both played by Frances O'Connor), and the story ends with the prospect of their union and a happy love life for Elliot.

The association of being genuine and "authentic" is not just a feel-good "be true to oneself" moral (a message found in so many mainstream movies) but also reflects an association of "authenticity" and "individuality" with the idea of the soul. In this view, bodies are merely the receptacles of soul, so that the devil can cause the protagonists' outward appearances to transform (as in *Damn Yankees*), while preserving the idea that the characters have retained their "true selves." Thus, while the protagonists find themselves in alternative universes where they essentially "play" different people, it is understood that in each case, the original character (soul) is still temporarily alive and intact, albeit sometimes in a different body. Hence, in *Damn Yankees*, the aging protagonist is given the body of a young athlete (Tab Hunter) so that not only can the Senators win the Pennant but so that old Joe can still be the one to make it happen.

As in *Damn Yankees*, OGYD employs two actors to make the point that no matter what the body looks like, the soul remains the same. In a variation of bodily transformation, here Bobby is turned into an existing rock star, Billy Wayne. In this case, however, the actor playing Bobby continues to play the protagonist so there is no disconnect for the audience in what our protagonist looks like. Instead, he appears to have switched lives with the former Wayne (Robert Desiderio) whose seven-year contract with the devil has just expired. The record executives and fans, among others, now believe that Bobby is the same rock star they have previously known, just as the actor playing Billy at the beginning of the film now fills Bobby's shoes in his former life, no longer aware that he used to be somebody else.

While the concept of soul as separate from the body provides a handy device for creating alternate scenarios for the characters, changeable bodies are also associated with something devilish and unhuman. Thus, not only can the devil take different physical forms, but in *Damn Yankees* and OGYD, the metamorphosis of the protagonists' bodies is both a ratification of their soul remaining intact (confirmed when they return to their former selves) and the kind of abomination of physical mutation long associated with the devil. As Marina Warner describes in her discussion of the damned in Dante's *Inferno*, "In medieval eschatology, metamorphosis by almost any process belongs to the devil's party; devils, and their servants, witches, are monstrously hybrid themselves in form, and control magic processes of mutation."[9] Even in the two *Bedazzled*s, not all of the alternate characters rely solely on the acting skills of Moore and Fraser. In the original, Stanley is temporarily turned into a cartoon fly (hence a double transformation—from human to insect and from live action to animation). In the remake, it is easy to identify the actor, Fraser, in each scenario, and yet his physical appearance is usually altered significantly as well. For example, his hair and the shape of his nose change when he becomes a Columbian drug lord, and his hair and his height change radically when he becomes a basketball player (as does the size of his penis, which the devil shrinks as part of her trick to make Elliot unattractive to Alison).

At the end of the film, Elliot doesn't magically win Alison's love but he *does* meet someone to whom he's immediately attracted to, as if there are different versions of Alison roaming around the world. This "doppelgänger" idea often plays into an eerie or uncanny feeling in movies but here it also taps into another facet of the body/soul conundrum that perhaps we are *not* unique individuals, but part of a larger cosmic play of bodies and souls. If "all the world's a stage," then here we might say that part of the "play" is this very interrogation of authenticity versus role playing, made so obvious in the original *Bedazzled* by the "skit" feeling of each alternate scenario. Just as acting is a kind of pretense or illusion, one can alternately see changes in physical appearance not as metamorphosis but as illusions, another common association with the devil's trickiness, and one featured in Goethe's version of *Faust* where the devil is not the all-powerful deity he seems and thus must resort to illusions for his trickery.

Another aspect of soul relates to music. In Thomas Mann's version of the Faust legend, Faust worries that he lacks a soul and so makes a pact with the devil in order to overcome what he perceives to be sterility in his music.[10] Here the idea of soulful music is equated with the cosmic notion of soul. So, in an ironic twist, the musician in OGYD seeks to acquire "soulful" success via a pact usually associated with *losing* one's soul. In Mann's *Faust*, the devil does not actually want Faust's soul. Instead, the pact consists of depriving Faust of love.

As we have seen, romantic love as well as sexuality and sexual attraction are components of these films. As in *Damn Yankees*, in *OGYD* Bobby is redeemed and ultimately saved by his preexisting love for his wife. This is so even though Bobby is shown enjoying his "montage" of drunken one-night stands with young female groupies. It is finally upon learning that his wife, Wendy (Roxanne Hart), is pregnant with his child that Bobby definitively realizes that he wishes to return to his old life. In *Damn Yankees*, however, Joe resists Lola's seduction, which is precisely why she comes to love him and betrays the devil, facilitating Joe's return to his wife.

In Goethe's *Faust*, Faust is a magician and scholar who wishes for knowledge to surpass his own limited abilities. Although in the movies discussed here, the main characters' desires seem more personal and unique to each situation, each personal dilemma is nevertheless inflected by the cultural milieu in which it appears. For example, the bargain in *Damn Yankees* is linked not just to a desire for youth and success, but to the idea that baseball is a potent symbol of US patriotism and evidence of the American Dream in action, where a talented kid from middle-America can become an overnight success. Patriotism and American can-do optimism appear in other movies that also suffuse baseball with supernatural elements such as *The Natural* (1984; ironically, not "Super-natural"), or *Field of Dreams* (1989). All three films reference the real-life Shoeless Joe Jackson, accused of throwing the 1919 World Series between the White Sox and the Cincinnati Reds. (Note that the devils in the comedies discussed here wear red, and the male devils wear red socks.) In *Damn Yankees*, not only is the young Joe referred to as "Shoeless Joe, from Hannibal MO," but when the devil realizes that the Senators are on their way to winning the Pennant, he attempts to ruin Joe's reputation by planting the notion that Joe is an infamous, corrupt player now operating under a pseudonym. *Damn Yankees* thus features a recurring tension between the characterization of baseball as a noble and almost mythic pastime, versus a potentially ruthless sport that tempts players to win unfairly, as in *Damn Yankees*, or for players to accept bribes to affect the outcome, as occurs to Roy Hobbs in *The Natural*, and in *Field of Dreams* (where Shoeless Joe's reputation is eventually redeemed).

While the sports metaphor in *Damn Yankees* provides a distinctly American version of success, in all of the movies discussed here, personal motivations (career success, desire for sex, love, and fame) are deeply imbricated in the ills of the modern industrialized world in more diverse ways.[11] In these films, we find explicit as well as implicit critiques of modern capitalistic enterprises, including the scourges of pollution, excessive and unbridled capitalism, and mass media and celebrity culture. Indeed, as Inez Hedges writes, while modern society places little stock in an actual devil, the phrase Faustian bargain still "seems to explain how success, power, and celebrity function."[12] For example, in OGYD Bobby erroneously believes that the devil is a music agent, a mistake to which the movie gives a sly nod when the devil alludes to the fact that most of the biggest rock stars have actually achieved their success only by making a deal with him. In *Damn Yankees*, the devil variously takes credit for crooked politicians and parking lot owners (not to mention seduced husbands), and harnesses sensational newspaper headlines about Joe's talent to stoke the Senator-fans' optimism. In the original *Bedazzled*, one of Stanley's wishes turns him into a televised rock star whose lyrics ("Love me!") and body language reflect his need for adoration. At first, he is surrounded by hysterical female fans, including Margaret. But in a commentary on both gender and fame, the devil steals the show with his own performance. He's so hip and cool that he shuns his female audience with his misanthropic and misogynistic lyrics ("I don't need you." "You fill me with inertia"), while his female backup singers whip the fans into a frenzy with the phrase, "You drive me wild!" Of course, being unattainable makes him much more desirable to Margaret and the other fans who immediately abandon the groveling and too-desperate Stanley. Raspberry!

As alluded to earlier, much of the humor in these movies comes from reenvisioning ancient notions of God and Satan in modern-day settings. Hence, as mentioned, the devil appears as a music agent in OGYD and as a baseball player's manager in *Damn Yankees*. Since the devil is known for his supernatural cleverness, it might be surprising that at the beginning of OGYD, "Mr. Tophet" uses a rather banal trick to demonstrate his devilish powers to Bobby at a wedding where Bobby has reluctantly accepted a gig. While the viewers see that a woman's escargots have magically come alive as squirming slugs, Bobby primarily witnesses a series of easily explained mishaps, beginning with the woman's scream, followed by a waiter's trousers falling down. This causes a chain reaction that results in the bride and groom falling into the swimming pool. Thus, Bobby remains understandably skeptical of the devil's so-called powers even though he cannot explain how Tophet's business card has responded to his remark that he must be "flipping out" by magically producing the words "You're not flipping out," when Bobby flips the card over.[13]

Likewise, in both versions of *Bedazzled*, the devil does his dirty work in distinctly modern, but often very pedestrian contexts—causing parking meters to expire, for example. It is in part, the mundane nature of these annoying pranks that creates humor. What we would expect to be a powerful, supernatural force of evil, is here often just the cause of pesky annoyances. This incongruity illustrates a widely believed theory of comedy that simple incongruities can cause humor.[14] Furthermore, in *Bedazzled*, while the devil can cause parking meters to expire with a magical snap of the fingers, many times the devil works his mischief the old-fashioned human way, such as physically scratching vinyl records or tearing out the last pages of mystery novels, as occurs in the original version. At the beginning of the movie, Stanley wishes for a demonstration of the devil's power and wishes for a Frobisher and Gleason raspberry ice pop—a rather silly and unambitious wish, fulfilled by having them jump on a bus in order to buy one. To make it funnier, the devil hits Stanley up for the requisite six pence. In the remake, the devil takes Elliot on a bus ride to a McDonald's to get him a hamburger and likewise stiffs him for the cost. In the original, when the devil finally does use his magical powers to instantly whisk Stanley to another location, Stanley remarks that his ice pop has melted. "You really *must* be the devil," he mutters pathetically, another instance of pairing devilish intent with a simple annoyance. In the remake, Elliot takes a jab at unhealthy fast food when he says of his Big Mac and Coke, "This truly is the work of the devil." Notably, in both movies we revisit the joke that the devil grants wishes through simple human methods when on their last wish the protagonists learn that they have already used up their seven wishes. As it turns out, despite the lack of any magic, the devil has counted the ice pop and the hamburger as the first of the seven wishes, thus actually making the first wish the final trick.

Both versions of *Bedazzled* and OGYD explicitly reference modern industrial and commercial culture along with its attendant environmental costs. In OGYD, near the end of the film when God gives Bobby a cosmic sign that he's listening to Bobby's prayers, he creates a rainbow outside of Bobby's hotel window. Bobby is alarmed when it disappears, fearing that God has left him, but God explains that he's just "saving on energy," a phrase very much of its historical moment. And when the devil loses his bet with God at the end of the original *Bedazzled*, he angrily threatens revenge in the form of more highways, more fast-food restaurants, and more pollution: "All right, you great git," he snarls at God, "You've asked for it. I'll cover the world in Tastee-Freez and Wimpy Burgers. I'll fill it with concrete runways, motorways, aircraft, television, automobiles, advertising, plastic flowers, frozen food and supersonic bangs. I'll make it so noisy and disgusting that even you'll be ashamed of yourself! No wonder you've so few friends; you're unbelievable!" In another scene, the devil explains how hard and interminable his task on earth has been, saying: "There was a time when I used to get lots of ideas. . . . I thought up the Seven Deadly Sins in one afternoon. The only thing I've come up with recently is advertising." While funny, the logic is also undeniable in suggesting that the devil could be responsible for an industry designed explicitly to tempt people and prey on their weakness.

In the original *Bedazzled*, the Seven Deadly Sins are also personified as the devil's helpers ("What terrible sins I have working for me. I suppose it's the wages"). Not only is advertising linked to the devil, but it turns out that his lawyer also happens to be the sin, Sloth, yet again pairing this age-old concept of sin with a modern suspicion of lawyers. We also see Anger as a burly bouncer at the devil's nightclub, and Gluttony stuffing her face on a carnival ride. Continuing the emphasis on sex as a powerful persuader, the devil tempts Stanley with Lust, "the babe with the bust," played by Raquel Welch, a cameo that plays upon her iconic status as a sex symbol. The devil quips that she's due down at the Foreign Office, thus taking a swipe at modern-day politics.

So, what's the deal with the devil? Even though all of these movies feature the devil as the personification of many ills—both large and small—all of them also implicitly or explicitly throw the ball back to ordinary humans by emphasizing that humans can make their own heaven or hell here on earth depending on the choices they make. Trying to be something you are not or to take shortcuts toward realizing your dreams is an invitation to the devil. Your best "bet" instead is to be true to yourself.

Notes

1. Lewis Hyde, *Trickster Makes This World: Mischief, Myth, and Art* (New York: North Point Press, 1998), 10.

2. Bronwyn Johnston, "Mephistopheles," in *The Ashgate Encyclopedia of Literary and Cinematic Monsters*, ed. Jeffrey Andrew Weinstock (Burlington, VT: Ashgate, 2014), 408.

3. For example, in the Christian tradition, in the fifth century, Saint Augustine declared suicide to be a sin of such seriousness that it would preclude a person's entrance into heaven.

4. In fact, the same could be said about Fraser's performance. Compared to Moore's understated performance, Fraser seems to be trying a bit too hard, often making his performance just as annoying as his character.

5. Peter Stanford, *The Devil* (New York: Henry Holt, 1996), 95.

6. Stanford, 109.

7. *Koyaanisqatsi* (Godfrey Reggio, 1982) is an independent film that uses a variety of cinematic techniques, including a sped-up camera to suggest that the modern, urban world is a "life out of balance," the meaning of the title word in Hopi.

8. While outside of the focus of this essay, it is interesting to observe that this is one of the few movies featuring a female devil, played here by Elizabeth Hurley.

What this highlights is the irony that, while the devil is associated with all things conventionally regarded as evil and taboo, these representations nevertheless have almost always been managed within a heterosexual framework—and one that typically avoids sexualizing the devil himself.

9. Marina Warner, *Fantastic Metamorphoses, Other Worlds* (Oxford: Oxford University Press, 2004), 35. Note that when Lola betrays him, the devil changes her appearance back to her formerly ugly self. While it seems as if she had sold her soul (having been working with the devil for centuries), she continues to root for Joe, hence an anomaly in the association of soul with one's "true" inner self.

10. Inez Hedges, *Framing Faust: Twentieth-Century Cultural Struggles* (Carbondale: Southern Illinois University Press, 2005), 55.

11. The other three movies are all set in large cities. The original *Bedazzled* is set primarily in London, whereas the remake is set in San Francisco. *OGYD* is set in Los Angeles.

12. Hedges, *Framing Faust*, 10.

13. The devil's business card reads Harry O. Tophet, the initials spelling "hot," while Tophet means Hell in Hebrew. In all of these movies, the devil introduces him- or herself with a business card. In *Damn Yankees*, the devil calls himself Mr. Applegate, perhaps a reference to the Garden of Eden.

14. While originally attributed to Kant and Schopenhauer, Marta Dynel notes that for theories of humor "most researchers concur that the main prerequisite is incongruity." See Marta Dynel, "Paragmatics and Linguistic Research into Humour," in *The Pragmatics of Humour Across Discourse Domains*, ed. Marta Dynel (Amsterdam: John Benjamins Publishing Company, 2011), 3.

His Father's Eyes: *Rosemary's Baby*

David Sterritt

Pray for Rosemary's Baby

—PARAMOUNT PICTURES

Satan is not among the dramatis personae named in the end credits of *Rosemary's Baby*, the classic 1968 movie adapted by writer-director Roman Polanski from Ira Levin's bestselling 1967 novel. The devil appears in only one scene, and even there he is pictured in fleeting, fragmented shots—first his monstrous hands and long-nailed fingers, then part of his face, and finally his piercing, slitted eyes—as he rapes the drugged, barely conscious Rosemary in order to impregnate her with a new embodiment of the ultimate evil that Satan has long stood for in the Western imagination. The eyes reappear in a quick, ghostly image when Rosemary gets her first glimpse of the baby near the end of the drama, but apart from these brief apparitions the face of evil stays modestly off the screen.

While he is elusive as a material presence, however, the Prince of Darkness is definitely not absent from Polanski's elegantly constructed film, in which every element contributes to the central idea that a physical reincarnation of the devil is entering our fallen world. Satan is the spirit presiding over the story, and he deserves much credit for its popularity. In fiction as in life, evil generally outpaces good in evoking strong intellectual and emotional responses. Just as the sinners and tortures on display in Dante's formidable *Inferno* have transfixed immeasurably more readers than their beatific opposites in the *Paradiso*, the thrillingly malevolent *Rosemary's Baby* was the bestselling horror novel of its decade, and the movie version became the

eighth-highest grosser of 1968, attracting a larger audience than such con-
ventional crowd pleasers as Franklin J. Schaffner's science-fiction epic
Planet of the Apes and Anthony Harvey's historical biopic *The Lion in Winter*.
Satan sells.

The Story

> Rosemary and Guy Woodhouse had signed a lease on a five-room
> apartment in a geometric white house on First Avenue when they
> received word, from a woman named Mrs. Cortez, that a four-room
> apartment in the Bramford had become available.
>
> LEVIN, *ROSEMARY'S BABY*[1]

Rosemary Woodhouse (Mia Farrow) is a bright, energetic young woman who
moved from the Midwest to Manhattan in search of contentment as a home-
maker and mother, readily finding the former role and hoping the latter will
soon follow. Her husband, Guy Woodhouse (John Cassavetes), is an actor
whose semi-promising career in commercials, television shows, and plays—on
Broadway he understudied Albert Finney in John Osborne's *Luther* and
appeared in Ronald Alexander's *Nobody Loves an Albatross*—has yet to produce steady employment or professional security. The young couple gets what
appears to be a lucky break when a roomy apartment becomes available in a
venerable apartment building called the Bramford, where an eighty-nine-year-
old tenant named Mrs. Gardenia has died after lying for weeks in a coma.
Inspecting the flat, Rosemary and Guy observe a few eccentric touches, such
as black curtains on the living-room window and a heavy piece of furniture
blocking a hallway closet, but the place impresses them with its spaciousness
and gravitas, and they seize the opportunity to rent it.

Signing the lease means overlooking two causes for concern: the sizable
cost of renting the place, and the anxiety expressed by their writer friend
Hutch (Maurice Evans), who warns them that the Bramford has a sinister history replete with pitch-dark doings. Its occupants have included the Trench
sisters, described by Hutch as "two proper Victorian ladies who . . . cooked and
ate several young children, including a niece," and Adrian Marcato, a practitioner of witchcraft who "made quite a splash in the eighteen-nineties by
announcing that he had succeeded in conjuring up the living Satan." Displaying "a handful of hair and some claw-parings" to prove his claim, Marcato
stirred up an angry mob that "attacked and nearly killed him in the Bramford
lobby," and although Rosemary discovers later that the attack really happened
outside the Bramford, this still seems too close for comfort.[2] The building was

nicknamed the Black Bramford in the 1920s, Hutch adds, and its "ugly and unsavory happenings" have continued into recent times; a dead infant was found in the basement not long ago, and an above-average number of suicides have occurred within its walls.[3] Indeed, the newly available apartment is vacant because of the previous tenant's death.

Captivated nonetheless by the Bramford's nineteenth-century charm, Rosemary and Guy move in. Soon they meet their nearest neighbors, Roman and Minnie Castevet (Sidney Blackmer and Ruth Gordon), ingratiating old folks who have taken a troubled young woman named Terry Gionoffrio (Angela Dorian) under their wing. Terry praises Roman and Minnie to the skies when Rosemary befriends her in the Bramford's dank laundry room. A few days later, however, Terry dies in an apparently suicidal leap from a seventh-floor window, a disturbing sign that the Bramford's balefulness is undiminished; significantly enough, Rosemary and Guy first meet Roman and Minnie amid the streetside confusion caused by Terry's horrible plunge. On a brighter note, Guy gets a career-boosting part in a forthcoming play. But here, too, darkness intrudes, since he receives it only after the producers' first choice for the role inexplicably goes blind; pleased with his good fortune, Guy nonetheless acknowledges that this is "a hell of a way to get it." Far worse, Hutch falls gravely ill for no discernable reason, sinking into a prolonged and ultimately fatal coma, the same fate that befell the late Mrs. Gardenia.

Although the latter developments hint that Hutch's warnings about the Bramford have at least a modicum of truth, they don't prevent Rosemary and Guy from enjoying life in their apartment and friendship with the quaint old couple next door. Minnie plays the amiable busybody with nonstop energy, bustling about and insisting that Rosemary wear a charm laced with tannis root, previously worn by Terry and smelling so bad that Rosemary stashes it in a jewelry box. Roman grows equally close to Guy, professing familiarity with his acting work and praising its "interesting inner quality," a phrase so vague that it's fair to wonder if the old guy knows what he's talking about.

Propelled by the opportunity that arose when the other actor went blind, Guy's career takes off, gratifying his pride at the expense of his warmth toward Rosemary, who finds him more vain and distracted than in the past—until he morphs again, now into a lavishly loving husband who floods their home with roses, announces his wish to have a baby without delay, and even pinpoints the dates when Rosemary's ovulation will be at its peak. The romantic prelude to the first of these evenings—dinner, candlelight, the works—is interrupted by Minnie, who pops in with cups of "chocolate mousse" that Guy insists they eat despite the "chalky undertaste" that induces Rosemary to scrape most of it into her napkin when he isn't looking. She eats enough however—if she threw away all of her mousse, Rosemary would not be narcotized enough to suffer the devilish rape that follows later in the night. Eating part of the drug-laced dessert throws her mind and senses into a state between waking and dreaming, compounding the physical impact of the monstrous assault with profound psychological effects that haunt her until the end.

The die is now cast. Rosemary gets pregnant and Minnie takes charge, setting up the expectant mother as a patient of Abraham Sapirstein (Ralph Bellamy), supposedly the finest obstetrician in the city. The pregnancy is fraught with pain, uncertainty, and fear, however, and Rosemary can't help remembering that she conceived the child not in an act of romantic intimacy with Guy, as she had hoped and expected, but during a hallucinatory night plagued by nightmarish visions of a hideous ravisher. Belatedly receiving and studying a book that Hutch obtained for her before his death, she eventually realizes that she is being victimized by a coven of witches, and that everyone important to her—her husband, her neighbors, her physician—is in on the conspiracy. Most horribly of all, their machinations are focused on the fetus in her womb, the most precious thing in her life. The exact nature and objectives of their plot remain unclear until the baby is born, spirited away from Rosemary, and reintroduced as an uncanny being in a cradle decorated with funereal crepe and an inverted cross. Only then do the implications of the unspeakable scheme become evident in all their apocalyptic horror.

The Production

The motion-picture rights to Levin's novel were owned by William Castle, who produced the movie and thought of directing it until Paramount Pictures chief Robert Evans intervened in Polanski's favor—a timely maneuver, since one shudders to think what the auteur of *The Tingler* (1959) and *Zotz!* (1962) might have done with the crafty nuances and multilayered meanings of Levin's narrative. Polanski was a new arrival in Hollywood with only four modestly budgeted features to his credit, including the 1965 psychological horror film *Repulsion*, where he had shown a flair for pitch-dark realism; when writing the screenplay for *Rosemary's Baby* he stayed almost entirely faithful to the novel, consulting with Levin by telephone even when changing details as minor as colors in the décor.[4]

Paramount was hesitant to release the film when it was finished, uncertain how to sell a story of contemporary terror at a time when supernatural cinema was dominated by Edgar Allan Poe adaptations and thrillers about monsters and vampires. The uncertainty cleared when advertising executive Stephen

Frankfurt designed a promotional blitz spearheaded by an eerie green poster showing Mia Farrow's face over a silhouetted baby carriage on a desolate crag, photographed in Central Park but looking like a blasted heath in an H. P. Lovecraft story. The image and its tagline, "Pray for Rosemary's Baby," worked wonders, helping to parlay the movie's $2.3 million budget into domestic grosses more than fourteen times higher. The movie premiered in June 1968, a few months before George A. Romero's very different horror landmark *Night of the Living Dead*, and the confluence is significant: *Rosemary's Baby* was arguably classical horror's last great cinematic hurrah before zombies, slashers, and splatter took control of the asylum.

Even with those changes in the genre, Polanski's film exercised considerable influence on horror in years to come, priming audiences for subsequent productions about Satanic and demonic doings, such as Piers Haggard's *The Blood on Satan's Claw* and Gordon Hessler's *Cry of the Banshee* (both 1970), and about children possessed by spirits and devils, such as William Friedkin's *The Exorcist* (1973) and Richard Donner's *The Omen* (1976). Other works along these lines include Larry Cohen's *It's Alive* (1974), Lee Philips's television movie *The Stranger Within* (1974), and Donald Cammell's *Demon Seed* (1977), which puts a computerized spin on the notion of devilish impregnation.

Its excellence and influence notwithstanding, *Rosemary's Baby* had no worthy offspring of its own. Levin published a flatly titled sequel, *Son of Rosemary*, in 1997, recounting the further adventures of Rosemary, who comes out of a twenty-seven-year coma in 1999 to find that her baby, now a grown-up spiritual guru with legions of followers all over the world, still seems to be a chip off the old Satanic block, laying plans for the apocalypse and whiling away the meantime with incestuous passes at his mom. The novel ends with the hokiest plot cliché of them all, revealing that its entire narrative has been a dream, and that the entire narrative of the original *Rosemary's Baby* was a dream as well! It is a dreary read from start to finish.

The only other spinoff project worth mentioning is the eponymous remake of Polanski's film, directed by Agnieszka Holland as a two-part TV miniseries broadcast by NBC in 2014. A gifted and versatile filmmaker, Holland turns a well-crafted but uninspired teleplay by Scott Abbott and James Wong into a well-crafted but uninspired entertainment. The cast includes Zoe Saldana and Patrick J. Adams as Rosemary and Guy, supported by Carole Bouquet and Jason Isaacs as the Satanists next door. The setting is now Paris and Minnie's name is now Margaux; in other respects, the remake is just a retread, with little of the resonance that Polanski's keen audiovisual sense imparted to the original.

The Style

In keeping with its imaginatively Satanic content, Polanski's film plays imaginative Satanic games with its audience, alternately deploying and subverting the conventions undergirding mainstream cinema's reality effect. The prevailing style kicks in at the very beginning, when a leisurely pan over the rooftops of Manhattan, accompanied by a female voice humming a soothing lullaby, gradually turns into a downward tilt, leading to a vertiginous top-down view of the Victorian Gothic building where the story will take place. The film is "determinedly realistic," Mikita Brottman observes, citing its real-world references to Broadway shows, Pall Mall cigarettes, Yamaha motorcycles, *Time* magazine, and the TV show *Open End* (1958–66).[5] Yet it is simultaneously "a challenge to realism, locating the ordinary world of plausible social interaction within a wider and more primitive universe of magic, sorcery, and supernatural forces."[6]

The film's narrative content and cinematic style find their most nearly perfect merger in the sequence representing Rosemary's semi-waking dream, which was influenced in part by Polanski's experimentation with hallucinogens. Seeking to evoke the feel of drug-induced hallucination in cinematic terms, Polanski combined painstakingly realistic elements—a team spent six weeks replicating a detail of the Sistine Chapel ceiling, for instance, complete with cracks and discolorations—with an eclectic array of expressionistic elements, fusing "images of the Pope and Michelangelo's 'Creation of Adam' from traditional Christianity, the Kennedy-like yachting captain from the modern myth of political power, with Satan and a coven of nude witches from the mythology of the demonic."[7] Polanski based his image of Satan on "a mask he made for himself as a child in Varsovie, with a long red tongue made out of candy wrappers and glowing eyes lit by a pocket torch."[8]

The result is as obscure as the most perplexing nightmare, yet concrete and tangible enough for Rosemary to declare in a momentary flash of crystalline lucidity, "This is no dream, this is really happening!" The real and the unreal are indissolubly linked in Polanski's vision, and as critic Karyn Valerius observes, both the narrative as a whole and the dream simultaneously depict reality and intertwine with it, digesting and rematerializing "historical events and discourses . . . as Gothic horror."[9]

The Criticisms

Not surprisingly, *Rosemary's Baby* was deemed offensive, immoral, irreligious, or all three by a variety of watchdogs. Objecting to "elements of kinky sex associated with black magic," the British Board of Film Censors demanded that fifteen seconds be cut from the rape sequence—not coincidentally, Satan's most important scene—before audiences in the United Kingdom could see the film. American theaters showed the movie as Polanski made it, but the National Catholic Office for Motion Pictures gave it a C or "Condemned" rating, citing "several scenes of nudity," a "perverted use . . . of fundamental Christian beliefs, especially the events surrounding the birth of Christ," and "mockery of religious persons and practices," all crafted with a "technical excellence" that serves "to intensify its defamatory nature."[10] Commenting from a more scholarly perspective, film critics Beverle Houston and Marsha Kinder contended that *Rosemary's Baby* is frightening because it suggests that "the Christian myth is certainly no more believable than its mirror image, and possibly less so."[11] The celebrated English theater critic Kenneth Tynan called *Rosemary's Baby* "one of the very few films that made one consider the possibility that there was any such thing as absolute evil," a fact that did not dissuade Tynan from collaborating with Polanski on the screenplay of *Macbeth* (1971), the director's next project.[12]

Such comments show how effectively *Rosemary's Baby* burrows under the skin, inducing fears of "black magic" and "absolute evil" in denizens of a presumably secular era. Since films dealing with the supernatural are customarily evaluated based on believability—the more credible the story and characters, the more effective the chills and thrills—the power of *Rosemary's Baby* would appear to be validated by both the queasy responses of moralistic critics and the thoughtful reflections of philosophical ones.

Interestingly, however, at least one influential critic argued that the film's very *persuasiveness* works against its efficacy as a horror tale. Describing it as "a highly serious lapsed-Catholic fable, going on the assumption that God is dead to imagine a Nativity for the dark powers," *New York Times* reviewer Renata Adler wrote that Rosemary's predicament is almost "the kind of thing that might really have happened to her, that a rough beast did slouch toward West 72nd Street to be born."[13] If the movie "doesn't seem to work on any of its dark or powerful terms," Adler continued, the reason is that "it is almost too extremely plausible. The quality of the young people's lives seems the quality of lives that one knows, even to the point of finding old people next door to avoid and lean on. One gets very annoyed that they don't catch on sooner. One's friends would have understood the situation at once."[14]

The Quotidian

Whether or not one's friends are as instantly astute as Adler seems to think, Levin steeped his novel in quotidian details precisely because he found the narrative's Satanic premise almost too implausible even for himself. "I anchored my unbelievable story in the reality of Manhattan in that season – as much to make myself believe it as to win the belief of readers," he wrote in the afterword to the book's 2003 edition. "I saved the daily newspapers, checking back through them [for facts] on the transit strike, the incoming shows, the mayoral election, writing always a few months ahead of Rosemary and Guy's calendar."[15] Beyond this, Levin was interested in horror less as a delivery system for thrills than as a vehicle for social and psychological commentary. Horror stories "touch our fears, anxieties, guilts," he told me in 1978. Engaging with them is "a way of exercising or exorcizing them."[16]

Polanski's film is similarly immersed in sociopolitical subtexts of the late 1960s. Rosemary's vulnerability, underscored by Farrow's understated performance, brings to mind her generation's uncertainties and trepidations about changes in gender roles and sexual norms, and her desire for pregnancy and tolerance of Guy's careerism bear traces of the backlash against feminism that was incipient in American culture even when the modern women's movement was still being born. More broadly, the movie's New York setting evokes the anxiousness felt by many people who reversed the post–World War II migration from big cities to nascent suburbs, instead moving from suburban or exurban communities into urban centers where strangers are everywhere, and predators can pose as friends.

Like most baby-boomers, Rosemary and Guy do little ruminating on earlier times or older generations; one of their first acts as young marrieds is to modernize and brighten their new home in an old building, and when the senior citizens next door ask them to dinner, their initial impulse is to dodge and hide. But their apartment and that of the Castevets used to be a single large unit, and even now the dwellings of the respective couples are divided by walls so thin that the most elusive sounds—ghostly strains of Ludwig van Beethoven's wistful "Für Elise," incantatory voices chanting some uncanny spell, enchantment, or hex—can penetrate it with ease. If evil influences lurk on the other side, these flimsy walls are no protection.

Nor does the Roman Catholic Church offer much security in the increasingly unspiritual 1960s—the decade when *Time* blazoned the provocative headline "Is God Dead?" on the cover of a 1966 issue that Rosemary sees in a physician's waiting room, and when the first-ever visit of a pope to New York could easily elicit the apathetic shrugs and mild mockery that *Rosemary's Baby* depicts. Guy and Roman declare that all religions are merely "show biz," confabulations of costumes, ritual, and flimflam. Satanism is itself a religion though, and Rosemary's vestigial respect for the pope does not prevent her neighbors' demonic faith—whose adherents substitute nudity for costumes and sinister rituals for sacramental rites—from infiltrating her marriage, compromising her well-being, and commandeering her womb.

The film's exquisite tension between worldly routines and otherworldly objectives is represented most compellingly by Roman and Minnie, an utterly commonplace couple with exceedingly uncommon interests that flicker into view as soon as they meet the new neighbors who become their new best friends. The same tension is evident in the other members of the coven, who either reside in the Bramford or presumably live nearby, able to scoot over when the baby is born and hang out in the Castevet apartment during the infant's early days, savoring their proximity to the supernatural presence they helped usher into the world. The secondary Satanists are sketchy presences in both Levin's novel and Polanski's film, and they seem rather silly as well; old Leah Fountain is easily tricked into falling asleep while monitoring Rosemary's postpartum bed rest, for instance, and Levin describes the chronically complaining Laura-Louise McBurney as a "dowdy" woman wearing a "Buckley for Mayor" button.[17] The coven is clearly fortunate to have energetic Minnie and personable Roman on hand to lure Guy into their scheme and dupe Rosemary into bearing Satan's child. Yet the Castevets are capable and appealing only by comparison with the rest of their bourgeois gang, and, setting aside their affable demeanor and offbeat spiritual pursuits, they are as ordinary as can be. At the Bramford, as in many other situations, evil is at once seductive, effective, and banal.

The Metaphysics

On their first neighborly get-together, Roman gives Rosemary and Guy well-filled glasses of a cocktail called the vodka blush, mentioning that Australians are especially fond of the drink. Rosemary asks if Australia is where he comes from. "Oh no, no," the host answers, "I'm from right here in New York City. I've been there, though. I've been everywhere, literally! You name a place and I've been there. Go ahead! Name a place!" Happy to play the game, Guy calls out Fairbanks, Alaska, and Roman replies, "I've been there, been all over Alaska," reciting a string of Alaskan place names to prove it. He is even more expansive in the novel, saying, "Every continent, every country. Every major city. You name a place and I've been there."[18] Asked about the nature of his journeys, Roman says that he has traveled for both work and pleasure, and in the novel he adds that he has been in just about every business as well. Quite a track record!

From all appearances, Roman is a mild-mannered senior citizen with a genial smile, a gentle demeanor, and a storehouse of anecdotes about the varied life he has lived in his seventy-nine years. But when it comes to having traveled "everywhere, literally" and engaged in all kinds of businesses, could his claim—could anyone's claim—possibly be true? Surely this is harmless hyperbole on Roman's part, a casual remark not meant to be taken at face value. Or could the friendly gent be other than what he seems, not a seasoned raconteur but a mendacious phony who can't be taken at face value himself? So far, the film has offered few clues to his nature, and those few are vanishingly small: the way Polanski's framing keeps him at a visual distance from Guy and Rosemary during their initial conversation, hinting at his psychological and spiritual distance from everyday people, and the way his boast about being skilled at bartending falls flat when he overfills the cocktail glasses and dribbles vodka blush onto Minnie's new carpet. By the story's end we know that these apparently insignificant signs are subtle indicators of the treachery and mendacity hidden by the witch's affable facades, but at this early point Roman's claim of ubiquitous voyaging seems to be merely a case of living-room exaggeration, an old man's transparent bid for attention from the younger set.

Alternatively, however, one can ask if Roman might personify some substance or represent some quality that has indeed been "everywhere, literally," extending its tentacles into all manner of activities while appearing ordinary or even humdrum to outward observers. Only something that exceeds or transcends the physical could operate in all possible places and every area of experience; but if that something is to have narrative impact, it must also be able to manifest itself in material form. In light of these considerations, it is reasonable to nominate *good* and *evil* as prime candidates for the element in question. These are philosophically abstract categories independent of time and space, yet they are nonetheless historically, psychologically, situationally, and existentially real, anchored in the deepest strata of human nature and operative in human affairs throughout the ages. Given their Satanic agenda, the Castevets and their coven can be identified as aggressively proactive agents of *evil* in its purest, most insidious form. In this sense, Roman and his ilk have indeed been everywhere and meddled in everything, in spirit if not actually in the flesh.

This said, the members of the coven do not *embody* evil as concretely and exhaustively as Satan and his spawn obviously do. The devil is literally identical with evil, and the same surely goes for Adrian, his son and reincarnation. Apart from this shared characteristic, the relationship between Satan and Adrian is somewhat complicated. The theology (or demonology) of *Rosemary's Baby* holds that they are at once distinct creatures *and* manifestations of each other, mystically unified beings who are simultaneously separate and fused, like distorted doppelgängers of the Father and Son in the Holy Trinity that

Rosemary's long-lapsed Catholic faith regards as the tripartite essence of God's ineffable personhood.

In the novel, Levin indicates the supernatural majesty of Satan and Adrian by putting uppercase initials on nouns and pronouns (Father, Son, Him, His) that refer to them. Like their authentically Christian prototypes, the story's aberrant counterparts of God the Father and Christ the Son are so preternaturally different from the stuff of ordinary experience that even a modality as compelling as modern cinema must represent them through circumlocutory glimpses and suggestions, lest they seem outlandish or unfathomable—hence Polanski's reticent depiction of Satan during the rape sequence and of Adrian during the cradle scene. And if the narrative's infernal trinity is rounded out by an unholy Holy Ghost, this must be the most indirectly represented manifestation of all: the invisible yet ubiquitous atmosphere of mendacity, treachery, misogyny, and cruelty that grows ever more intense as the narrative unfolds. The devil is everywhere, even when he isn't clearly perceptible to the senses or apparent to the conventionally attuned mind of the film's beleaguered heroine.

And much is anticipated from Satan and company in the new age that is dawning, as witness the triumphal exclamations with which the Lucifer-worshiping witches greet the newborn member of the team. "He shall overthrow the mighty and lay waste their temples," Roman exults. "He shall redeem the despised and wreak vengeance in the name of the burned and the tortured. Hail Adrian! Hail Satan! God is dead! Satan lives! The year is 1!"[19] These predictions suggest that Adrian will do the sorts of things that Jesus was expected to do—redeem the lowly, humble the powerful, redress perceived injustice—when he trod the earth in the original Year 1. Also, like Jesus, he will perform his miraculous feats on behalf of his father, with whom he is presumably conjoined as intimately as Jesus was conjoined with *his* heavenly parent when he declared in John 10:30, "The Father and I are one."[20]

It is a bit of a stretch for Roman to count the members of the coven among the burned and tortured of the earth, but evidently an upside-down hubris enables them to see themselves as victims and martyrs instead of upper-middle-class New Yorkers with swell Manhattan apartments. In any case, their efforts to bring Adrian into the world bring genuine victimhood and martyrdom to quite a few people, including the kindly and prescient Hutch; the supposedly self-destructive Terry; the actor whose sudden blindness gives Guy his big break; the woman who occupied 7E in the Bramford before the Woodhouses moved in; and, of course, Rosemary, a credulous innocent exploited by people in whom she has placed her deepest trust. As the infernally chosen vessel for Satan's renewed presence on the earth, she is unwittingly turned into an irreligious proxy for the Virgin Mary, and in Levin's novel (although not in Polanski's film) she is saluted with cries of "Hail Rosemary" by celebrants of the unholy birth.[21]

Rosemary's decision not to reject her (extremely) illegitimate child is virtuous by the standards of conventional morality, marking a victory for the maternal instinct in the old-fashioned sense of that term. But before she makes this choice, seemingly irrefutable evidence—comments from members of the coven and a glimpse of the infant himself—lets her know that he is unquestionably the devil's progeny. Arguing that *Rosemary's Baby* posits a critical view of its main character, Valerius points out that she could choose to terminate this "satanic contamination of white, bourgeois maternity" but decides not to ("I won't have an abortion!") despite the fact that her condition involves three commonly adduced justifications for legal termination of a pregnancy: she was raped, her physical health is endangered, and her fetus—which causes excruciating pain—shows clear signs of abnormality.[22]

Although she is the protagonist, therefore, Rosemary is not the heroine of the story, which has no heroine and no hero. The witches who engineer the birth of Satan's mystic son are aiming to augment and accelerate the potency of evil, transforming it from a diffuse, unfocused influence into a tangible, concentrated force. As she comes to sense the baby's nature, Rosemary's inclination to embrace and nurture him indicates that the Satanic invasion of her body has somehow blighted her soul as well. Roman has been everywhere and done everything as Satan's emissary, and now Satan's contagious malignity has directly infected Rosemary's spiritual bloodstream. She is an honorary member of the coven, if not (yet) a card-carrying affiliate.

Conclusion

Evil's ability to pollute, pervert, and corrupt whatever it touches is the central theme of *Rosemary's Baby*, manifested in Rosemary's sad experience and symbolized by the setting of that experience: the quintessential American city in the famously swinging 1960s, when the certainties of religious faith and its attendant values seem to be losing more of their normative power with every passing day. A pope pays a visit and nobody cares, allies and enemies are impossible to tell apart, occultism thrives in the apartment next door. Anxieties about gender, sexuality, careerism, and other unsettled areas of contemporary life revolve around the narrative like dark Satanic moons, affording a ripe environment for the devil's most poisonous project since antiquity.

This said, the film's purposefully disorienting style is paralleled by the story's susceptibility to multiple interpretations that are neither "correct" nor "incorrect" nor mutually exclusive. Rosemary may indeed be the prey of genuine witches whose Satanic machinations are as authentic and efficacious as the rock-solid foundations on which the Bramford has rested for all these many decades. Alternatively, she might be a gullible naïf in the clutches of a delusional cult that dupes her meagerly talented husband, enacts a brutal rape during a costume-party orgy, poisons her pregnancy with herbs and potions, and rejoices when she gives birth to a deformed infant. Or perhaps she is simply suffering from what Guy calls the "pre-partum crazies," an escalating psychosis that the audience vicariously shares by perceiving events through the filter of her increasingly distressed consciousness.

The nonsupernatural interpretations link *Rosemary's Baby* with Polanski's earlier features—*Knife in the Water* (1962), *Repulsion*, *Cul-de-sac* (1966), and even the comic *Dance of the Vampires* (1967, aka *The Fearless Vampire Killers*)—in an ongoing exploration of sexuality as a form of power ritual. Rosemary's fictional travails are surrogates for the anxieties of everyday moviegoers, "ordinary people who cast out their own demons in the forms of film narratives, scapegoats, rumors, urban legends," and other stand-ins for the not-believed-yet-still-believed presences that were once called witches, warlocks, and Satanic visitations.[23]

In sum, *Rosemary's Baby* can be understood in many ways: as "a modern-day tale of witchcraft and demonic pregnancy, a Faustian story of destructive ambition, a tribute to *Dracula* in which the unborn rather than the undead perniciously feed off the living, and a perversion of the Christian narrative of the Immaculate Conception in which Satan impregnates a mortal woman in order to become human and intervene in world history."[24] No matter which hermeneutic trail one chooses to follow, however, one is sure to encounter the manifold sins of patriarchy along the way. Minnie's chattering presence notwithstanding, the force bedeviling Rosemary is a predominantly masculine mystique, as Leslie H. Abramson points out, describing Rosemary's imprisonment within "dark structurations of patriarchy" administered by "her enigmatic husband and the mysterious impenetrabilities of masculine culture, all of which constantly undermine her perceptions."[25]

Rosemary's Baby takes a strong stand against these forces, portraying them as indisputably evil, and Polanski extends the critique by linking the patriarchy depicted in the film with the patriarchy of the film industry itself. The traditional studios amount to a coven of corporate culture, as Abramson suggests, and the Bramford is a storehouse of old-school Hollywood spookiness, populated by a band of movie veterans—Bellamy, Blackmer, Elisha Cook Jr. as a real-estate agent—with long-familiar screen personalities. Discombobulating these well-worn presences, Polanski stirs things up with the forward-looking personae of Cassavetes, a maverick actor-filmmaker whose independent production *Faces* also appeared in 1968, and Farrow, a new kind of star with a "nonclassical" beauty resembling "that of European art cinema actresses."[26]

A holdover from Old Hollywood in some respects and a harbinger of New Hollywood in others, *Rosemary's Baby* traverses the passageway between pre-1960s and post-1960s values much as Rosemary traverses the architectural passageway between apartments, and Satan's seed traverses the biological passageway to Rosemary's womb, and Minnie's noxious brew traverses the umbilical passageway linking the pregnant mother with her malevolent fetus, and Adrian traverses the passageway between preternatural imminence and corporeal immanence. None of these crossings would have happened if a more fundamental passage—between the spiritual insights of the intuitive past, on one hand, and the materialistic prejudices of the scientistic present, on the other—were not so willfully blocked in the contemporary world. As noted earlier, Rosemary and Guy are young sophisticates with little patience for the lessons of older generations, earlier epochs, or history itself. Blindness to the past is the linchpin of *Rosemary's Baby*. The title character, remember, has his father's eyes.

Notes

1. Ira Levin, *Rosemary's Baby* (New York: Pegasus Books, 2010), 1.
2. Levin, 15–16.
3. Levin, 17.
4. David Sterritt, "*Rosemary's Baby*," *Cineaste* 38, no. 3 (Summer 2013): 53.
5. Mikita Brottman, *Hollywood Hex: Death and Destiny in the Dream Factory* (Powder Springs, GA: Creation Books, 1999), 40.
6. Brottman, 40.
7. Brottman, 44.
8. Brottman, 44.
9. Karyn Valerius, "*Rosemary's Baby*, Gothic Pregnancy, and Fetal Subjects," *College Literature* 32, no. 3 (Summer 2005): 124.
10. James Marriott, *Horror Films* (London: Virgin Books, 2007), 121.
11. Beverle Houston and Marsha Kinder, "*Rosemary's Baby*," *Sight & Sound* 38, no. 1 (Winter 1968–69): 17.
12. Kevin Hagopian, "*Macbeth*," *Film Notes*, n.d., accessed October 18, 2020, http://www.albany.edu/writers-inst/webpages4/filmnotes/fns98n3.html.
13. Renata Adler, "Rosemary's Baby," *New York Times*, June 13, 1968, accessed October 18, 2020, https://www.nytimes.com/1968/06/13/archives/the-screen-rosemarys -baby-a-story-of-fantasy-and-horror-john.html.
14. Adler.

15. Ira Levin, "'Stuck with Satan': Ira Levin on the Origins of *Rosemary's Baby*," *Current*, November 5, 2012, accessed October 18, 2020, https://www.criterion.com/current/posts/2541-stuck-with-satan-ira-levin-on-the-origins-of-rosemary-s-baby.

16. David Sterritt, "What's Involved in Concocting a Thriller," *Christian Science Monitor*, September 14, 1978, 18.

17. Levin, *Rosemary's Baby*, 66.

18. Levin, 54.

19. Levin, 236.

20. *The Gospel According to John*, in *The New Oxford Annotated Bible: New Revised Standard Version*, ed. Michael D. Coogan, 4th ed. (Oxford: Oxford University Press, 2010), 1900.

21. Levin, *Rosemary's Baby*, 244.

22. Valerius, "Rosemary's Baby," 125.

23. Brottman, *Hollywood Hex*, 40.

24. Valerius, "Rosemary's Baby," 118.

25. Leslie H. Abramson, "1968: Movies and the Failure of Nostalgia," in *American Cinema of the 1960s: Themes and Variations*, ed. Barry Keith Grant (Camden, NJ: Rutgers University Press, 2008), 202.

26. Abramson, 202–203.

From the Eternal Sea He Rises, Creating Armies on Either Shore

The Antichristology of the Omen Franchise

R. Barton Palmer

In a decade of Hollywood filmmaking dominated by a young generation of film school graduates infatuated with the international art film, one of the more surprising developments was the commercial success achieved by a classy, but very much old-school thriller. *The Omen*, directed by Richard Donner and released in 1976, offered viewers a modern and substantially secularized version of the Antichrist legend, accommodating the ancient tale about "end times" to horror film conventions. Producer Harvey Bernhard commissioned David Seltzer to write a treatment on the subject, which had been suggested to him by a born-again friend, Bob Munger. Munger correctly saw commercial film possibilities in the fact that his coreligionists were increasingly convinced by various "signs" or "omens" that the millennium was fast approaching.

High-Concept Religious Horror

Bernhard's brief pitch impressed Warner Bros., which had recently had a huge success with another religious horror release, *The Exorcist* (William Friedkin, 1973), but Twentieth Century Fox quickly signed up the project after Warner Bros. hesitated. Crucial to green-lighting the project was that Seltzer's proposed narrative traced how a father is brought to the inescapable conclusion that his adopted son is in fact the Antichrist. More horrifyingly, events then reveal it is also up to him to kill the boy. Only in this way can humankind prevent God's enemy from proceeding with plans to defeat a revenant Christ in battle and claim the created order for Satan. Even if not based on a presold literary property, *The Omen*, or so Bernhard argued, would tell such an innovative and compelling story that it was certain to appeal to filmgoers. Popular enthusiasm for religious-themed horror thrillers had been revealed by the unexpected box office success of *The Exorcist*. Events proved Bernhard correct. *The Omen* would become the second film in the religious horror production cycle that would dominate the late eighties and early nineties. Both *The Omen* and *The Exorcist* soon gave rise to profitable franchises, while also inspiring a series of less successful imitations (e.g., Taylor Hackford's *The Devil's Advocate* [1997]).

The Exorcist's shocking, even pornographic, depiction of demonic possession and priestly efforts to relieve it pushed the horror genre in a direction that Harvey Bernhard was eager to follow. He, too, aimed at delighting audiences with unusually staged graphic violence and with an intriguing depiction of how metaphysical forces, as understood within the Judeo-Christian tradition, could unpredictably intrude upon an only apparently desacralized modernity. And yet there were significant differences between the two films. *The Exorcist* focuses on a spiritual illness that has been nearly forgotten in contemporary Christianity but not officially abandoned as superstition. Something less dramatic than the priestly intervention at the film's center is still practiced, mainly in the Catholic Church, while exorcism holds a marginal place in Islamic and Jewish traditions as well.

The Omen, in contrast, probes more deeply into Christian history and belief, literally unearthing what has become a "buried" and forgotten past for most contemporary adherents of the faith. Perhaps most American Christians would be unfamiliar with either the prophecies about the advent of the Antichrist contained in the Book of Revelation or the long history within Christian culture of the refiguring of these prophecies in contemporary experience, with an important instance being Martin Luther's denouncing of Pope Julius II and his successors as avatars of the Antichrist. And yet this past, both scriptural and material, has recently come back into theological and historical focus, as *The Omen* itself suggests. The narrative's emphasis on exploration and discovery invites being read as a mise en abyme for this larger cultural recapturing of a sacralized history. Crucial to Donner's tale are sequences depicting ongoing archaeological explorations in the ancient city of Megiddo, now in Israel, where the final battle between Christ and Antichrist (Armageddon) will take place according to the Book of Revelation. For years preceding the film's production, digs had gone on in the city's substantial ruins conducted by famed Israeli historian Yigael Yadin, who appears in *The Omen* disguised as archaeologist Carl Bugenhagen (Leo McKern). Location shooting at the site provides an important link between the fictional story and the ongoing search for the meaning of the past it evokes.[1]

Beyond its contribution to the developing cycle of religious horror films pioneered by *The Exorcist*, the *Omen* films, and the novelizations that imitated the process in another medium, established narrative patterns, themes, and marketing strategies that would soon be followed by others. The first part of this essay is devoted to the production history of the *Omen* franchise (the original film, two sequels, and a remake, as well as two unsuccessful TV series). The second part pays attention to the idiosyncratic ways in which the filmmakers and screenwriters involved in the series developed, while modifying, traditional understandings of the Antichrist, especially his "parental" connection to Satan as God's enemy. The *Omen* films, like the novelizations that followed, succeed at providing engaging entertainment in a familiar genre. But it is also true that in drawing on a nexus of traditional religious themes, beliefs, and practices, they constitute a modern reversioning that invites a serious cultural analysis. These texts, both cinematic and literary, propose that human efforts to resist ultimate evil must end in failure, as the dark forces of the universe represented by Satan and the Antichrist prevail for the most part, to be defeated in the end only by lucky accident.

Creating a Formula

Not being based on a popular novel proved no bar to *The Omen*'s popularity and profitability. Quite the opposite, for both the film and its sequels generated novelizations, reversing how adaptation has usually worked in Hollywood. It was also no problem that the script lacked the literariness of *The Exorcist*. There were no round characters like Blatty's priest, Father Karras (played in the film by Jason Miller), who experiences a profound crisis of faith when faced with the agonizing fact of demonic possession. And yet *The Omen*'s flat surface provided the filmmakers with an advantage, allowing viewers to focus elsewhere. As Justin Wyatt suggests, the success of such productions depends not on dramatic interchanges but on "a simplification of character and narrative and a strong match between image and music soundtrack throughout."[2] Unlike *The Exorcist*, which is to good dramatic effect largely dependent on dialogue, *The Omen* provides suspenseful action that plays out in an immensely varied number of real locations. The film opens in Rome with a speeding taxi ride, moves on to London, then to Israel, and finally ends, after another desperate chase, in an English church with the failure of the desperate father to kill his child and the survival of Satan's child. Even with this complex and frenetic narrative, however, the tale of the Antichrist remains only partly told by film's end, an incompletion that immediately invited sequelizing.[3]

Confined for the most part to a single interior set, Friedkin's *Exoricst* was dependent on unusual action scenes, elaborate makeup, and special effects. With the possessed young girl freed from her devil at the cost of her exorcist's life, the film was not structured toward generating multiple refashionings; at least at first it seemed to fit better into another production trend characteristic of the era: the blockbuster.[4] But then it, too, albeit with struggle and controversy, underwent franchising, with *The Omen* series serving as something of a model. Two *Exorcist* sequels and two prequels of varying quality and box office success were produced and released over the next three decades. A TV series (*Exorcist*) was broadcast by Fox in 2016 and generally well received; a second season debuted in September 2017. The novel has been turned into a play, which premiered in 2016 at the Birmingham Repertory Theatre in the United Kingdom. The *Exorcist* films, however, do not have a strong soundtrack tie-in.

The success enjoyed by *The Exorcist* was surprising only by its scale. The emerging popularity of the horror/thriller using Judeo-Christian material, however superficially, had been established by *Rosemary's Baby* (Roman Polanski, 1968). Polanski's film cost three million dollars to produce and earned more than thirty-three million dollars in its initial release, while also garnering Academy and Golden Globe nominations and awards. These were unusual accolades for what the industry in previous years would have considered a genre piece. Based on Ira Levin's bestseller of the same name, *Rosemary's Baby* depicts the predicament of an upscale New York woman (Mia Farrow) who is drugged and then impregnated by Satan with the connivance of her husband and a coven of devilish minions; intriguingly, these are professional and artistic types who live in her Upper East Side apartment building. Polanski's tale combines elements of demonic possession (literally "from within") with a vaguely evoked version of the Antichrist legend. Despite Polanski's art house stylings, *Rosemary's Baby* was a conventional Hollywood project intended to be unique and firmly anchored to a pre-sold property.

The film evokes the Antichrist tradition, including an incarnation mirroring that of Christ, but Polanski's interest (as in his earlier film *Repulsion* [1965]) is in tracing Rosemary's gradual, horrific discovery that she is carrying Satan's child. In the end, despite her protestations and resistance, even the Antichrist's hitherto anguished involuntary mother reconciles herself to what the film presents as an ontological inevitability. Satan's newly born son is hailed by his New York City disciples as the expected one who will deliver the world to Evil. It seems clear that Seltzer recycled principal elements of the film in preparing the script for *The Omen*, especially the narrative focus on a horrified parent eager to destroy his own child after learning the truth of his origin.

The Omen cost less than three million dollars to produce and earned its producers over sixty million dollars in its initial releases, making it one of the highest grossing films that year.[5] The film's success was due at least in part to the studio's decision to make the project an "A" production, casting stars Gregory Peck and Lee Remick in the featured roles as the parents, Robert and Katherine Thorn, of their adopted son, Damien (Harvey Spencer Stephens), the son of Satan whose birth mother is a jackal. The film also featured two well-known British performers, David Warner and Billie Whitelaw, in important supporting roles (Jennings and Mrs. Baylock, respectively). Many sequences were shot at various locations in London and the United Kingdom as well as in Jerusalem and Rome, lending what might have been a studio-bound genre piece a strong sense of authenticity (and qualifying the film for UK tax breaks).

Crucial to the film's success, as it had been the year before for Steven Spielberg's *Jaws*, was a musically simple soundtrack main theme (written by Jerry Goldsmith) that is established early on, in the Wagnerian manner, as the *leitmotif* for the unseen Satanic force that propels the narrative. The score's complete form plays over the credits as a fully orchestrated faux Gregorian chant. This hymn praises Satan's spawn, who, incarnated, will soon descend to earth. The ungrammatical Latin text, intoned by a presumed mass chorus of his earthly supporters, imparts a medieval tone to a film otherwise set in the contemporary world. If the score's driving beat, separated as a brief musical figure, is an appropriately modern and pulse-quickening accompaniment for the film's fast-moving horror narrative, the chant also ironically invokes a distant, but not entirely noncontemporary, form of Christian devotion in the Anglican, Catholic, and Orthodox traditions. The current Evangelical preoccupation with "end times" to which the film appeals is here clothed and stylized in more ancient forms of Christian practice and culture. The advantage of the approach the filmmakers take is not only to authorize an engagement with Gothicness in all its senses (allowing the devilish to emerge in familiar forms) but also that viewing the end times through this particular Christian lens also allows the filmmakers to summon up an institutional church with ancient roots. If this church still holds true to its Petrine mission, including providing the sacraments that ensure salvation, it also harbors Satanists, seduced (as the narrative hints) by promises of personal advantage, who are eager to subvert it through support of God's ontological foes. This vision of a church divided against itself—full of wolves in sheep's clothing and containing the very opposition that might destroy it—dates to ancient times. It arose in the second and third centuries because of several fundamental doctrinal controversies that for more than three centuries roiled the early history of institutional Christianity.

Heresy, or false belief, created communities that some influential Orthodox thinkers understood as reflecting the premillenarian mission of incarnated Antichrists, born before the Antichrist proper appears, as foretold in the Book of Revelation, in order to contest its possession with the revenant Christ, as discussed shortly.[6]

With its praise of God's enemy intoned by an unheavenly chorus of presumed devil worshippers, some of whom play roles in the film's narrative, the chant, *Ave Satani* or "Hail Satan," evokes this history, with Evil conceived in mirror terms of the divine, including the key role played by adoptive parents. In the manner of much film music, the chant (which sometimes invoked only a few bars of music and no voices) indicates the normally unrevealed underside of the complacent, largely secular modernity that the film otherwise depicts. Jerry Goldsmith won the Oscar that year for best original score, providing the franchise with a simple musical signature as distinctive and recognizable as the two-note theme for *Jaws* composed by John Williams, who himself understood that the threat posed by the killer shark could be evoked musically as well as visually. A few bars of the soundtrack worked a similar marketing magic for *The Omen*, providing it with a shorthand "signature" that aided in it becoming one of the decade's most discussed event films.[7]

As in the case of *The Exorcist*, *Omen*'s producers quickly responded to a receptive marketplace. *The Omen* became a franchise as two sequels followed in quick succession: *Damien: Omen II* (Don Taylor, 1978) and *Omen III: The Final Conflict* (Graham Baker, 1981). These carried the story of the Antichrist's advent through Damien's adolescent embrace of his identity and subsequent failed effort to rally forces against a Jesus who (in a striking revision of biblical materials) is once more born in human form. Damien finds himself defeated, but not by God. Instead, just as he is making plans to finish off the newly born Savior, he is killed by one of his erstwhile followers, who sees through his false promises to create a new order that will save the world from the mass starvation that, as Damien has arranged, will soon threaten it. And so, a collective human problem finds a solution more or less by good luck, as there is only a limited and essentially ineffective intervention on the part of the organized church, while the heavens remain silent. David Seltzer turned his script into a novel, while novelized versions of the scripts for the two sequels were turned out by Joseph Howard and Gordon McGill, respectively. McGill would go on during the 1980s to write a fourth and fifth *Omen* novel—neither book was connected to a film, and these later entrants sometimes deviate from the narrative through-line of the trilogy. The *Omen* novel series (released between 1976 and 1985) has proved successful with horror/thriller fiction enthusiasts, making the *Omen* one of the most successful of

the transmedia franchises based on films that emerged to cultural prominence in the 1970s.[8]

A faithful remake of the original *Omen* was released in 2006 (John Moore),
while Bernhard tried to exploit in a TV production what remained of the
popularity of the story materials by penning a spin-off. *Omen IV: The Awakening* (Jorge Montesi and Dominique Othenin-Girard, 1991) featured the
rebirth of the Antichrist, the son of Damien, who was implanted as an embryo
within a young girl, Delia (Asia Vieira), and subsequently reimplanted within
her mother. The Antichrist, in short, appears as a pair of fraternal twins.
Otherwise, the film follows much the same narrative structure as the original
film. *Omen IV* never garnered a theatrical release, much to Bernhard's
disappointment.

Unsurprisingly, the later entrants in the *Omen* franchise did not achieve
the popularity that the original did, even though *Damien: Omen II* was also
given "A" picture treatment by Warner Bros. *Omen II* featured impressive
location shooting (in Israel and many sites, public and private, in the US
Upper Midwest), as well as star performances (William Holden and Lee
Grant appeared in the roles of Damien's foster parents). The sequel recycles
with interesting variations much of what had made the original popular, with
the destruction of his family by the Antichrist-to-be and his minions once
again constituting the main plot. Elaborate action sequences added to the
increased audience interest as the film's engagement with the battle of good
versus evil became even more spectacular. An adolescent Damien (Jonathan
Scott-Taylor), now aware of the destiny to which he had been born, takes part
in the struggle against those in his own family who would expose and thwart
him. By film's end, with the death of his adoptive parents, he has become the
protagonist, which is the role he plays out fully in the final film of the original
trilogy.

Why was this franchise successful with filmgoers? For one thing, the producers benefitted from scripts that were uniformly workable, occasionally
excellent in terms of creating and sustaining a pervasive atmosphere of threat
and apprehension, with easy-to-read and fast-paced narratives that were easily
summed up iconographically and thematically. As Wyatt observes, it is this
sense of an appealing "matter" and "style" rather than character and plot that
filmgoers find compelling; they are "sewn into the surface of the film," which
in the case of the *Omen* franchise includes, as discussed below, the particular
spin imparted to traditional materials belonging to what might best be termed
Christian legend rather than belief or doctrine.[9] Much the same might be
said, *mutatis mutandis*, of the novelizations and original works in the fictional

series, all of which enjoyed substantial popularity with millions of copies distributed and read worldwide.

More remarkable is that the 2006 remake, with featured Hollywood performers rather than stars in the principal roles and production values that were hardly equivalent to either those of the original or even of *Damien: Omen II*, took in almost $120 million on a budget of $25 million in worldwide release; the movie became one of the most profitable of the many remakes characteristic of the New Hollywood production, and rebooting the franchise for further exploitation on either the big or small screen. This seems in fact to have happened. The TV series *Damien* was picked up by the A&E network for the 2016 season and eventually renewed for another season.[10] And as of this writing, a prequel, to be produced by Fox and tentatively titled *The First Omen*, has stalled, but not been canceled.[11]

The not-yet exhausted success of the *Omen* media franchise is indeed a New Hollywood story, reflecting how those in the business learned during the 1970s to nurture and then handle to best advantage the blockbuster films that were found to be so profitable to make, including exploiting different platforms (film and print) to build and sustain interest. A carefully calculated TV ad blitz campaign for *The Omen*, imitative of the one that had been so successful the year before in drumming up enthusiasm for *Jaws*, was largely responsible for its initial excellent box office. Both films opened "wide" in the nation's theaters, then a still-controversial exhibition strategy, and *The Omen* grossed more than four million dollars in its opening weekend, then a quite remarkable figure, if not up to the seven million dollars earned by *Jaws*. And once the original release proved to be a hit, the filmmakers decided almost immediately on a sequel, once again following then-current evolving industry practice. As Wyatt observes, "a film recombining other financially successful films possesses built-in marketing hooks," including its "look and sound," and this pattern was followed throughout the original trilogy, albeit neither for *Omen IV* nor for the 2006 remake because of contract restrictions.[12]

A Post-Christian Reimagining

However, there is another explanation for the success of the *Omen* films. These films offer a strikingly revisionist version of the Antichrist story that connects at key points to an important and ancient strand within the evolving tradition itself, intellectual ambitions for which screenwriters (and subsequently novelizers) David Seltzer, Gordon McGill, and Joseph Howard are responsible. This critical engagement with Christian tradition differentiates the franchise from the other religious-themed horror films of the 1970s. To be sure, the *Exorcist* franchise focuses on demonic possession by opportunistic demons, the minions of Satan, a phenomenon accepted as an element of the created order by the Catholic Church. But demonic possession is hardly a central element of the Christian worldview, beyond its confirmation that evil and opposition to God are not only elements of human depravity but also ontological facts that can be glimpsed in the extraordinary phenomenon of such demonic possession. What we might call Antichristology is more central to Christian thought and tradition. According to historian Bernard McGinn, the figure of God's enemy offers "a mirror for conceptions and fears about ultimate human evil . . . based on the conviction that that evil can be realized in a human individual and even in a human collectivity."[13] Surveying the depth of the Antichrist materials, including their contemporary representation in popular culture, McGinn, however, underestimates the cultural value of the *Omen* franchise when he asserts that the films simply exemplify "the banality of Hollywood's view of evil."[14]

On the contrary, the *Omen* films can be read as thoroughgoing rejections of the belief that an existential enemy in human form will arise only to be defeated, as he contests the dominion over a transforming ultimate order of existence that God has granted to the revenant Jesus. In the first two films of the trilogy, Damien, with the aid of dedicated followers, defeats attempts to kill him. To be sure, the franchise, as I have suggested, draws for its thematic "surface" on the current preoccupation of certain segments of the Evangelical community with the events of the "end times," which many within that community think imminent. The resurrected Jesus and his rescue of the faithful from the era of tribulation that will precede the final establishment of the heavenly Jerusalem are the focus of a powerful and immensely popular tradition of hopeful, if admonitory fiction, perhaps the most influential strain of popular Christian literature to emerge over the last century.

In contrast, as Robert M. Price observes, "*The Omen* portrays the coming of Antichrist as an inexorable doom, the scourge of humanity."[15] In these films, the church is a seldom-glimpsed presence that possesses no powers to deliver humanity from a collective fate that, until the closing minutes of the third installment of the narrative, no individual proves able to prevent. And this is true even though ancient lore, passed down to the present by those eager to uncover the ancient sources of evil, offers the means to destroy the Antichrist before he can mature and fulfill predictions that he will seize control of the world after killing the newly reborn Jesus. In this way, as the mature Damien predicts in the series finale, he will end the two-thousand-year reign of stultifying goodness, giving him and his father Satan a chance to impose a new order, one that elevates evil to a place of satisfying prominence. In a striking scene, Damien dialogues with a life-size crucified statue of Jesus, bringing tears to roll down its wooden face as he celebrates a triumph that God seems unable to prevent. But it is not to be. The pretender to universal rule is stabbed to death by a woman he had earlier bedded, enraged that he caused her son to be killed to save himself from assassination.

The promised confrontation between cosmic forces ends in a small-scale and all-too-human melodrama, even as a vision of the resurrected Jesus fills the screen to provide the semblance of a conventional conclusion. In this version of the final struggle against evil, God is essentially a no-show, little more than an offstage presence, a quite remarkable revision of the account offered in the Book of Revelation. And yet in shifting the focus of the Antichrist's machinations earthward, the *Omen* franchise engages with a long-established tradition of apocalyptic thought that focuses on the need for a communal resistance to the establishment of the kingdom of evil.

Multiform Antichrists

Surveying the immense body of Christian traditions, historian Wilhelm Bousset observes that, "no popular myth can compare with that of the Antichrist legend in general interest, widespread diffusion, and persistence, from a hoar antiquity down to the present time."[16] As he details, some important elements of the ever-expanding and transforming narrative took their initial shape "prior even to the Old Testament records themselves," while stories about the Antichrist continue to fascinate even in what many might call a post-Christian world, adding a considerable number of fictionalized treatments to a huge, complexly interconnected body of tales and lore.[17] Over the centuries, interest has waxed and waned in these traditions of a supernatural agent, the son of Satan, who comes to earthly power in order to oppose a transfigured Christ charged by the Father with judging humanity and establishing a realm of eternal blessedness for the elect.[18]

Since the 1940s, theological and devotional developments within the Anglo-American evangelical community have increasingly focused attention on these "end times" in which the Antichrist will be a central figure, with "the rapture" (or the exemption of the virtuous from the conflict, death, and destruction involving his struggles with a returning Christ) gaining attention as a crucial aspect of the salvation guaranteed by strong faith and moral probity. Reflecting this interest, Christian Zionist Hal Lindsey wrote *The Late Great Planet Earth* (1970), which, in addition to summarizing biblical and other accounts of the end of the world, offered a detailed reading of recent history that, Lindsey argued, suggested that more ancient prophecies were about to be fulfilled. The book, at a time when apocalyptic visions of our collective human future were enjoying a bull market (see Paul Ehrlich's 1968 bestseller *The Population Bomb*), attracted a huge readership, with more than thirty million copies of the book eventually sold. With the end of the world approaching, it was time for a spiritual renewal, or so Lindsey argued. This was also the evangelizing message of preacher-turned-novelist Tim LaHaye, whose series of sixteen *Left Behind* novels (1995–2007) likewise found a huge readership, with the focus very much on the unfortunate destinies of those who find themselves suffering the fate described in the series title when the righteous, spared horrific deaths, are suddenly transported heavenward before the earth is consumed in apocalyptic struggle. The Antichrist is a Romanian politician named Nicolae Carpathia, who is supported in his attempt to take over the kingdom promised to Christ by a worldwide organization named Global Community, first founded in connection with the United Nations. Carpathia is opposed in his plotting by the so-called Tribulation Force, whose members are born again Christians, drawn from a population only some of whom find themselves fully committed to faith in Christ's return and the rejection of secular values and lifestyles.

No doubt, the works of Lindsey and LaHaye succeeded in their missioning intentions, popularizing the most important tenets of their brand of end times thinking (technically speaking premillennial, pretribulational dispensationalism), while also providing information about important Christian traditions to less informed believers. As far as biblical versions of this threat are concerned, the Antichrist, of course, is ultimately defeated, as the most elaborated mythological version of his emergence and flourishing in John's Book of Revelation proclaims. John's purpose, as scholars such as Elaine Pagels recognize, was to provide an optimistic form to ancient traditions during the early decades of the faith's crisis-filled expansion following the destruction of the Temple in 70 CE. The Book of Revelation, she writes, was to create a powerful form of "Anti-Roman propaganda" that celebrated the victory of a revenant Jesus over forces of ontological chaos and their representatives in an empire that claimed sovereignty over many peoples, including those that God had "chosen."[19] However, John's version of the ancient story refers to contemporary events and only indirectly to the precarious situation of the Jesus movement. The book's aesthetic is allegorical not historical, with its reference to a time beyond this time giving a futurist twist to a primordial mythology and ending with a potent vision of collective salvation in the heavenly Jerusalem that both fulfills and displaces historical experience.

The canonical account of end times in the Book of Revelation has been read as focusing on the emergence of two powerful foes of God, summoned into existence by a fearsome dragon, usually identified as an avatar of Satan, so that they might take part in the coming battle against a returning and aggressive Savior. The first named of these Satanic minions is a beast that comes up from the sea, replete with seven heads, ten crowns, as well as a form that recalls, in its different parts, the leopard, lion, and bear. To this beast, the dragon gives dominion over all the nations and peoples of this world, powers to be shared by a second fearsome monster that arises from the land and is charged with marking all the inhabitants of the earth with the mark of the beast, which is 666 and, as John mysteriously affirms, a human number.

In the Book of Revelation, the term *Antichrist* is not used to refer to either of these beasts (whose origin, like that of the dragon, lies in Middle Eastern myths of great antiquity); the term does occur in 1 John 22, but as designation more generally for the enemies of God who deny Christ. However, the New Testament offers a complementary, if brief and much vaguer, account of the emergence of a new ontological order in Paul's letter 2 Thessalonians. This narrative centers on a human figure referred to as the Final Enemy, an author of wickedness, whose presence was hitherto occulted, but who will come forward to be destroyed, along with his devoted followers, before this world makes way for the next. During the next century or so, as Christian apocalypticism gained new energy from increased Roman persecution, the Antichrist became identified as an actor in human affairs, in the view of many appearing as the emperor Nero but representing the secular order more generally as well. In this developing tradition, Irenaeus, bishop of Lyon, turns out to be a central figure. As Elaine Pagels explains, Irenaeus specifically links John's "beast from the sea" with the "deceiver" from John's gospel and Paul's Final Enemy. He argues that even before the end times begin, Antichrist "now rules the world with his host of demonic spirits. He deceives, dominates, and terrorizes all nations," providing another version of the Fall's effect on human history, and what the Second Coming might mean in terms of the restoration of moral order in the face of enduring opposition from both Satan and Antichrist.[20]

The essential quality of the Antichrist in Revelation and 2 Thessalonians is his ontological opposition to the incarnated divine, the Word made flesh, of whom he is conceived as a negative mirror image. Completing the parallel is that the archenemy Satan is usually said to be his father. John agrees with Paul in stating that Antichrist only emerges after a series of prophecies and omens foretelling his arrival in a postapocalyptic order of cosmic upheaval. His cosmic purpose is to contest possession of the renewed eternal kingdom promised to Christ, as foretold by him according to the Gospels. For Paul, the reappearance of the transfigured Jesus will be sufficient to defeat the final enemy. The very breath of the Savior will rob him of the power to establish an earthly kingdom to rival that promised by God to his Son. For John, however, the Antichrist and the evil that he epitomizes and defends, including his father Satan, are not so easily defeated, and the emergence of an order in which virtue enjoys a final triumph over evil is much more problematic.

As John understands it, in fact, the earthly kingdom must be won in a titanic struggle against elements of chaos and resistance, whose scope and nature are meant to amaze and horrify. His tale is meant to convince Christians of the immense power arrayed within the cosmos against God. At one point, in this account, God charges vultures with devouring the mountains of corpses that cover the battlefield. John's account otherwise emphasizes a bewilderingly diverse gallery of monstrous beings opposing Jesus and his army of angels, suggesting a realm of physical and cosmic disorder at least initially beyond the regnant reach of God and his warrior angels. This frightening vision of incipient dissolution contrasts with John's account of a heaven in whose transcendent spirituality and promise of eternal blessedness reflect a divine order to be perfected by the Creator's final act: the shaping of a heavenly Jerusalem. Once concluded by the destruction or banishment of all that is evil, including the Antichrist, the war between claimants to the seat of human power makes possible John's imagination of a thousand years during which Jesus reigns over a world restored to a state of moral goodness. At the end of this era, which will witness the resurrection of all the virtuous from past ages, Jesus will sit in judgment over the "living and the dead," with the morally unclean sent into the lake of fire along with Satan, the Antichrist, and their minions, while those judged virtuous ascend with a victorious Savior into a reconstituted Jerusalem.

Conceived as the negative image of the redeemer sent by God to put right a world in moral and political disarray, the figure of the Antichrist gives expression to a moral dualism that Christianity, with its post-Nicene insistence on divine omnipotence and singularity, officially rejected. And yet Christianity never separated itself completely from those source traditions (notably Manichaeism and Neoplatonism) that were crucially dependent on such metaphysical oppositions. These traditions promoted, as does the Book of Revelation, a collective form of purification and transcendence, one that is a feature of the Jewish and Babylonian myths about cosmic struggle that John as well as other authors in the apocalyptic tradition (of whom there were a good many) drew on deeply.[21] Understanding itself as charged by God to help those who receive its sacraments attain to salvation and eternal life, the post-Constantine church by the fifth century had accepted a version (often termed Semi-Pelagianism) of the doctrinal explanation of depravity developed in the Augustinian notion of Original Sin. This key teaching identifies man himself as responsible through the exercise of free will for a disposition toward evil transmitted from one generation to the next by the necessarily sinful acts of intercourse that lead to conception.[22] As a doctrine, it was formulated and widely endorsed as orthodox only after rancorous debate over the human capacity and need for right action and precise nature (destined or otherwise) of the complementary role played by divine grace in the individual struggle for salvation that is the drama of every *individual* Christian life. Ontologically speaking, evil did not exist; it was the absence of virtue, a void that could only be filled through God's grace. Yet, as Elaine Pagels recounts, "Augustine acknowledges . . . that Christians in this world still struggle against evil in ways that they experience as demonic attack."[23]

For Augustine, the world is filled with Antichrists, those who oppose the church and its teaching. The Antichrist, in short, might be more than a horrific beast as the end times play out. What if he also manifests himself as a seemingly ordinary member of human society connected, if in mysterious ways, to the created order more generally? What if, in short, the conflict between good and evil also is staged in human affairs, forecasting the ultimate cosmological struggle John describes? If so, vexing questions are raised, or so thought the leaders of the then-outlawed Christian community as they sought to fix the place of resistance to divine will within the still not completely revealed moral structure of the universe. The most important of these questions addresses the role that members of the Christian community are to play in this contest between the Savior and his ontological opposite, whose story, in the view of the church father Irenaeus of Lyon, must "recapitulate evil, just as Christ recapitulates all good."[24] The story of the Antichrist, then, must parallel that of the Savior. In McGinn's description of Irenaeus's influential reformulation, "As the Word truly became flesh in order that the human might become God . . . so too Antichrist must come in the flesh as the one who sums up all the evil that separates humanity from God."[25] And this would be because, as McGinn suggests, "the returning God-man would have to encounter the epitome of human opposition to goodness in order to realize the fullness of his reign on earth."[26]

But this struggle can be imagined historically as well as in terms of eschatology. Or rather, it can be imagined in both ways simultaneously. If the Antichrist is man as well as beast, perhaps even a series of men and an anti-culture eager to displace the Christian order, then his identification and destruction might well depend at least in some measure on human action, on some among the community of believers recognizing the danger in their midst and taking the appropriate measures for its extirpation. This rededication to the centrality of the metaphysical in human experience would include a renewal of faith in the presence of a God who might call upon his creatures to make the most difficult of sacrifices. Embroiled in the never-ending whirl of the worldly, they would be forced to recognize the brittle falseness of "ordinary" appearances, whose underlying truth is revealed by signs and then events whose purposeful extraordinariness cannot be denied even by those most determined to dismiss any explanation for phenomena not amenable to a logical positivist exegesis. *The Omen* dramatizes this awakening with a biblical figure, as Richard Thorpe, like Abraham, is moved to slaughter his own son on an altar to further the will of God. Like Abraham, he also fails to draw the blood of his own flesh, acting against every human instinct. But Thorpe is prevented from this horrific act not by God but by the Satanic power of the infant Antichrist appealing to the father's paternal feelings. The rejection of the efficacy of human actions is in many ways the main intellectual theme of all the *Omen* films. This dark view of human possibility runs counter to the optimism of contemporary millenarianism in the evangelical community, with its emphasis on what we might call fast-track salvation, or dispensationalism. The *Left Behind* novels trace the horrific suffering of those with weak faith, while offering a reassuring vision of the assumption of those chosen to be saved. Tellingly, this company of God's elect is absent from the visions of end times evoked by the *Omen* films.

Unsurprisingly, Antichrist becomes a more central figure in Christian culture when expectations about the end of the created order become more compelling and influential. We have been living in such a period now for two centuries. The advent in the 1830s of dispensationalist apocalypticism among English, and then American, evangelicals gave rise to enthusiastic speculations about the end times that only grew more intense in the post–World War II era. There were historical reasons for this development, which is connected to certain readings of those signs or omens that tradition predicted would forecast the beginning of the events prophesied in the Book of Revelation. The dispensationalists believe that the prophecies in the Revelation were postponed by the destruction of the temple in Jerusalem (first century CE) only to be put back into motion when the Jews returned definitively to the Holy Land (the state of Israel was established as a Jewish homeland in 1948).

The advent of the Antichrist would mean for the faithful accepting acting in complete disregard of the most basic of human emotions and feelings to endorse the irresistibility of an all-superseding divine will. The story of the Antichrist as a threat acting in historical time thus poses a test to those "called" to knowledge that the most basic of moral struggles is unfolding. In the first two *Omen* films, this recognition is forced by signs and the irrefutable testimony of personal experience on, first, his original adoptive parents and then, with their death, on his uncle and aunt who assume responsibility for the orphan. Forced to acknowledge that their beloved child is the Antichrist, the fathers in each case do not act swiftly enough to kill him in the prescribed manner (using a set of special sacred knives). Resistance, though aroused, fails; in *The Final Conflict*, a company of monks, reading the signs in the heavens, likewise are defeated by unseen powers in a series of ingenious attempts to assassinate the enemy of God. The world is saved not by a returning Christ wielding a sword but by lucky chance. And yet, as *The Awakening*, aptly titled, demonstrates, the seed of the Antichrist is not easily destroyed. This film, too, ends with the horrific death of the parent who would kill her child to save the world and an Antichrist, present in the two unnaturally related "twins," who will presumably grow into their prophesied role as destroyers of the divine order.

The franchise has at this point reached a provisional end (the possibility of extension has not been foreclosed) in which human efforts to prevent the very worst of outcomes for the created order have once again failed. It seems appropriate that in this latest installment the would-be defender of righteousness kills herself, surrendering to the hopelessness that she sees in her world. Once again, as Price suggests about *The Omen*, "a sense of fatalistic foreboding builds as the story progresses, as attempt after attempt to stop the child fails . . . the countdown is underway and no one can avert it."[27] Thus, the faux biblical prophecy recited in that film by the renegade priest Father Brennan (Patrick Troughton) comes to pass, reversing the victory recorded in Revelation and, more recently, in the *Left Behind* novels, among other hopeful evangelical fiction about the end times:

When the Jews return to Zion,
And a comet rips the sky,
And the Holy Roman Empire rises,
Then you and I must die.
From the eternal sea he rises,
Creating armies on either shore,
Turning man against his brother,
Till Man exists no more.

Notes

1. For information on these excavations today, see Israel Finkelstein, "Megiddo 3" (review), Bible History Today, January 14, 2012, accessed May 13, 2021, http://digs.bib -arch.org/digs/megiddo.asp.

2. Justin Wyatt, *High Concept: Movies and Marketing in Hollywood* (Austin: University of Texas Press, 1994), 16.

3. Wyatt,15.

4. Wyatt,78.

5. All box office figures in this essay are from Box Office Mojo, accessed May 13, 2021, http://www.boxofficemojo.com/.

6. For details, see Bernard McGinn, *Anti-Christ: Two Thousand Years of the Human Fascination with Evil* (New York: Harper, 1994).

7. For a discussion of the importance of music as sound "icon" for high concept releases), see Wyatt, *High Concept*, 1–22.

8. For a historical sketch of this development, see Barry Langford, *Post-Classical Hollywood: Film Industry, Style, and Ideology since 1945* (Edinburgh: Edinburgh University Press, 2010).

9. Wyatt, *High Concept*, 60.

10. See the Damien Disciples Facebook group, accessed May 13, 2021, https://www.facebook.com/DamienDisciples.

11. See Abdullah Al-Ghamdi, "The Omen Prequel Movie Will Reveal Damien's Origin," Screen Rant, September 10, 2020, accessed May 13, 2021, https://screenrant.com/omen-movie-prequel-damien-origin-story-details/.

12. Wyatt, *High Concept*, 16, 15.

13. McGinn, *Anti-Christ*, 2–3.

14. McGinn, 272.

15. Robert R. Price, "Antichrist Superstar and the Paperback Apocalypse," RMP, accessed February 21, 2017, http://www.robertmprice.mindvendor.com/art_antichrist_superstar.htm.

16. Wilhelm Bousset, *The Antichrist Legend* (London: Hutchinson, 1894), xi.

17. Bousset, xi.

18. For a detailed history of the sources and subsequent developments, see McGinn, *Anti-Christ*, and Bousset, *Antichrist Legend*.

19. Elaine Pagels, *Revelations: Visions, Prophecy, and Politics in the Book of Revelation* (New York: Penguin, 2012), 16.

20. Pagels, 115.

21. For details, see Bousset, *Antichrist Legend*.

22. For an interesting and detailed account of his negative views of human sexuality, see Geoffrey R. Stone, *Sex and the Constitution* (New York: W. W. Norton, 2017), 7–23.

23. Elaine Pagels, *The Origin of Satan* (New York: Random House, 1995), 182.

24. Quoted in McGinn, 59.

25. McGinn, *Anti-Christ*, 59.

26. McGinn, 3.

27. Price, "Antichrist Superstar," 9.

The Weird Devil

Lovecraftian Horror in John Carpenter's Prince of Darkness

Carl H. Sederholm

At first glance, it seems only natural to include a discussion of John Carpenter's *Prince of Darkness* (1987) in a collection focused on representations of Satan in Western cinema. The film's title, a recognized synonym for the devil (one used by Shakespeare, Milton, and many others), might suggest a narrative concerning a Judeo-Christian devil and its attempts to possess, manipulate, or otherwise control a film's characters within recognizable genre conventions. By 1987, audiences already familiar with the array of horror films that built on the success of *The Exorcist* (William Friedkin, 1973), *Rosemary's Baby* (Roman Polanski, 1968), and *The Omen* (Richard Donner, 1976) might reasonably expect *Prince of Darkness* to light out for well-trodden territories. But *Prince of Darkness* has little explicit interest in understanding (or even representing) the devil or his activities through familiar cultural, theological, or ideological perspectives.

By appearance alone, Carpenter's devil is hardly the *sui generis* figure found in Judeo-Christian teachings, let alone the often-mocked cartoonish imp in red tights, armed with a sneer and a pitchfork. Instead, the film confronts viewers with a devil in the shape of a billowing green liquid trapped in a large container and held in the basement of an abandoned church. This unconventional devil is nothing less than a swirling and pulsating enemy that is both uncanny and all too real. As Kendall Phillips describes it, Carpenter's Satan is a "cosmic force," one with explicit thematic ties to the director's most memorable villains, Michael Myers in *Halloween* (1978), the vengeful spirits terrorizing Antonio Bay in *The Fog* (1980), or the shape-shifting monstrosity in *The Thing* (1982).[1] Although Phillips correctly describes these antagonists as cosmic forces, his discussion is more concerned with how they fit within

Prince of Darkness's unique representation of the Devil as green liquid.

Carpenter's film career rather than with developing the implications of a broader cosmic outlook, one that readily falls not only within Lovecraftian conceptions of the weird but also within the purview of the philosophical thinking associated with weird realism. Given Carpenter's long-standing interest in powerful outside Others, cosmic forces beyond human ken, we must turn greater attention to the ways *Prince of Darkness* addresses encounters with these Others and how they shed light on the ways of approaching the unthinkable. As Eugene Thacker writes, "horror is about the paradoxical thought of the unthinkable" in that it engages explicitly with the limits of human understanding and the impossibility of representing reality as it really is.[2] To understand the green liquid Satan from *Prince of Darkness* requires much greater attention to the film's thematic ties to weird realism precisely because this Satan is strange and unknowable but no less real. Only in that light can we begin to explore Carpenter's larger approach to thinking about the unthinkable and its implications on how human beings grapple with reality. Only then can we give this liquid green devil his due.

Weird Realism

My approach to *Prince of Darkness* suggests that the film is symptomatic of a larger turn to the weird, both in philosophy and in culture, a turn discussed by philosophical thinkers such as Graham Harman, Eugene Thacker, Dylan

Trigg, and others. As Thacker writes, the everyday world as human beings currently experience it does not lend itself to easy explanation. In his words, "the world is increasingly unthinkable—a world of planetary disasters, emerging pandemics, tectonic shifts, strange weather, oil-drenched seascapes, and the furtive, always-looming threat of extinction."[3] Understanding a world in commotion and disastrous events stretches conventional wisdom and requires confronting the paradox of thinking about the unthinkable. Put another way, if the world can no longer be understood through conventional means, how can we ever begin to understand reality?

Even though horror films like *Prince of Darkness* are not, strictly speaking, philosophical texts, they nevertheless provide an insightful means of approaching the problem of the unthinkable. In *The Philosophy of Horror* (1990), Noël Carroll argues that horror challenges limits of human understanding by introducing monsters that "breach the norms of ontological propriety presumed by the positive human characters in the story."[4] Horror suggests the existence of creatures (or of circumstances) that cannot be subsumed within any preexisting philosophical, scientific, or metaphysical program. In Thacker's terms, horror films routinely address the "absolute limit[s]" of human comprehension, usually by introducing situations, events, or beings that defy representation.[5] In that sense, horror suggests that reality itself is not only stranger than people can think but also stranger than they can represent.

Outside of introducing monsters that have no place in conventional taxonomies, horror also routinely creates epistemological dread by manipulating the tension between what appears on the screen and what lurks outside of one's frame of reference, "just beyond the borders of the frame."[6] Even though a film's main characters do not always realize what dangers await them, audiences are usually acutely aware of unseen threats and anxiously scan the screen with the expectation that something hides just beyond what they can see or understand. To watch a horror film is to engage with the possibility that one's commonsense expectations about the world, especially things in everyday life, may change in a heartbeat.

Prince of Darkness approaches these limits of human understanding by challenging conventional wisdom in both science and theology. The film's reflections on the nature of God and of Satan ultimately suggest material realities that defy all human understanding. If objects and events within the world seem increasingly impossible to comprehend, how might someone come to grips with a devil in the shape of a swirling mass of green liquid?

Prince of Darkness demands that audiences confront the possibility that scientific studies do not bring about any obvious meanings, at least not in terms of what can be thought, measured, or understood. If reality is thus no longer conventionally thinkable, it may also exceed the bounds of human representation, let alone human understanding. As Harman writes, "reality itself is weird because reality is incommensurable with any attempt to represent or measure it."[7] Instead of a philosophy that seeks intelligible correlations between the mind and the world, connections that seem warranted by scientific or other kinds of understanding, weird realism stresses the ways reality is unthinkable and unknowable, something that is stranger, weirder, and less prone to representation than human beings have imagined. In Harman's terms, "when it comes to grasping reality, illusion and innuendo are the best we can do."[8] As with Carpenter's impossibly strange green devil, human beings may initially rely on measurements, formulae, equations, assumptions, translations, beliefs, and rituals, only to discover that objects exist independently of human interaction, understanding, or intention.

Prince of Darkness exacerbates the problem of thinking about the unthinkable by imagining a devil that is not only explicitly real but whose reality also subverts all human understanding—especially those stemming from science and theology—concerning the nature and purpose of evil, its relationship to human beings, and its place in the world. In this light, Carpenter's film is the kind of horror film that engages with "the paradoxical thought of the unthinkable."[9] Instead of simply upending religion, however, the new insights about Satan subject everything else to question. For instance, when Brian Marsh (Jameson Parker), one of the science graduate students in the film running tests on the green liquid Satan, begins to summarize his findings, he cautions the others that the plot "gets a little wild here." By "wild," he means that the details that follow are beyond conventional expectation, that they press the limits of human understanding, and that they risk dismantling everything people expect about the workings of the universe. Although the film's overall narrative is characterized by similarly wild gaps in understanding and logic, a point that likely prompted John Clute and Peter Nicholls's dismissal of the film as "inept and barely coherent," these gaps have a larger philosophical purpose.[10] Against Clute and Nicholls, I argue that the film's apparent lack of narrative cohesion reinforces its thematic emphasis on the problem of addressing the significant gaps between objects (e.g., a green liquid devil) and the power of human language or wisdom to understand it. In this light, Carpenter's film falls within the tradition of the speculative realists.

The Lovecraftian Weird

Not surprisingly, speculative realism borrows much of its dominant assumptions from the work of H. P. Lovecraft, the pulp writer whose popularity has grown rapidly in the twenty-first century. As Harman characterized H. P. Lovecraft, "No other writer is so perplexed by the gap between objects and the power of language to describe them, or between objects and the qualities they possess."[11] Lovecraftian assumptions may even take on the quality of a "background enthymeme," a compelling and persuasive proposition that nothing is quite as it seems and that reality ultimately exceeds the powers of representation.[12] As Lovecraft suggests in "The Call of Cthulhu" (1928), "The most merciful thing in the world, I think, is the inability of the human mind to correlate all its contents. We live on a placid island of ignorance in the midst of black seas of infinity, and it was not meant that we should voyage far."[13] For Lovecraft, such ignorance may be bliss because deep exploration usually entails discovering that reality is not what it seems. In Lovecraft's terms, knowledge risks opening up "such terrifying vistas of reality, or our frightful position therein, that we shall either go mad from the revelation or flee from the deadly light into the peace and safety of a new dark age."[14]

In another familiar passage for Lovecraft fans, Lovecraft explains that weird narratives function best precisely when they suggest the possibility of those terrifying vistas opening up. Weird narratives must consistently reach beyond convention and cliché in order to develop "a certain atmosphere of breathless and unexplainable dread of outer, unknown forces."[15] For Lovecraft, weird tales depend on the destabilizing suppositions of such moods because they help audiences experience the possibility that life, the universe, and everything are subject to radical suspension or change, suggesting realities far beyond what human beings have conventionally claimed to understand.

To a large extent, *Prince of Darkness* represents one of Carpenter's best forays into Lovecraftian horror.[16] Carpenter reread Lovecraft as part of his preparation for the film; he especially wanted to borrow from the author's ability to create the kind of atmosphere, mood, and pacing that would result in a final, terrifying "gasp."[17] In an interview with Gilles Boulenger, Carpenter suggests that he especially admires Lovecraft's early tale "The Outsider" because of its sudden concluding twist.[18] Throughout his career, Lovecraft created such powerful affective states not through mundane or clichéd scares but by balancing the right atmosphere with enough realism so that whatever strange or improbable conditions he would introduce might seem plausible. In his "Notes on Writing Weird Fiction," Lovecraft cautioned would-be weird writers to introduce fictional marvels "impressively and deliberately—with a careful emotional 'build-up'—else it will seem flat and unconvincing."[19] Each narrative element must work together to create a climactic suspension of disbelief so powerful that it also gives the illusion that the so-called laws of the universe—not to mention human epistemological and ontological assumptions of human beings—may be subject to radical suspension or alteration. *Prince of Darkness* arguably operates on a similar level. From its long title sequence to its slowly unfolding plot, the film follows Lovecraft's technique of creating fear and anxiety by building things slowly, ever pushing toward that final, dreadful, climax.

Despite the film's explicit debts to Lovecraft, *Prince of Darkness* is not simply an extended nod to the author. Instead, it pushes the weird in directions similar to those found in weird realism, or the human inability to represent reality in precise and ultimately meaningful ways, a problem that suggests all commonsense notions of observation, objectivity, or reality are bound to fail. Despite all the efforts of scientists, theologians, and others to understand Carpenter's green Satan, the result is less a series of new insights into familiar questions but a terrible realization that nothing may be as it seems and that most things—the world, the cosmos, human life, and so on—are increasingly unthinkable. With *Prince of Darkness*, Carpenter ultimately suggests that the devil is not in the details but is the main attraction in an impossible attempt to come to grips with commonsense notions of reality. Carpenter's swirling green Satan is nothing less than a weird devil.

Something Is All Wrong

Despite its use of visual and narrative gaps, there are enough details in the film to piece together part of the cosmic scheme driving the overall plot. Satan, viewers learn, is actually the son of Anti-God, an embodied evil that can only be understood through the insights of theoretical physics. Against all odds, human beings somehow banished this Anti-God to another dimension thousands of years ago. Buried in the Middle East by his father, Satan is eventually discovered and held under guard by a secret Catholic sect known as the Brotherhood of Sleep. *Prince of Darkness* opens just as the last surviving member of this brotherhood is dying, never having passed on his secret to others. When the unnamed Priest character (played by Donald Pleasance) learns of the man's death,[20] he quickly discovers in Father Carlton's journals and other documents what was long kept hidden: that Satan is physically real, that his strength is growing, and that he is determined to set free the Anti-God. Realizing that he cannot fight Satan without help, Priest enlists the help of Professor Howard Birack (Victor Wong), a prominent physicist who brings along with him a team of doctoral students who will help him understand the enemy and then defeat him, thereby saving the world from destruction.

Carpenter's story (written under the pseudonym Martin Quatermass, one of many nods to Nigel Kneale and the *Quatermass* films) is by turns compelling, vague, exciting, confusing, implausible, and insightful; however, the film's strength comes from its blending of outside doom with key thematic questions concerning the nature of evil, the status of human beings in the cosmos, and the limitations of human intelligence. As Harman writes (in a discussion of "The Call of Cthulhu"), "nothing could be more threatening than the notion that something is 'all wrong' in the presumed spatial contours on which all human thought and action is based."[21] A similar point may be made about *Prince of Darkness*, especially the awful sense that everything is "all wrong" both in the way humans understand the world and in how this sense takes characters to the edge of human understanding.

As the film's plot unfolds, Carpenter routinely suggests that human understanding is little more than a series of long-standing superstitions and misunderstandings; moreover, he shows that human beings are largely insignificant, weak, and helpless against the larger plots of supernatural beings. Even though the film is ultimately more invested in science rather than religion, Carpenter is careful to avoid the trap of placing them into an interminable tug of war. Instead, he shows off their strengths, weaknesses, and ultimate helplessness before the vastness of the cosmos.

Likewise, *Prince of Darkness* takes viewers even more deeply into a novel and unconventional exploration of good and evil, one that is both uncanny and unnerving. Indeed, long-standing Christian teachings begin to fall apart as soon as Priest learns that Satan is a material entity that operates at the quantum level and infects all matter throughout the universe. In response to the question, "How did the Roman Catholic Church manage to keep this a secret for 2,000 years?" Priest suggests, "Apparently, a decision was made to characterize pure evil as a spiritual force, even within the darkness in the hearts of men. It was more convenient. In that way, man remained at the center of things. A stupid lie. We were salesmen, that's all." No less devastating, Priest also discovers that Jesus "was of extraterrestrial ancestry" and was sent to earth specifically to warn human beings about Satan and his growing power. Following Jesus's death, his disciples determined to withhold his message from the world "until man could develop a science sophisticated enough to prove what Christ was saying." But science, as everyone quickly discovers, only provides even more evidence of unthinkable problems.

Weird Science

Carpenter's dream for *Prince of Darkness* was to combine elements of horror with the controversial insights of quantum physics in order to frighten audiences intellectually more than his other films had. As he explained to Gilles

Boulenger, "I wanted to do a movie that worked here [Carpenter points to his brain] as opposed to working out here [Carpenter looks around]."[22] Carpenter began studying quantum physics around the time he was making *Big Trouble in Little China* (1986).[23] His initial plan for *Prince of Darkness* was to develop a project that would include "some sort of ultimate evil and combine it with the notion of matter and anti-matter." He continues, "Since there is a mirror of anti-matter for every particle of matter, I thought it would be great to have an anti-God, namely a mirror opposite of God, that would be totally evil."[24] Carpenter was largely influenced by popular scientific texts such as Heinz Pagels's *The Cosmic Code* (1982) and Paul Davies's *God and the New Physics* (1984); he also studied work by John Wheeler, one of the most respected scientists of the postwar era. Carpenter additionally adapted portions of Gregory Benford's science fiction novel *Timescape* (1980), a text that imagines the possibility that tachyons—particles that travel faster than the speed of light—could be used to convey warnings from the future.[25]

By turning to quantum physics, Carpenter hoped to frighten audiences by introducing a series of ideas that would shake up everyday understanding in ways that suggest forms of knowledge far outside of human capacities, thereby upsetting commonsense notions of order and reality. As Dylan Trigg writes, "Carpenter presents this disturbance of reality as a confrontation with a cosmos that is at best indifferent, at worst opposed to humanity."[26]

On its own, quantum mechanics challenges classical physics by taking aim at the idea of an orderly universe defined by observable phenomena, rational laws, and predictable forces. Instead, quantum reality attempts to make sense of things that "cannot be visualized," let alone be explained, using conventional wisdom or science.[27] According to Heinz Pagels, quantum physics is so disconcerting that its insights produce a discomfort he describes as "quantum weirdness," precisely because of the way it replaces traditional notions of order with something much more difficult to comprehend, let alone explain.[28] The insights of the new physics were both exciting and controversial given the implication that they could permanently transform classical notions of some of the broadest topics, including the nature of reality, life, matter, energy, and the universe. For some, quantum physics appeared as a threat, one that held the power to upend all other sources of knowing by introducing the unknowable into the picture. As Arkady Plotnitsky writes, these "nonclassical theories" could "radically redefine the nature of knowledge by making the unknowable an irreducible part of knowledge, insofar as the ultimate objects under investigation by nonclassical theories are seen as being beyond any knowledge or even conception, while, at the same time, affecting what is knowable."[29] Quantum mechanics pushes the boundaries of what can be understood by making the universe less susceptible to fixed laws. Moreover, it changes the ways people perceive reality, rendering the everyday world at best uncanny and at worst unknowable. As Harman explains about weird realism, certain objects, experiences, or events begin to feel as though they "resist all description" even though they are real.[30]

The new physics was not just shaking up the world of science; it was also challenging long-held theological assumptions concerning the process of creation, the purpose of life, and the nature of God, something Carpenter develops in his film through his challenging of conventional theology and his representation of Satan as liquid matter. In his discussion of quantum physics, Paul Davies suggested that "science offers a surer path to God than religion," because it was more likely to offer an accurate picture of the universe.[31] Put another way, physics might even supersede religion as the major source of insight relative to understanding the cosmos. Similarly, Pagels suggests that the new physics could cause a "conversion of our imaginations" precisely because of its power to challenge commonsense notions of reality.[32] In *Prince of Darkness*, Professor Birack explores these implications by telling his students: "Say good-bye to classical reality, because our logic collapses on the subatomic level into ghosts and shadows. From Job's friends insisting that the good are rewarded and the wicked punished to the scientists of the 1930s proving to their horror a theorem that not everything can be proved, we've sought to impose order on the universe. But we have discovered something very surprising. While order does exist in the universe, it is not at all what we had in mind." To say "good-bye to classical reality" is to face the possibility that the world was not designed solely for human beings in the first place and that people must therefore develop a new means of understanding the world and its objects. As Trigg writes, people may even have to embrace the insight that "human beings are not and never were at the centre of things."[33]

In *Prince of Darkness*, the main characters are not only unprepared to face new conceptions of reality but must also face the unexpected consequences of grappling with the all-too-real presence of Satan as a disembodied mass of green liquid. This Satan is frightening precisely because he is "a materiality outside of humanity," a living substance with a will and a consciousness that disregards any human attempts to understand or control his powers.[34] In an intriguing scientific analogy, Professor Birack suggests one way of coming to grips with this new reality: "Suppose what your faith has said was essentially correct. Suppose there is a universal mind controlling everything, a god willing the behavior of every subatomic particle. Now every particle has an antiparticle, its mirror image, its negative side. Maybe this universal mind resides in the mirror image instead of in our universe as we wanted to believe."

If Satan operates at an inverted and subatomic level, then he can no longer be understood as a shrewd tempter or a metaphor for human evil; instead, he is, as the film calls him, the Anti-God, the source of all negative power throughout the universe. Borrowing from Mary Midgley's description of the demon Mephistopheles in *Wickedness: A Philosophical Essay* (1984), this Anti-God may be described in part as "simply anti-life": "Whatever is arising, he is against it. His element is mere refusal."[35] Even though Midgley is not describing Carpenter's Anti-God, her point about "mere refusal" nevertheless plays into the film's larger sense that everything has its opposite and the Anti-God always presses against whatever God chooses to do. Horror itself may be generally described as "the experience of inversion, a disordering of interiority and exteriority, until nothing remains except materiality rendered spectral / spectrality rendered material."[36] In this sense, the Anti-God may be understood not only as a "disordering" power but one that is also just as real and as material as anything else.

Unfortunately, *Prince of Darkness* does not completely explore the implications of the Anti-God, its power, or its purposes. Likewise, the film—by Carpenter's own admission—does not wrestle with quantum physics as much as it could have.[37] As with much of Carpenter's work, audiences were not quite ready for his signature blend of intelligence, pessimism, and horror, not to mention his willingness to explore realities outside of human understanding.

Uneasy Being Green

In *Prince of Darkness*, the most prominent reminder of "realities that are impossible to describe" is the presence of the green liquid Satan.[38] When Carpenter reveals the swirling liquid for the first time, he does so in a sequence in which Priest and Professor Birack descend into the basement of an abandoned Los Angeles church to look at it together. Though neither man seems afraid, they both appear awestruck, unsure what to make of the incongruous majesty of the enormous vat of swirling green liquid positioned where a sacred altar should be. Just as impressive, the room is adorned with hundreds of crucifixes, large and small, that not only surround the container but also help ward off its growing power. The room is lit by hundreds of wax candles that create a bold and impressive chiaroscuro, one that adds even greater mystery contained within this strange pillar of liquid. This play of light and shadow, however, is not just a striking effect; it is also symbolic of the ways the uncanny green liquid upends human understanding. In Harman's terms, this is a chiaroscuro within "reality itself," one that points to the impossibility of representing things as they really are.[39] Put another way, Carpenter's devil suggests unthinkable realities, things that can only be understood through inference, allusion, or symbolization.

In a handful of impressive wide shots, Carpenter captures the awful majesty of the cylinder as it appears in the basement of an old Los Angeles church. These shots, though uncommonly highlighted, effectively demonstrate how Carpenter's design and *mise-en-scène* lends magic and mystery to its representation of the film's antagonist. The play of light and shadow, not to mention the restlessness and power of the swirling green liquid, helps portend something truly awful, something unknowable by conventional sources of information, including those from science and religion.

In terms of its impact on human understanding, Carpenter's pillar of green liquid may be compared to Lovecraft's strange and uncanny meteor from "The Colour Out of Space" (1927), especially because both Satan and the meteor use color to suggest realities beyond human understanding—what Harman calls the "unintelligible but real."[40] In Lovecraft's tale, the colors connected to the meteor are actually impossible to describe through any appeal to scientific or other kinds of human knowledge. Lovecraft signals this impossibility by suggesting, "it was only by analogy that they called it colour at all."[41] That is, the titular color out of space exceeds the bounds of human language and human understanding but gestures toward realities impossible to comprehend within current circumstances. Such a color would be impossible to portray on film; nevertheless, Carpenter's use of green helps to convey a sense of mystery, disgust, and the unknowable. As Lovecraft writes in "The Colour Out of Space," "It was nothing of this earth, but a piece of the great outside; and as such dowered with outside properties and obedient to outside laws."[42] In *Prince of Darkness*, the green liquid Satan certainly counts as "a piece of the great outside," something impossible to represent in human terms and something that points to realities beyond human understanding.

In horror films, color is routinely exploited to create key symbolic, affective, or thematic conditions.[43] For Carpenter, green takes on multiple values that, taken together, point not only to the real presence of Satan but also to the ways his existence suggests other impossible realities and significant liminal spaces.[44] During the Middle Ages, green was regularly understood to be a sign of the devil. In folkloric traditions, for example, the devil was associated with green because green was "the traditional color of the hunter's clothing" and Satan was believed to be a hunter after human souls.[45] As D. W. Robertson Jr. explains, the devil as a hunter in green even finds its way into Geoffrey Chaucer's "Friar's Tale."[46] Moreover, as Michel Pastoureau demonstrates, green devils sometimes appeared in stained glass windows and illuminated texts, usually in the company of demons, serpents, or dragons that were also represented as green.[47] Together, these creatures made up a "green bestiary" that contributed to expanding the negative associations with green in general, especially when it was tied to representations of dragons, serpents, crocodiles, frogs, and other similar creatures.[48] Green dragons were especially bad, their scaly green coloring contributing to their overall "slimy, pustular, gleaming, and fiery" appearance.[49] According to Ruth Mellinkoff, the painter Matthias Grünewald signals the presence of Satan in the *Isenheim Altarpiece* through the "greenish cast of his hands," using the color as a sign of the devil's theological connections to death and decay.[50]

Although *Prince of Darkness* is a twentieth-century film and not a medieval work of art, its use of green to represent Satan is nevertheless consistent with the color's historically negative associations. By representing Satan through a color, however, Carpenter draws on traditions drawn from folklore and from the visual arts and not from theological discourse. His devil, like the strange and uncanny creatures in medieval art and folklore, maintains the power to evoke powers and purposes that lie beyond human understanding. More to the point, Carpenter's Satan is a real substance, "a materiality outside of humanity" that overturns every human attempt to understand evil.[51] Because Carpenter's Satan is real, it always suggests the possibility that "something is 'all wrong' in the presumed spatial contours on which all human thought and action is based."[52] Put another way, Carpenter's devil evokes the "terrifying vistas of reality, and of our frightful position therein" that Lovecraft mentions in "The Call of Cthulhu."[53] In this case, however, the terrifying vistas risk upending everything human beings once believed about evil, the creation, and the purpose of human life.

In a few key moments, Carpenter also uses green to highlight the ways conventional approaches to science and religion are subject to radical change. In this light, he may have borrowed Dario Argento's own use of green in the film *Inferno* (1980) to suggest liminal spaces, particularly the strange and porous border between the conscious and the unconscious.[54] As with the green liquid Satan in *Prince of Darkness*, Argento uses green liquid in *Inferno* to highlight the transition from knowing to unknown. In that film, green marks liminal spaces, particularly the strange and porous border. In a famous sequence from *Inferno*, Rose Elliot (Irene Miracle) descends into a mysterious flooded underground ballroom and swims around slowly in search of a lost set of keys. When she ascends to take a breath, the water at the point of entry is green, suggesting that she has been swimming in a place outside of the constraints of human reason.

Outside of the green liquid, the color also appears at several interesting places in *Prince of Darkness*. Catherine (Lisa Blount) wears a green blouse while attending Professor Birak's lecture about the principles of quantum physics and their significant challenge to classical reality. Likewise, when Priest first reads the diaries from the Brotherhood of Sleep, he does so in a darkened room, lit only by a green lamp. And, in a comic scene, Dr. Paul Leahy (Peter Jason) juggles a green apple prior to his own expanded understanding of Satan, the Anti-God, and the plot against humanity. Obviously, none of these varied uses of green should be understood to underscore a singular, dominant use of the color. And yet, these seemingly small uses of green appear at moments in which characters come to a greater understanding that the nature of reality is nothing like they had assumed. In that sense, green might be read as a symbol of larger realities that are impossible to describe, let alone understand. Given that Satan also appears as green liquid, the appearance of green elsewhere in the film might also suggest that his influence is expanding to other parts of the world and that nothing is completely free of evil.[55]

In a more playful scene, Carpenter shows Walter (Dennis Dun) watching a Tom and Jerry cartoon entitled "Heavenly Puss." For a few moments, Carpenter frames the television in the center of the shot so that viewers can see exactly what Walter sees: a sequence in which Tom (a cat) falls into a trapdoor that plunges him downward into hell where he subsequently lands inside a cauldron being stirred by Spike the dog. Though this scene may be little more than a funny cartoon parody of a literal belief in hell as a place of fire and brimstone, there are nevertheless at least three details from the short scene that underscore symbolic associations between the color green and the devil: the floor of hell is green, Spike prevents Tom from escaping by threatening him with a green pitchfork, and the smoke billowing from the cauldron is also green. In this hell, as in *Prince of Darkness*, green suggests a transition from a state of security to a state of insecurity. Whereas in the cartoon Tom eventually escapes, the characters in *Prince of Darkness* must continue to wrestle with an overwhelming sense that things will never be the same again, that religion, science, and reality now lie far beyond human understanding.

Carpenter has a long-standing fascination precisely with such moments, especially when they challenge everyday notions of truth and reality. As Robert Cumbow explains, Carpenter's films broadly address the implications of such sudden dramatic reversals or subverted expectations. In his words, "Carpenter's films are populated by seekers whose quest for meaning is usually rewarded, but who often discover an order quite different from the reassuring one they set out to find."[56] These outcomes cut to the heart of human experience. As Cumbow writes, "This is the far deeper, more devastating (and sometimes transfiguring) experience of finding that the order in accord with which one has lived one's life is *not the right one*; that some *other* order altogether controls—and perhaps has always controlled."[57] Such reversals are devastating because they suggest the possibility that any attempts to understand, measure, or represent reality are far more challenging than anyone suspected.

In *Supernatural Horror in Literature*, Lovecraft argued that weird tales must not recreate clichés nor dwell on questions of morality but should frighten readers by exploring circumstances that could lead to "a malign and particular suspension or defeat of those fixed laws of Nature which are our only safeguard against the assaults of chaos and the daemons of unplumbed space."[58] In that light, *Prince of Darkness* certainly qualifies as a weird tale, but it is more than just a Lovecraft-inspired narrative. Instead, *Prince of Darkness* tests the limits of scientific and theological discourse to suggest that human attempts to understand—or to represent—reality are ultimately impossible. The approach to the weird *Prince of Darkness* takes shares with speculative realism a fascination with exposing the unknowable, questioning the knowable, and challenging the status of human beings within the cosmos. In the end, nothing is so weird as reality itself.

Notes

The author would like to thank Robert Colson for commenting on multiple drafts of this paper and for his always-helpful suggestions

1. Kendall Phillips, *Dark Directions: Romero, Craven, Carpenter, and the Modern Horror Film* (Carbondale and Edwardsville: Southern Illinois University Press, 2012), 144.

2. Eugene Thacker, *In the Dust of This Planet: Horror of Philosophy* (Winchester, UK: Zero Books, 2011), 1:9.

3. Thacker, 1.

4. Noël Carroll, *The Philosophy of Horror; or Paradoxes of the Heart* (New York: Routledge, 1990), 16.

5. Thacker, *Dust of This Planet*, 1.

6. Lester Friedman, David Desser, Sarah Kozloff, Martha P. Nochimson, and Stephen Prince, *An Introduction to Film Genres* (New York: W. W. Norton, 2014), 388–389.

7. Graham Harman, *Weird Realism: Lovecraft and Philosophy* (Winchester, UK: Zero Books, 2012), 51. Harman's work on H. P. Lovecraft has been wildly influential, especially among critics who embrace his object-oriented ontology. Among other places, this influence appears throughout my coedited volume *The Age of Lovecraft*, ed. Carl Sederholm and Jeffrey Andrew Weinstock (Minneapolis: University of Minnesota Press, 2016). Harman's article—"On the Horror of Phenomenology: Lovecraft and Husserl," *Collapse* 4 (2008): 333–364—was expanded and developed into the book *Weird Realism: Lovecraft and Philosophy*.

8. Harman, *Weird Realism*.

9. Thacker, *Dust of This Planet*, 9.

10. John Kenneth Muir, *The Films of John Carpenter* (Jefferson, NC: McFarland, 2000), 133.

11. Harman, *Weird Realism*, 3.

12. Harman, 23.

13. H. P. Lovecraft, "The Call of Cthulhu," in *The Call of Cthulhu and Other Weird Stories*, ed. S. T. Joshi (New York: Penguin, 1999), 139.

14. Lovecraft, 139.

15. H. P. Lovecraft, *Supernatural Horror in Literature* (New York: Ben Abramson, 1945), 15.

16. Gilles Boulenger, *John Carpenter: The Prince of Darkness* (Los Angeles: Silman-James Press, 2001), 97. For most viewers, Carpenter's 1995 film *In the Mouth of Madness* is the one that is most obviously and explicitly indebted to H. P. Lovecraft. My purpose here is not to ignore that connection but to point out the ways *Prince of Darkness* not only works out many of those themes even earlier but also how it reaches beyond them in ways that connect with speculative realism.

17. Boulenger, 204.

18. Boulenger, 204.

19. H. P. Lovecraft, "Notes on Writing Weird Fiction," in *Collected Essays*, vol. 2: *Literary Criticism*, ed. S. T. Joshi (New York: Hippocampus Press, 2004), 177.

20. Although the film never specifically grants Priest a proper name, he is known popularly as Father Loomis, a playful nod to Pleasance's character in *Halloween*. For convenience and clarity, I will refer to this character simply as Priest.

21. Harman, *Weird Realism*, 71; brackets in the original.

22. Boulenger, *John Carpenter*, 203.

23. Robert C. Cumbow, *Order in the Universe: The Films of John Carpenter*, 2nd ed. (Lanham, MD: Scarecrow, 2000), 180.

24. Boulenger, *John Carpenter*, 201.

25. Sandy King, email response to author, January 20, 2016. While writing this paper, I wrote to Sandy King Carpenter with some questions about *Prince of Darkness* and she was kind enough to have John Carpenter respond to those questions. I would like to thank both John Carpenter and Sandy King Carpenter for their help.

26. Dylan Trigg, *The Thing: A Phenomenology of Horror* (Winchester, UK: Zero Books, 2014), 92–93.

27. Heinz R. Pagels, *The Cosmic Code: Quantum Physics as the Language of Nature* (Mineola, NY: Dover, 1982), 64.

28. Pagels, 64.

29. Arkady Plotnitsky, *The Knowable and the Unknowable: Modern Science, Nonclassical Thought, and the "Two Cultures"* (Ann Arbor: University of Michigan Press, 2002), xiii.

30. Harman, *Weird Realism*, 234.

31. Paul Davies, *God and the New Physics* (New York: Simon and Schuster, 1983), ix.

32. Pagels, *Cosmic Code*, 13.

33. Trigg, *The Thing*, 3.

34. Trigg, 96.

35. Mary Midgley, *Wickedness: A Philosophical Essay* (New York: Routledge, 1984), 15.

36. Trigg, *The Thing*, 53.

37. Cumbow, *Order in the Universe*, 180–181.

38. Harman, *Weird Realism*, 234.

39. Harman, 79.

40. Harman, 235.

41. H. P. Lovecraft, "The Colour Out of Space," in *The Call of Cthulhu and Other Weird Stories*, ed. S. T. Joshi. (New York: Penguin, 1999), 176.

42. Lovecraft, 176.

43. Brigid Cherry, *Horror* (New York: Routledge, 2009), 78–79.

44. When I asked Carpenter whether there was any deliberate symbolic purpose behind his use of green in the liquid, his response was "No. No symbolic value" (King, email to author). His answer surprised me, particularly given the historical associations of green with Satan. And yet, Carpenter's remark is a reminder that this film has no easy symbolic value, nothing that simply points to a core message or moral overall. In that sense, my discussion that the green liquid points to complex realities beyond human understanding should be understood as complicating the symbolic possibilities of green in the film.

45. Jeffrey Burton Russell, *Lucifer: The Devil in the Middle Ages* (Ithaca, NY: Cornell University Press, 1984), 69.

46. D. W. Robertson Jr., "Why the Devil Wears Green," *Modern Language Notes* 69, no. 7 (1954): 470–472.

47. Michel Pastoureau, *Green: The History of a Color*, trans. Jody Gladding (Princeton, NJ: Princeton University Press, 2014), 89.

48. Pastoureau, 93–94.

49. Pastoureau, 94.

50. Ruth Mellinkoff, *The Devil at Isenheim: Reflections of Popular Belief in Grünewald's Altarpiece* (Berkeley: University of California Press, 1988), 22.

51. Trigg, *The Thing*, 96.

52. Harman, *Weird Realism*, 71.

53. Lovecraft, "Call of Cthulhu," 139.

54. Carpenter suggested to me that "the real inspiration for *Prince of Darkness* was a movie by Dario Argento called *Inferno*. There was a narrative freedom to Dario's movie that inspired me." King email.

55. Given Carpenter's love for Alfred Hitchcock, we might possibly connect the heavy use of green in *Prince of Darkness* to the scene in *Vertigo* when Judy (Kim Novak) transforms into "Madeline" (also Kim Novak) right before Scottie's (Jimmy

Stewart) eyes. In this scene, a hazy green light—coming into the room from a bright neon sign—fills the room. The same green light also appears to surround Madeline as she approaches Scottie. In this scene, green could also be read as a metaphor not only for transition but also for the ways human beings sometimes rely on self-deception when they don't want to face difficult realities. I am grateful to my colleague Roger Macfarlane for making this connection for me.

56. Cumbow, *Order in the Universe*, 2.

57. Cumbow, 2.

58. Lovecraft, *Supernatural*, 15.

Narration and Damnation in *Angel Heart*

Murray Leeder

The devil is a plum part for an actor. Georges Méliès knew this early on, enacting Mephistopheles before his camera many times; and the better part of a century later, method actors like Robert de Niro, Al Pacino, and Jack Nicholson would all have their turns to play the Prince of Darkness. But where Pacino and Nicholson played their versions of Satan with scenery-chewing abandon, de Niro's "Louis Cyphre" in Alan Parker's *Angel Heart* (1987) is a surprisingly restrained and low-key devil, played with quiet authority, a simmering edge of rage, and a wry undercurrent. Based on William Hjortsberg's novel *Falling Angel* (1979), *Angel Heart* follows the classic structure of a detective film impeccably but arrives at a conclusion quite atypical for—or even anathema to—the genre: one that obligates the audience to accept a supernatural explanation more characteristic of the horror genre—literally, "the devil made me do it." Any film that builds to a shocking narrative twist requires a careful withholding and disclosure of narrative information, but in *Angel Heart*, the process of narration is explicitly diabolical, being managed by the devil himself. I will argue here that the devil is not merely a character in *Angel Heart* but is constructed as diegetic incarnation of the implied author, and as such is an evolution of the Mélièsian author-devil of early cinema who works tricks not only of light and shadow but of narrative manipulation.

Detection and Damnation

Since *Angel Heart* builds to an important twist that forces a reconsideration of everything prior, it is vital to begin with a plot summary. *Angel Heart* tells the story of Harry Angel (Mickey Rourke), a private investigator working in 1955

New York. He is hired by the mysterious Louis Cyphre to locate Johnny Liebling, a crooner who performed as "Johnny Favorite"; Cyphre had a contract with Johnny that was interrupted when Johnny was shell-shocked during World War II. Harry's investigation leads him to numerous old associates of Johnny. First, he confronts Albert Fowler (Michael Higgins), a doctor who has been falsifying Johnny's records for money; Harry finds Fowler dead from a gunshot immediately afterward. Following the trail to New Orleans, Harry meets Johnny's old lover Margaret Krusemark (Charlotte Rampling), a former society fortune-teller and witch, as well as two voodoo practitioners: a bluesman who played with Johnny named Toots Sweet (Brownie McGhee), and Johnny's illegitimate daughter, Epiphany Proudfoot (Lisa Bonet).[1] Toots and Margaret are both brutally murdered, and Harry confronts Margaret's father, Ethan Krusemark (Stocker Fontelieu), who reveals that Johnny used an occult ritual in an attempt to renege on the deal with the devil that brought him success. They kidnapped a soldier celebrating New Year's Eve of 1943 in Times Square and sacrificed him, with Johnny subsequently taking on his life.

That soldier was Harry Angel. Having lost any knowledge of himself as Johnny, Harry has been unwittingly tasked with finding himself. Only at the end of the narrative does Harry realize the truth. Cyphre appears and confirms the story; he has contrived events in order to retrieve Johnny Favorite's stolen soul, hidden within Harry. What's more, the recent murders were actually committed *by* Harry in a dissociative state. Discovering Epiphany, both his daughter and his lover, killed using his gun, Harry gives himself up to the police, acknowledging that he is destined for punishment both on Earth and in Hell.

The familiar Russian formalist distinction between story (*fabula*) and plot (*syuzhet*) has proved broadly influential on studies of the narrative film and of the detective film more specifically; predictably, it proves particularly relevant to *Angel Heart*. The fabula "embodies the action as a chronological, cause-and-effect chain of events occurring within a given duration and spatial field."[2] A film's syuzhet, in contrast, is "the actual arrangement and presentation of the fabula within the film"[3] which is not held to chronological order and may obscure cause and effect through selective omissions. While all narrative films and indeed narratives of any medium have a fabula and a syuzhet, detective stories are considered remarkable because they foreground the working of a syuzhet on a fabula, since unanswered questions about cause and effect drive the narrative and provide suspense. In *Angel Heart*, the question "Where is Johnny Favorite?"—a mystery to Harry and the audience alike—drives the early part of the syuzhet, swiftly accompanied by other questions, including "Who is murdering Favorite's associates?"

Syuzhets are distinguished by relative degrees of restriction—what do we know and what do we not know. Bordwell contrasts *Rear Window* (1954), which largely (though not entirely) confines itself to Jeff's (James Stewart) perspective, with *The Birth of a Nation* (1915), where the sprawling, unrestricted narration follows many characters with relative psychological shallowness.[4] In *Angel Heart*, narration is restricted to the extent that we gain information almost exclusively as Harry Angel gets it. The first-person narrator of the novel, Harry is in every scene in the film (save for the symbolic introduction and a few later intercuts coded as memories or hallucinations), and the perspective of the audience is firmly wedded to his, reinforced by frequent point-of-view shots from his perspective (an early scene of Harry searching Fowler's dwelling approaches the pure POV camerawork of *The Lady in the Lake* [1947] or *Dark Passage* [1947]). Bordwell's observation that both *The Big Sleep* (1946) and *Murder My Sweet* (1944) restrict audience knowledge to that possessed by the detective applies to *Angel Heart*.[5] Viewers may occasionally suspect more than Harry does, especially if they decipher the significance of the name "Louis Cyphre," but only reach certainty when Harry does.

Angel Heart introduces so many characters and colorful details that it discourages the viewer from speculating about the really important question until near the end: "Who is Harry Angel?" The treatment of Harry is simultaneously close and distant. We know little enough about his backstory, yet we witness his private moments and even his dreams. Genre conventions often supply viewers with information that does not need to be validated in any other way, and the fact that a film noir detective rarely has an intricate backstory combines with the typecasting of Rourke as this rough-hewn Brooklynite to discourage speculation about Harry's true identity. We seem to have all the information about him required: only in retrospect do his brief recollections about getting "a little fucked up" during the war prove narratively relevant.

Bordwell represents a detective story's fabula with this schema:

CRIME
cause of a crime
commission of crime
concealment of crime
discovery of crime

INVESTIGATION
beginning of investigation
phases of investigation
elucidation of crime
identification of criminal
consequences of identification[6]

It is generally the case that the "crime" phase will occur before the syuzhet begins, or early in the syuzhet with a partly occluded presentation. In *Angel Heart*, the "crime" is the 1943 kidnapping and ritual murder of the real Harry Angel, motivated by Johnny Favorite's attempt to renege on the promise of his soul to the devil. It is two crimes in one: the earthly crime of murder and the metaphysical crime of grand theft soul. The concealment of the crime is so complete that the killer himself lacks knowledge of it. The "discovery of the crime" stage belongs only to Cyphre, whose true motivations are only clear at the end of the film.

The "investigation" phase dominates *Angel Heart*, with the twist being that Harry's investigations lead him to an intolerable self-realization. Harry's motion toward the truth is accompanied by his growing increasingly unhinged, perhaps sensing the truth on a semiconscious level—hence his smashing of his reflection in the mirror following intercourse with Epiphany, his daughter. In the final confrontation with Cyphre, Harry's repeated cries of "I know who I am!"—each less convincing than the prior—underscore the fact that, until recently, we thought we knew who he was too. Simultaneously, Harry/the audience realize that he is a different person than he/we had thought, and that the syuzhet has until then omitted key information, not only about the "crime" phase (as is expected) but about the "investigation" phase too, because Harry, the character to whom our perspective is limited, has failed to retain it. He murdered five people himself but did not know it at the time, so neither did we. We glimpse the omitted events of both phases only through flashback-coded intercuts late in the film, a matter to which I will return.

If one canonical Western literary work underpinning *Angel Heart* is surely *Faust*, the story of a deal with the devil,[7] another is Sophocles's *Oedipus Rex*, the story of a man unwittingly investigating himself.[8] Trying to solve the problem of a plague on Thebes, Oedipus searches for the murderer of King Laius, but he is that murderer. Unwitting incest is, of course, a motif in both stories as well. The film foregrounds this link by the placing of the line, "How terrible is wisdom if it brings no profit to the wise," in Cyphre's mouth in his last scene; this line paraphrases words spoken by the blind prophet Tiresias in *Oedipus Rex* (and is the epigraph to Hjortsberg's novel). *Angel Heart* builds on an ur-work of the genre, in which the question, "What happened in the past to make the present as it is?" is inseparable from the question, "Who am I?"[9]

The Genres of *Angel Heart*

To ask a related question: What kind of film is *Angel Heart*, generically speaking? While it is structured as a detective film, the revelation that Cyphre is the devil and that Harry is Johnny falls well outside what a detective story traditionally permits. To explore the generic implications of the film's twist, I will first turn to Tzvetan Todorov's categories of the fantastic, the marvelous, and the uncanny. This triad is drawn from a set of epistemological distinctions about the narrative worlds of given stories, what rules prevail in them, and how they are different from rules of the reader's world. The mode Todorov values the most heavily is the fantastic, which he describes thus:

> In a world which is indeed our world, a world without devils, sylphides, or vampires, there occurs an event which cannot be explained by the laws of this same familiar world. The person who experiences the event must opt for one of two possible solutions: either he is the victim of an illusion of the senses, of a product of the imagination . . . or else the event has indeed taken place. Either the devil is an illusion, an imaginary being; or else he really exists, precisely like other beings— with this reservation, that we encounter him infrequently.[10]

Todorov's fantastic mode obliges the reader to vacillate between naturalistic and nonnaturalistic explanations for narrative phenomena, and that this hesitation is generally (though not necessarily) shared by one or more characters.[11] While some works, like James's *The Turn of the Screw* (1898), maintain the fantastic mode throughout, most either resolve in the uncanny mode (strange but not supernatural) or the marvelous mode (legitimately supernatural, and thus presumably different from the reader's world).

Todorov notes that while detective stories often come close to the *effects* of fantastic literature, they are rarely fantastic in themselves because the audience is not given to seriously suspect legitimately supernatural explanations to be valid.[12] Indeed, part of the "Detective Story Decalogue" prepared by Father Ronald A. Knox in 1929 was "all supernatural or preternatural agencies are ruled out as a matter of course."[13] *Angel Heart* clearly does not hold to this rule, but Harry operates under the misplaced certainty that he is in a narrative of the Todorovian uncanny, full of the strange, but not the supernatural. He even accuses Cyphre of merely impersonating the devil during the final confrontation, because his worldview aligns with the presumptive materialism of a detective story, rather than a supernatural horror story about the devil. When Cyphre wonders, "If I had cloven hooves and a pointed tail, would you be more convinced?," the line confronts both Harry and any audience members with lingering fantastic hesitation about whether he is the real devil; the demonic yellow eyes that appear on both Cyphre and Epiphany's son serve to erase any ambiguity.

Angel Heart is best located within the Todorovian fantastic-marvelous. The audience initially hesitates between naturalistic and nonnaturalistic

Louis Cyphre's yellow eyes reveal his diabolical nature in Alan Parker's *Angel Heart.*

accounts of the story's events (the fantastic), but in the end it is obliged to accept a supernatural explanation (the marvelous)—as is Harry. Does this shift from the fantastic to the marvelous also constitute a change in genre from the detective film to the Gothic horror film? Or does it instead reveal that *Angel Heart* was always a horror film? Does it even constitute a critique of the detective story and the rationalistic worldview that undergirds it? This last question is somewhat beyond the scope of this essay, but others have interpreted *Falling Angel* and *Angel Heart* as a postmodern "metaphysical" detective story that parodies or subverts the genre's conventions,[14] or as an "anti-detective narrative."[15]

Since genres are not defined only through narrative but also through style and tone, it is also noteworthy that while *Angel Heart* is full of traditional film noir aesthetics (chiaroscuro lighting, rundown urban spaces, rain, mirrors, stairways, mournful saxophones, etc.), these coexist with a different set of stylistic principles, more drawn from horror conventions that "inject supernatural emanations into the noir story."[16] The key examples are, in one direction, the black-clad, genderless figure that makes fleeting appearances both in scenes coded as reality and in dream sequences, and the film's gore, beyond what's typical of a film noir. The two are linked: the shadowy figure is introduced cleaning blood from a wall. Fred Botting observes that the "punctuations" of Gothic imagery herald the eventual supplanting of "the detective story . . . by a Faustian tale of diabolical repression."[17]

I would suggest, however, that *Angel Heart* literalizes Gothic and horrific subtexts within film noir. The downbound elevator connoting Brigid
O'Shaughnessy's (Mary Astor) damnation in *The Maltese Falcon* (1941)
becomes a literal trip to Hell.[18] Noir subjects like amnesia and plastic surgery
get supernatural twists in *Angel Heart*.[19] The best example of a noir image
turned to supernatural horror is ventilation fans, a common sight in the over-
heated and cramped cityscapes of many film noirs. *Angel Heart* repeatedly
displays them to look like pentagrams, hexagrams, and swastikas.[20] Throughout the film the viewer is given to wonder whether such imagery is pure symbolism or something more, and in retrospect we can read it as the film (or
Cyphre, Harry Angel's puppet master and, we shall see, a figure of narration
itself) tipping its hand repeatedly about the true, supernatural, character of
the film's world.

On both formal and narrative levels, *Angel Heart* proves to be less a competition between the detective story and the horror story so much as a demonstration of their commensurability (unlike, say, the mix of film noir and magic
realism in *Rough Magic* [1995]).[21] It is not an either/or: It is both, though *Angel
Heart*'s status as a horror film only becomes fully evident at its end, as it moves
to Todorov's marvelous. This trajectory mirrors the audience's understanding
of Louis Cyphre himself: Wealthy, cultured, calculating, and brilliant, he is
akin to Caspar Gutman (Sidney Greenstreet) in *The Maltese Falcon*, Waldo
Lydecker (Clifton Webb) in *Laura* (1944), and Noah Cross (John Huston) in
Chinatown (1973), with their figurative devilry made literal.[22] Cyphre also
looks ahead to Keyser Söze in *The Usual Suspects* (1995), likened repeatedly to
the devil. Like Cyphre, Söze is a narrator who works his diabolical manipulations not just on characters but on the audience as well. (In the final section I
will argue that Cyphre's narrator qualities are the key to understanding the
film and link him to a long association between cinema and the devil.)

The Moving-Picture Devil

John Grierson, popularizer of the term *documentary* and the fabled father of
documentary traditions in both Canada and the United Kingdom and with
influence far beyond them, lamented how cinema's realist potential was
swiftly redirected—or misdirected—into Hell: "Hardly were the workmen out
of the theatre and the apple digested than [cinema] was taking a trip to the
moon, and only a year to two later, a trip in full colour to the devil. The scarlet
women were in, and the high falsehood of trickwork and artifice was in, and
reality and the first fine careless rapture were out."[23] Geoff Brown notes that
Grierson's Calvinist upbringing underpins this construction of cinematic

formalism as paradise lost: "Imagine the shudder . . . when instead of docu-menting places, people and their workaday lives, cinema took off to visit the devil's lair itself"[24]—Grierson likely was referring to Méliès's *Les quat'cents farce du diable / The Merry Frolics of Satan* (1906). In 1913, in "Making the Devil Useful," Robert W. Neal assured his readers that, "the moving picture is not an invention of the devil." He continued, "There is a great deal in it, at the present stage of its development, that we have to think of with all optimis-tic faith summonable in order not to regard it as excessively satanic."[25] Both Grierson and Neal thought that cinema was salvageable for social or pedagog-ical purposes but couched this optimism with the discourse of condemnation that "the moving-picture devil" had attracted.[26]

These iconophobic treatments of cinema can be attached to a much longer narrative in Western culture of the distrust of systems of the visual, where the cultural imagination has often located the devil. According to Marina Warner, "The devil's medium was enigma, illusion, darkling sight. In medieval Chris-tian tradition, he is a mimic, an actor, a performance artist, and he imitates the wonders of nature and the divine work of creation. But unlike God, St. Augustine decided, the devil cannot perform real miracles or alter real phe-nomena. He is merely the ape of God, the master of lies, of imitating and simulating and pretending."[27] This conception of the devil is memorably evoked in Marlowe's *Dr. Faustus*, as Faustus confronts a shade of Helen of Troy conjured by demonic powers: The answer to Faustus's famous question "Is this the face that launched a thousand ships?" is probably "no"—Helen's shade is an illusion conjured by Mephistopheles's magic.

As early cinema's great illusionist, Georges Méliès is an appropriate Satan figure for the realism-minded Grierson. Méliès was a magician and impre-sario whose principal interests lay in exploiting cinema's potential for appear-ances, disappearances, transformations, and the construction of radically artificial screen worlds that expanded the magical arts through film's trickery. In keeping with the diegetic openness that is a feature of early cinema, the cheerfully anticlerical Méliès often played an internal incarnation of the magician-auteur, and he enacted Mephistopheles in many films, including *Le manoir du diable* (1896), *Le Chaudron infernal* (1903), *Le cake-walk infer-nal* (1903), *Le roi du maquillage* (1904), and several largely Gounod-derived adaptations of the Faust legend: *Le Cabinet de Méphistophélès* (1897), *Faust aux enfers* (1903), and *Damnation du docteur Faust* (1904). The devil's powers of illusion are thus tied to those authorial powers of the cinemagician himself.[28]

In André Gaudreault's terminology, Méliès was a *monstrateur* or exhibitor: His sometimes-Mephistophelean presence within his own films extends his extradiegetic authorial role as a conjurer and furnisher of attractions. Kevin Heffernan cleverly repurposes the term *monstrateur* to describe the presence of magician/author figures in horror cinema, which he sees as an evolution of Méliès's internal avatars: "In many horror films, the narrative's storytelling process is often enacted in a magician or trickster figure who accompanies his acts of sorcery with elaborate gestures to the audience that have their origins in the deliberately distracting sleight-of-hand of the stage magician."[29] Heffernan describes this figure as both a master of shocking display and a storyteller, like Henry Jerrold (Vincent Price) in *House of Wax* (1953).

The literary Cyphre is more obviously a monstrateur than his cinematic equivalent. He performs both as "El Çifr, Master of the Unknown,"[30] a faux-Arabic magician who wears a turban and blackface, and as "Dr. Cipher," a traditional evening-ware clad magician.[31] Among Dr. Cipher's props is a case containing performing mice costumed as *commedia dell'arte* characters, which he claims are souls enchanted to perform for all eternity . . . rather like the images captured by a movie camera.[32] The literary Harry even likens himself to "the rube on this macabre midway, dazzled by the lights and sleight of hand. The shadow-play events screened manipulations I could barely discern."[33]

The magician dimension of Cyphre is removed in *Angel Heart*, I suggest, because it is redundant. There is no need for him to stage such trickery within *Angel Heart*; *Angel Heart* is his trick. Cyphre is an evolution of the Méliès-style Mephistopheles/showman/auteur for classical narrative cinema. He has no need to enact the role of magician: He *is* a magician. His influence is felt on the level of sound and image—the film's whole sickly tone is attributable to the fact that it is filtered through Cyphre's narration—but also through the unfolding of narrative. Arguing for continuities between the trick film and later narrative cinema, Karen Beckman reminds us, "continuous narrative *is* a trick,"[34] a fact that *Angel Heart* makes plain. The fact that de Niro appears to be impersonating his friend and frequent collaborator Martin Scorsese, at least in terms of Cyphre's look,[35] is thus more than trivia. Asked about this impersonation, Alan Parker replied, "Yeah, maybe that's how he sees the devil, I don't know!"[36]

However, Cyphre is less tied to the specific authorial powers of a director like Scorsese or Parker than to the more abstract and depersonalized authority of a cinematic narrator. Here I do not mean narration in the aural sense of the word, though, interestingly, we hear Cyphre whisper "Johnny" at the beginning of the film, well before we see his image; later, his voice plays as a series of auditory flashbacks over Harry's drive to Poughkeepsie. The disembodiment of the voice is a feature of Michel Chion's *acousmêtre*, the voice that is heard without being connected to a body on-screen and therefore attains the impression of omnipresence and invincibility—certainly characteristics of Cyphre. Rather, "narrator" here refers to an agent responsible for the unfolding of a film's syuzhet. Bordwell cites Walter Booth's conception of the "implied author": "the invisible puppeteer, not a speaker or visible presence but the omnipotent artistic figure behind the work."[37] Bordwell argues that this is not a useful concept in most narrative films: "In watching films, we are seldom aware of being told something by an entity resembling a human being. . . . No trait we could assign to an implied author of a film could not more simply be ascribed to narration itself: it sometimes suppresses information, it often restricts our knowledge, it generates curiosity, it creates a tone, and so on. To give every film a narrator or implied author is to indulge in an anthropomorphic fiction.[38]

I propose that in *Angel Heart*, however, Cyphre *is*—or very nearly is—an anthropomorphic incarnation of the implied author. Cyphre is a visible and audible presence, yes, but it's also clear that the embodied presence that interacts with Harry is an illusory and temporary manifestation that fails to convey the devil's true nature.[39] He is an invisible puppeteer who scripts and guides all of Harry's actions; as he tells Harry in the last scene, the numerous murder victims were "All killed by your own hands. Guided by me, naturally." Where puppet-master villains like Gavin Elster (Tom Helmore) in *Vertigo* (1958) or Lee Woo-Jin (Yoo Ji-tae) in *Oldboy* (2003) carefully manage what appears to be their victims' free will, Cyphre truly obliterates Harry's agency. In hindsight we realize that Harry's narrative agency (bolstered for instance by his ability to relocate the narrative to Poughkeepsie or New Orleans as he moves his investigation, or to draw audience attention to objects through a POV shot) is merely the appearance of agency. The same is perhaps also true of all film characters, all of whom are slaves to the forces of narration but is more reflexively the case with Harry.

One could ask why Cyphre needs Harry to go through the investigation in order to learn his true identity as Johnny Favorite. In other words, what prevents Cyphre from simply reclaiming Johnny's soul from Harry at the beginning of *Angel Heart* (or for that matter, before the film even starts)? One of Cyphre's first lines to Harry is "Do you by any chance remember the name Johnny Favorite?"—presumably Cyphre wants or needs Harry to reach self-realization at the culmination of his investigation before he reclaims the purloined soul, that this is part of his punishment. The other reason is, of course, narrative delay: Cyphre could hypothetically divulge everything he knows in his first scene, but then there would be no further story. The plot needs the kind of "arabesque or squiggle" that Peter Brooks ascribes to narratives in order to "avoid reaching the end too precipitously."[40] One of the implied narrator's functions, more obvious in a detective film than other genres, is to dole out narrative information slowly but steadily, and perhaps misleadingly, before leading to a climax and closure. Here, this carefully modulated plotting is attributable to Cyphre's grand showman persona.

In his last scene, Cyphre playing one of Favorite's records seems to trigger playback of another kind: images of Harry murdering Fowler, Toots, and the two Krusemarks, all lacking diegetic sound and intercut with Harry's anguished expression as he confronts his reflection in a mirror. As his face begins to reflect resignation to the truth of who he is and what he has done, the film cuts to Epiphany screaming as Harry chokes her—now with diegetic sound that bridges back to when we return to Harry. He turns around and Cyphre is gone, and he rushes back to his hotel room to find Epiphany murdered. These intercut images echo the earlier scene where Ethan Krusemark informs Harry about the ritual sacrifice Favorite conducted in 1943. Ethan's description of their victim as "Just a soldier celebrating New Year's Eve in Times Square" triggers the visual of a soldier seen from behind, and his reference to the hotel where the ceremony took place triggers an exterior view of a window, followed by intercut images of the ritual and its bloody aftermath, as well as a quick cut of Harry's first meeting with Cyphre. Some of these images also appeared earlier in the film too, coded as nightmares and hallucinations. They are images of earlier events in the fabula, providing evidence of events that the syuzhet elided. Are they Harry's or Johnny's suppressed memories returning to him (some images, the POV of a hand reaching out to touch the soldier's shoulder, cannot logically be Harry's memories)? Or his mental visualizations of what Cyphre has told him? Or do they exist only for the audience's sake? I would suggest that it doesn't really matter—that however we read these images, they are triggered both by narrative necessity (they are images that we and Harry need to see to confirm that what Cyphre is saying is true) and by Cyphre's will, and indeed collapse the distinction between the two.

Appropriately, the film's climax breaks with restricted narration only with Cyphre's manifestations. A medium close-up of Cyphre's cane (echoing his introduction) is followed by a pan to Cyphre's face; we know he is present in Margaret's residence before Harry does. A series of close-ups reveal Cyphre's presence before Harry sees him. The final sequence contains another intriguing detail: as Harry rushes to his hotel room, he passes a seated figure in black, the final appearance of this recurring image. We see in medium close-up that the figure turns to watch as Harry rushes past—and it is a (clean-shaven) de Niro. This shot lasts three seconds before the film cuts to Harry reaching the murder scene.

This moment reinforces the theme of Harry continuing to miss what's hidden in plain sight (overlooking the significance of the name "Louis Cyphre," and blind to his own real nature). When we see the devil in this guise, *Angel Heart* gives us information that Harry lacks altogether. It thus breaks with the restricted narration it had upheld up to that point. Rather as *Citizen Kane* (1941) ends by moving away from a tightly restricted narration focused on the investigator Thompson (William Alland) to give us information that no character has, we are now shown something only the omniscient devil-narrator knows—we are finally, perversely, unpinned from Harry's perspective and drawn into the confidence of the diabolical narrator himself.

Closure and Apocalypse

Closure, the target of a traditional narrative, means the closing-off of chains of causality and the answering of relevant narrative questions. *Angel Heart* ends as a detective story is supposed to—with the apprehension of the criminal and his punishment. Only this time, the criminal and the detective are one and the same. Harry turns himself in to the pair of grotesque New Orleans cops, who tell him, "You're going to burn for this." Harry answers, "I know. In Hell." Harry, who is two men in one, is simultaneously guilty and innocent. His punishment is both just and undeserved. The ending thus provides closure but not catharsis.

Closure is Cyphre's explicit goal since it means retrieving the soul. Earlier, Cyphre remarked, "I don't like messy accounts"—indeed. Virtually everyone connected to Johnny Favorite is now dead, the guilty and the innocent (Epiphany) alike. Soon, Harry—Johnny—will join them, probably executed for the murder of Epiphany. What's more, the implication is that Harry's fate was inevitable: Cyphre tells him, "You were doomed from the moment you slit that young boy in half." *Angel Heart* is fatalistic even by the standards of film noir (see Pippin), since it appears that nothing Harry ever could have done would have saved his soul.[41] Carrol L. Fry claimed in 1991 that, "in no recent horror film does Satan win so convincingly as in *Angel Heart*,"[42] and I will go further: He does not win because there is no real competition. He does not play the game so much as control it. In *Angel Heart*, then, the classical narrative's motion toward closure inevitably edges up against theological questions about fate and free will.

Closure, as Bordwell has noted, is more properly seen as a "closure effect" or "pseudo-closure,"[43] and *Angel Heart* works to expose that distinction. One cryptic image works against *Angel Heart*'s sense of closure: the glowing yellow eyes on Epiphany's son as he looks emotionlessly on Angel being arrested for

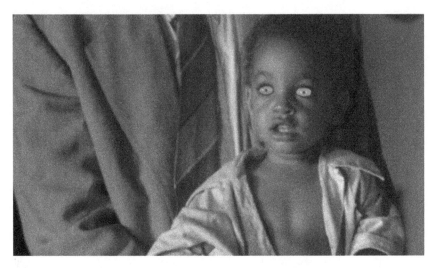

Epiphany's son shares yellow eyes with his father in *Angel Heart*.

his mother's murder while her body lies across the room. Epiphany earlier claimed to have been impregnated by spirits during a voodoo ceremony, but perhaps the unseen father was actually Cyphre. The linkage with Cyphre's own eyes (perhaps referencing *Rosemary's Baby* [1968]: "He has his father's eyes") suggests that the boy, descended from both the devil and Johnny Favorite, may be the Antichrist.[44] In its last perverse gesture, *Angel Heart*'s closure effect is punctured by this gesture toward a continuing demonic scheme to which the relatively closed saga of Johnny Favorite and Harry Angel is marginal. This apocalyptic addition, small enough to be easily ignored by most scholars but vast in its implications all the same, suggests that the final image might allegorize not only Harry's descent into Hell, but that of all mankind.

Notes

1. *Angel Heart*'s peculiar racial politics, especially where voodoo is concerned, have attracted much scholarship. See Robert R. Means Coleman, *Horror Noire: Blacks in American Horror Films from the 1890s to Present* (London: Routledge, 2011), 154–155; and Douglas Keesey, "Black Magic and White Guilt: Voodoo in *Angel Heart*," *Psy Art* 10 (2011): n.p. See also Tanya Krzywinska, *A Skin for Dancing In: Possession, Witchcraft, and Voodoo in Film* (Trowbridge, Wiltshire: Flicks Books, 2000), esp. 182–185; and Kameelah L. Martin, *Envisioning Black Feminist Voodoo Aesthetics: African Spirituality in American Cinema* (London: Lexington Books, 2016), 51–74. *Angel Heart* also cites the Tommy/Robert Johnson narrative of a

bluesman selling his soul to the devil, here displaced onto the white crooner. See Jon Michael Spencer, *Blues and Evil* (Knoxville: University of Tennessee Press, 1993), esp. 30–31.

2. David Bordwell, *Narration in the Fiction Film* (London: Routledge, 1985), 49.

3. Bordwell, 50.

4. Bordwell, 57–58.

5. Bordwell, 65

6. Bordwell, 64.

7. For a discussion of *Angel Heart* as a Faustian narrative, see Robert Lewis Singer, "Cinematic Representations: The Merlin/Faust Archetypes in *Excalibur* and *Angel Heart*," in *Merlin vs. Faust: Contending Archetypes in Western Culture*, ed. Charlotte Spivack (Lewiston, NY: Edwin Mellen Press, 1992), 95–111. Singer affiliates the film more with the Marlovian tradition of Faust than the later Goethean tradition, in which Faust's soul is redeemed.

8. Rabel gives a thorough account of the influence of *Oedipus Rex* on *Falling Angel* and *Angel Heart*. Robert J. Rabel, "Murder at the Crossroads: *Oedipus Rex, Falling Angel* and *Angel Heart*," *Classical and Modern Literature* 23, no. 1 (2003): 33–48.

9. For a discussion of *Oedipus Rex* as an ancestor of the modern detective novel, see John Scaggs, *Crime Fiction* (New York: Routledge, 2005), 9–12.

10. Tzvetan Todorov, *The Fantastic: A Structural Approach to a Literary Genre* (Cleveland, OH: Press of Case Western Reserve University, 1973), 25.

11. Todorov, 33.

12. Todorov, 49–50.

13. Ronald A. Knox, "A Detective Story Decalogue," in *The Art of the Mystery Story: A Collection of Critical Essays*, ed. Howard Haycraft (New York: Carroll, 1983), 194. Todorov and Knox necessarily ignore the long-standing subgenre of supernatural detective stories. See A. B. Emrys, "Introduction: From Psychical Investigation to Paranormal Detective," *Clues: A Journal of Detection* 30, no. 2 (2012): 5–9.

14. Patricia Merivale and Susan Elizabeth Sweeney, "The Game's Afoot: On the Trail of the Metaphysical Detective Story," in *Detecting Texts: The Metaphysical Detective Story from Poe to the Postmodern*, ed. Patricia Merivale and Susan Elizabeth Sweeney (Philadelphia: University of Pennsylvania Press, 1999), 5.

15. Stefano Tani, *The Doomed Detective: The Contribution of the Detective Novel to Postmodern American and Italian Fiction* (Carbondale and Edwardsville: Southern Illinois University Press, 2008), esp. 108–109; Debra A. Moddlemog, *Readers and Mythic Signs: The Oedipus Myth in 20th Century Fiction* (Carbondale: Southern Illinois University Press, 1993), 140–141n22.

16. Foster Hirsch, *Detours and Lost Highways: A Map of Neo-Noir* (New York: Limelight Editions, 1999), 312.

17. Fred Botting, *Gothic* (London: Routledge, 1996), 176.

18. Later texts would reuse the elevator to Hell imagery either metaphorically (*The Grifters* [1990]) or literally (the *Angel* episode "Reprise" [2001]).

19. *Somewhere in the Night* (1946), the story of a man unwittingly pursuing himself, strikingly anticipates *Angel Heart*. See Eddie Muller, *Dark City: The Lost World of Film Noir* (New York: St. Martins Press, 1998), 132.

20. Carrol L. Fry, "The Devil You Know: Satanism in *Angel Heart*," *Literature/ Film Quarterly* 19, no. 3 (1991): 200–201.

21. Stevenson's *The Strange Case of Dr. Jekyll and Mr. Hyde* (1886) is also structured as a detective story, only revealing other generic affiliations (both the gothic novel and science fiction) at its climax—and it, too, is a tale where two men prove to be one. For more on horror/detective story links, see Tony Magistrale and Sidney Polger, *Poe's Children: Connections Between Tales of Terror and Detection* (New York: Peter Lang, 1999); and Paul Meehan, *Horror Noir: Where Cinema's Dark Sisters Meet* (Jefferson, NC: McFarland, 2011). *Alias Nick Beal* (1949) reworked *Faust* within a noir idiom.

22. For an attempt to situate *Angel Heart* within the American hard-boiled detective film, see Stephen Cooper, "Sex/Knowledge/Power in the Detective Genre," *Film Quarterly* 42, no. 3 (Spring 1989): 23–31. For the metaphorical devils of detective fiction, see Stacy Gillia and Philippa Gates, eds., *The Devil Himself: Villainy in Detective Fiction and Film* (Westport, CT: Greenwood Press, 2002).

23. John Grierson, *Grierson on Documentary*, ed. Forsyth Hardy (London: Collins, 1946), 132.

24. Geoff Brown, "Paradise Lost and Found: The Course of British Realism," in *The British Cinema Book*, 3rd ed., ed. Robert Murphy (London: BFI, 2008), 28.

25. Robert W. Neal, "Making the Devil Useful," *English Journal* 2, no. 10 (December 1913): 658.

26. Neal, 658. See also Tom Gunning's account of the understanding of the cinema as evil: Tom Gunning, "Flickers: On Cinema's Power for Evil," in *Bad: Infamy, Darkness, Evil, and Slime on Screen*, ed. Murray Pomerance (Albany: State University of New York Press, 2004), 21–38. See also Erik Barnouw's comparison of "the new industrialized magic" of narrative cinema to "black magic" in Eric Barnouw, *The Magician and the Cinema* (New York: Oxford University Press, 1981), 112.

27. Marina Warner, *Phantasmagoria: Spirit Visions, Metaphors, and Media into the Twenty-First Century* (Oxford: Oxford University Press, 2006), 123. See also Simon During, *Modern Enchantments: The Cultural Power of Secular Magic* (Cambridge, MA: Harvard University Press, 2002), 33–34.

28. For more on Méliès and devilry, see Michael Mangan, *Performing Dark Arts: A Cultural History of Conjuring* (Bristol: Intellect, 2007), 134–139.

29. Kevin Herffernan, *Ghouls, Gimmicks, and Gold: Horror Films and the American Movie Business, 1953–1968* (London: Duke University Press, 2004), 26.

30. Herffernan, 136.

31. Herffernan, 172–173.

32. For an account of cinema as an inheritor to the "device of wonder," see Colin Williamson, *Hidden in Plain Sight: An Archaeology of Magic and the Cinema* (New Brunswick, NJ: Rutgers University Press, 2015).

33. Williamson, 137.

34. Karen Beckman, *Vanishing Women: Magic, Film, and Feminism* (Durham, NC: Duke University Press, 2003), 131.

35. Andy Dougan, *Untouchable: A Biography of Robert de Niro* (New York: Thunder's Mouth Press, 2002), 188–189.

36. John Gallagher, *Film Directors on Directing* (Westport, CT: Greenwood Press, 1989), 190.

37. Bordwell, *Narration in the Fiction Film*, 62.

38. Bordwell, 62.

39. Note that Cyphre's climactic fourth scene finds him sporting hair substantially longer than in the earlier three, even though not much time has passed. His fingernails also grow visibly in each successive scene.

40. Peter Brooks, *Reading for the Plot: Design and Intention in Narrative* (Cambridge, MA: Harvard University Press, 1984), 104.

41. One wonders, however, if Harry missed a chance at salvation when he refuses Cyphre's offer of a soul/egg.

42. Fry, "The Devil You Know," 197.

43. Bordwell, *Narration in the Fiction Film*, 159.

44. Fry, "The Devil You Know," 5.

The Devil's in the Details

Devilish Desire and Roman Polanski's The Ninth Gate

Jeffrey Andrew Weinstock

Roman Polanski's *The Ninth Gate*, his 1999 adaptation of Arturo Pérez-Reverte's 1993 novel, *The Club Dumas*, is a film about the devil in which the devil never appears. As such, it is less about the devil himself than about modern desire for him and, through verification of his existence, confirmation of what Victoria Nelson refers to in *The Secret Life of Puppets* as the "transcendental," the coexistence of an invisible world above, below, and imbricated with the material world of the senses.[1] The approach the film adopts toward expressing this desire is one that has been curiously congenial to postmodern sensibilities: close textual exegesis as the key to lost or forbidden knowledge of this other world. As in such blockbusters and bestsellers as Stephen Spielberg's *Raiders of the Lost Ark* (1981), Dan Brown's *The Da Vinci Code* (2003), and Jon Turteltaub's *National Treasure* (2004), the protagonist of *The Ninth Gate*, Dean Corso (Johnny Depp), is an unorthodox scholar-turned-detective whose knowledge of Latin and arcane lore allows him to solve a puzzle, the implications of which then force upon him a reconceptualization of the universe. Corso's cracking of the code and confirmation of the devil's existence shatters his religious skepticism and, with it, modern repudiation of the transcendental.

In an interesting twist, this resurrection of a premodern conception of the universe in which the devil exists, forbidden books can conjure him (or at least allow access), and the supernatural is an active force in the world is paralleled with Corso's assumption at the end of a conventional model of manhood. The film thus overlays three metaphorical journeys on top of the physical journey depicted—the movements from ignorance to knowledge, from unbelief to belief, and from impotence to manhood—as it turns the scientific method back on itself, showing how a process of logical deduction leads to a conclusion undermining that same process: the existence of the devil. The film thereby enacts a curious inversion wherein skepticism and rationalism are ultimately conceptualized as ignorance, while belief in the irrational is established as knowledge.

In the end, through Corso's overlapping journeys to knowledge, belief, and manhood, the film constructs a kind of fantasized nostalgia for an older world of arcane lore, secret sects and cults, and belief in the invisible world of demons and the devil in which men can assert agency by controlling forbidden knowledge. *The Ninth Gate* thus supports Nelson's contention that demonology in modern culture is "the only avenue open to the transcendental" as it suggests that the supernatural is superior to unbelief even if it culminates in damnation. Better to believe in the devil, implies the film, than nothing.[2]

Ignorance to Knowledge

The Ninth Gate is a film about knowledge and its attainment that ironically may be particularly appealing to those least likely to give credence to the supernatural—scholars, bibliophiles, and collectors of rare books—as the film focuses on those who covet antique tomes and those who possess specialized knowledge concerning them. Depp's character, Dean Corso, is a procurer of rare volumes whose means of obtaining them are at times suspect if not outright mercenary. At the start of the film, for instance, having beaten his competition to the library of a book collector who has recently committed suicide, Corso intentionally undervalues a rare edition of Cervantes's *Don Quixote* that he desires while overvaluing the rest of the collection to facilitate his deception and flummox his competitors. During a brief exchange with one of his opponents whom he has beaten to the New York apartment, the man characterizes Corso as a "vulture" and pronounces him "unscrupulous, thoroughly unscrupulous." While perhaps not necessarily on the path to perdition at the start, Corso is certainly no angel.

While Corso's ethics may be questionable, what he indisputably possesses is a vast erudition concerning rare books, particularly those related to the occult—and part of the appeal of the film for those who enjoy it is its showcasing of this specialized knowledge possessed by Corso and others for the viewer. Bookseller Bernie Feldman (James Russo), who serves as a middleman locating buyers for Corso's acquisitions, for example, lovingly scrutinizes Corso's Cervantes prize, identifying it for the viewer as "The Ybarra 'Don Quixote,' 1780, all four volumes" and adding, "Sonofabitch, fantastic, fantastic. You are the best." Later, when summoned by ultra-rich book collector Boris Balkan (Frank Langella) to his private library, Corso again demonstrates his encyclopedic knowledge of rare occult books. When asked by Balkan if he is familiar with *The Nine Gates of the Kingdom of Shadows*," Corso replies immediately, "Yes. Venice, 1666. The author and printer Aristide Torchia was burned by the Holy Inquisition, together with all his works. Only three copies survived." Balkan corrects him, stating that only one copy survived, to which Corso replies, "The catalogs list three copies surviving in private ownership: the Fargas, the Kessler, and the Telfer." "True, you know your business," acknowledges Balkan before going on to explain the shady business in which he seeks to enlist Corso's aid.

As this early scene in the film develops, it continues to emphasize the depths of Corso's specialized knowledge concerning rare books. First, Corso's command of Latin is demonstrated. Balkan has obtained a copy of *The Nine Gates*—the Telfer copy, owned by the man whose suicide starts the film—and, as Corso examines one of the engravings, Balkan speaks aloud the caption: *SI.VM E.T A.V . VM* (*"silentium est aureum"*). Corso then offers his translation: "Silence is golden." Second, when the possibility that the Telfer copy of *The Nine Gates* is a forgery is introduced, Corso examines the book and listens to the quality of the paper by putting his ear to the book and riffling the pages with his thumb. "It doesn't appear to be," he responds. "Even the paper sounds kosher." Corso knows "the catalogs" by heart, can quickly discriminate between rare and more common volumes in a large library, speaks Latin, and can tell a forgery by the sound the pages make when riffled.

Also reemphasized in the early scene in Balkan's library is Corso's willingness to utilize ethically questionable tactics to achieve his goals. Balkan's purpose in summoning Corso is to engage his services. He explains to Corso first that the engravings in *The Nine Gates* were adapted by its author from a book reputed to have been written by the devil himself, the *Delomelanicon*, and that the images "form a kind of Satanic riddle." While Corso believes the *Delomelanicon* to be a myth, Balkan asserts that it existed and further claims of the engravings in *The Nine Gates* adapted from it that, "Correctly interpreted with the aid of the original text and sufficient inside information, they're reputed to conjure up the Prince of Darkness in person." The problem for Balkan, however, is that his copy of *The Nine Gates* hasn't worked—the devil hasn't appeared—so he suspects the book may not be authentic. Corso's job is to compare Balkan's copy with the two other extant copies and, if one of the others turns out to be the genuine one, to "get it . . . at all costs, never mind how." When Corso hesitates, "'Never mind how' sounds illegal," Balkan responds, "It wouldn't be the first time you've done something illegal." "Not that illegal," rejoins Corso. "Hence the size of the check," replies Balkan. When Corso expresses his disbelief that Balkan would allow him to leave with his copy of *The Nine Gates* unless something were wrong with it, the scene ends with Balkan's pronouncement, "I have the utmost faith in you, Mr. Corso. There's nothing more reliable than a man whose loyalty can be bought for hard cash." Corso, we understand, possesses vast knowledge concerning rare occult books and few scruples when it comes to obtaining them for interested buyers.

Despite his expertise, however, Corso nevertheless starts from a position of ignorance as he is confronted with two puzzles: first, how to ascertain which copy of the *Nine Gates* is authentic and, second, how to make sense of the discrepancies he finds among the three copies. Thus begins Corso's literal journey to Europe seeking out the other copies. At each stop, he visits extensive libraries and consults with bibliophiles and experts on rare books. He begins in Toledo, Spain, by consulting the twin Ceniza brothers (both played by José López Rodero)—previous owners of the Telfer copy of the *Nine Gates* and experts on rare books—about the possibility that the Telfer copy could be a forgery. This line of inquiry allows the brothers to explain for Corso (and the viewer) the difficult art of forgery: The paper and binding materials must be from the same period, and the watermarks, inks, typefaces must match. "Too expensive to be profitable," explains Pablo, although they admit it can be done. Considering the Telfer edition of the *Nine Gates*, however, they explain, "We had ample opportunity to examine it thoroughly. The printing, the binding are magnificent examples of seventeenth-century Venetian craftsmanship. . . . If this is a forgery, or a copy with pages restored, it's the work of a master." What the brothers then do is to supply additional information about the *Nine Gates* and to fill in one piece of the puzzle. They point out to Corso that only six of the nine engravings are signed with the initials of Aristide Torchia. The other three are provocatively signed "LCF." "Lucifer?" questions Corso—to which the brothers respond, "Torchia was burned alive because he wrote this book in collaboration with someone else. . . . The man who wrote this did so in alliance with the Devil and went to the stake for it. Even Hell has its heroes, Señor."

This scene with the Ceniza brothers propels the plot along by providing Corso with several valuable clues that assist him on his journey from ignorance to knowledge: First, it focuses his attention on the engravings rather than the text itself. This emphasis on the visual importantly also engages the viewer's participation as it conveniently allows the viewer, who may not know Latin, to confirm the differences between engravings—we can visually identify the differences being highlighted. Second, it introduces the idea that each

"Venture too far and danger may descend on you from above." One of the engravings from
The Nine Gates in Roman Polanski's *The Ninth Gate*.

engraving itself is a kind of puzzle requiring interpretation. Considering one
engraving of a man approaching a bridge as an angel—or God?—takes aim
with a bow and arrow from above, Pablo offers that it "could be interpreted as
a warning. 'Venture too far,' it seems to say, 'and danger will descend on you
from above.'" "These types of books often contain little puzzles," he adds. The
engravings as "little puzzles" add an additional layer of complexity to Balkan's
pronouncement earlier that the engravings "form a kind of Satanic riddle."
Puzzles within a larger puzzle: One must first correctly interpret the Tarot-like
individual images of the individual engravings before fitting them together as
pieces of another riddle.

The scene with the Ceniza brothers, however, in addition to moving the
plot forward, functions in another capacity as well—in keeping with the film
as a whole, it seeks to impress the viewer and engage their interests through
the foregrounding of highly specialized erudition. For the viewer unaware of
the difference between rag paper and wood pulp, the prohibitive expense of
forgery, and the symbolism of medieval and early modern engravings, the

introduction of such information, together with other such details and the overall fetishization of rare books, functions as a kind of lure. The excessiveness of such knowledge, combined with the effortless way in which it is introduced, overflows its diegetic function and becomes itself a form of spectatorial enjoyment—the film's knowledge becomes the viewer's pleasure. This aestheticization of knowledge—a variant of what we may wish to consider the "informational sublime" elicited by *too much* knowledge—then culminates in the summoning of the devil, whose initials lurk in the details of the engravings. The devil, suggests the film, is conjured by the pleasure of the gratuitous detail, the decadent flourish, the superfluous paraph. The devil is literally in the details—and the pleasure we take in the gratuitous detail then becomes central to the summoning of him.

Now keeping occasional company with a mysterious, unnamed young woman—The Girl (Emmanuelle Seigner)—that he first noticed in New York and then reencounters on the train to Portugal, Corso travels to view the Fargas copy of *The Nine Gates* and discovers a mansion almost emptied of belongings and in a sad state of repair reflecting the owner's reduced circumstances. What remains in the home is primarily Fargas's book collection: "There they are, eight hundred and thirty-four of them," Fargas (Jack Taylor) tells Corso. "A pity you didn't see them in better times, in their bookcases. I used to have five thousand. These are the survivors." Considering the remaining collection, Corso observes that if Fargas sold the rest, his financial difficulties would be alleviated. "I know," Fargas replies, "but if I sold them all I'd have no reason to go on living." His collection of books is what makes life meaningful for Fargas. He points out to Corso some of his particularly rare volumes and then realizes that Corso has a copy of *The Nine Gates* with him. Considering the Telfer copy, he points out details and imperfections present in his own copy, making clear that he is intimately familiar with the tiny details of the text, which has been scrutinized. "Look at this imperfection in the fourth line here—the damaged S," he says. "The same type, the same impression." Fargas clearly knows the book by heart. Corso's comparison of the Telfer and Fargas versions, however, confirms his suspicion that the discrepancies among copies pertain not to the text but to the engravings—as with the Telfer copy, three of the nine engravings in the Fargas version are signed "LCF." They are a different three however, and these three possess other minor differences as well. "Well, I'll be damned," mutters Corso humorously foreshadowing the film's conclusion as he discovers these small discrepancies.

After Fargas dies under mysterious circumstances, Corso and The Girl travel from Lisbon to Paris to consider the Kessler copy, owned by the imperious Baroness Kessler (Barbara Jefford). Like Balkan, Kessler fancies herself an expert on occult matters in general and the devil in particular. Kessler rejects out of hand the possibility that her copy of *The Nine Gates* is not authentic, telling Corso arrogantly, "My knowledge of this book is profound." She then reveals for the viewer that she has authored a biography of Aristide Torchia, reconfirms Balkan's explanation of *The Nine Gates* as Torchia's adaptation of the "dread *Delomelanicon*" written by Lucifer himself, and adds that, following the burning of Torchia at the stake, a secret society, the Order of the Silver Serpent—"a kind of witches coven"—was established to read from *The Nine Gates*, preserve its secrets, and "worship the Prince of Darkness." Although initially unwilling to allow Corso to examine her copy once she learns he is in the employment of Balkan, she relents after he elaborates on the variations he has discovered in the Telfer and Fargas copies and permits him to consider hers—although her forbearance does not extend to allowing him to smoke in her library. (Corso, as we shall see, is associated with smoke and fire throughout.) The result is the same: Three of the nine engravings are signed "LCF" and differ in minor details. "Maybe Torchia hid the secret of *The Nine Gates* in three books, not one," correctly concludes Corso.

It is, however, Balkan who assembles the engravings into a single narrative for Corso and the viewer. Believing himself through Corso's aid to have obtained the authentic nine engravings signed "LCF," he pieces them together into a narrative: "To travel in silence . . . by a long and circuitous route . . . to brave the arrows of misfortune and fear neither noose nor fire . . . to play the greatest of all games and win, foregoing no expense . . . is to mock the vicissitudes of fate and gain at last the key . . . that will unlock . . . the ninth gate." The puzzle is seemingly solved; Balkan however fails to conjure up the devil and, erroneously believing himself to have been endowed with superhuman powers, presumptuously sets himself on fire. Corso then kills Balkan (although it can be construed as a mercy killing since Balkan has set himself aflame and is in agony) and, against the suitably hellish backdrop of a burning castle, has sex with The Girl—or, perhaps more accurately, she has sex with him as he lies prostrate and seemingly mesmerized.

The next day, The Girl reveals to Corso that the ninth engraving possessed by Balkan was a forgery. Corso expresses his desire for the real one and, stopping to put gas in his car, returns from paying to find The Girl gone and a note on the forged ninth engraving directing him back to the Ceniza Brothers' shop. He returns to Spain and discovers the shop empty and being cleaned out by workmen. As the workers remove a large bookcase, a piece of dusty parchment slips from the top and magically falls at Corso's feet: the ninth engraving, which features a likeness of The Girl astride a seven-headed beast, suggesting that she is the Whore of Babylon. With a complete set of authentic

The ninth engraving suggests that The Girl is the Whore of Babylon.

engravings in hand and having knowledge of the narrative they construct, Corso returns to the castle that was the scene of Balkan's demise and walks, upright, through the gates that open for him and into the light. He has solved the puzzle introduced by Balkan at the start, and the answer has forced upon him a reconceptualization of the universe. From a man whose only faith was in money, he has transformed into one who now believes in a larger universe of powers and forces, including Satan and presumably God.

Unbelief to Belief

Corso's shift from ignorance to knowledge is paralleled by a metaphorical movement from cynicism concerning the supernatural to acceptance of the transcendental. Corso's initial belief system is concisely expressed during his early interview with Balkan. In response to Balkan's question, "Are you a religious man, Mr. Corso?" he replies, "I believe in my percentage." Corso is thus positioned at the start as a materialist who rejects that which he cannot confirm with his own eyes—a position that is then repeatedly challenged by the interactions he has with believers over the course of the film. Put differently: Corso is shown to know a lot but to believe nothing—and his failure to believe in the end is what marks his having been ignorant all along. Having pointed out the "LCF" signature on certain engravings, the Ceniza brothers explain that Torchia was burned alive because of his "collaboration" with Lucifer—a proposition that Corso rejects: "Come on. You can't honestly believe . . ." In Portugal, Fargas tells him, "Some books are dangerous. Not to be opened with impunity." Corso agrees with this proposition, but his sincerity is in doubt since he wants to get on with his work. Baroness Kessler tells him that she saw the devil when she was fifteen years old, "as plain as I see you now" and that it was "love at first sight." When asked by Corso whether she truly believes in the devil, she replies, "Enough to devote my life and my library to him. Not to mention many years of work. Don't you?" Corso's response here, "Almost," suggests some wavering of his initial rejection of the supernatural; however, when the baroness explains that *The Nine Gates* requires "a certain amount of faith," he replies that, "I'm afraid my faith is in short supply these days." Corso knows but does not believe. Consequently, he does not fully understand, and, in the absence of understanding, he becomes a pawn in someone else's game, acted upon rather than an actor.

While this shared belief in the devil on the part of the wealthy and educated individuals with whom he engages may play some role in the shifting of Corso's attitude, it is arguably his interactions with The Girl and the supernatural aura surrounding them—and her—that most fully precipitate first his questioning and then his revision of his belief system. The Girl, who Corso first notices at a lecture by Balkan on the occult, is present in the film even before he is commissioned to compare the *Nine Gates* texts and is initially assumed by Corso to be in Balkan's employ. She is a source of mystery throughout as she is never named and evades all his questions. When asked if she is a student, she replies, "So I am. In a way. I like books." To Corso's question of whether she has been traveling long, she replies ambiguously, "A while." Increasingly, Corso is unsettled by her knowledge of events. In Portugal, she awakens him early in the morning in his hotel room to tell him he should go see Fargas again, whom they find dead. "It's come to my attention that you know too goddamn much," he berates her. When he later adds that he could end up dead as well, she replies, "Not with me around to look after you." "Oh, I see. You're my guardian angel then," he retorts. "If you say so," she responds. She does, however, literally rescue him on multiple occasions. She scares off attackers both in Portugal and Paris and flies down from a second story balcony at a Satanic gathering to prevent Corso from killing Balkan. Her supernatural nature is then developed more fully when her eyes glow with a kind of hypnotic desire during their sexual encounter, when she disappears from the car leaving directions as to where to find the authentic ninth engraving, and when her likeness is featured on the ninth engraving astride a seven-headed beast.

In the end, because of his journey toward knowledge and the ministrations of The Girl, Corso abandons his materialist position and embraces a transcendental belief system validated by the film's conclusion as correct. No longer concerned merely with his percentage, he desires the ninth engraving as the key to a puzzle he wishes to solve on his own. And, as the gates of the castle open before him at the end of the film and he walks toward the light, he evidences no surprise or hesitation as it is now the anticipated culmination of his journey. In the end, he embraces that which he rejected at the start. "Well, I'll be damned," he mutters as he observes the discrepancies between the Telfer and the Fargas copies—and at the conclusion his prophecy is fulfilled as he walks, upright and confident, through the gates of hell. The film in this way is ironically nostalgic for the possibility of damnation—better Satan than nothing.

From Impotence to Manhood

While Corso's metaphoric journeys from ignorance to knowledge, and from skepticism to belief are tightly coupled—he doesn't truly know until he believes—his journey toward a conventional model of masculinity on the face of it seems more incongruous. What the film establishes however is that with knowledge and belief comes power congruent with stereotypes of masculinity. This desire for power works to "naturalize" Corso, even as it renders the female characters "unnatural." Part of the film's nostalgia for an earlier conceptualization of the universe is thus also its desire for conventional gender roles aligning men with mind and action and women with body and passivity.

It is worth noting that there is a "devilish" aspect to Corso who is in some ways "coarse" from the start. He is ethically suspect, he possesses vast knowledge of occult books, he is associated throughout with smoke and fire, he fashions his facial hair in a Van Dyke style often associated with Satan— perhaps there are even resonances of "devil" or "devil of course" in the name Dean Corso. But what Corso lacks until the very end of the film is stereotypically masculine assertiveness. To begin with, he is repeatedly rescued by the attractive but much more competent and active Girl. This happens first at night outside the Fargas mansion when, inverting conventional gender expectations, she rides up on a motorcycle scaring off a potential assailant. She comes more directly to his rescue later in Paris when he is being assaulted, literally flying down a set of stairs and fending off his assailant—the first unambiguously supernatural event in the film. She comes to his aid a third time in the Telfer chateau when, again descending magically from a height, she prevents Corso from shooting Balkan in front of a group. Corso throughout the film is a sort of damsel in distress, rescued repeatedly by the assertive Girl.

Corso also lacks stereotypical masculine assertiveness in sexual situations. Indeed, he is seduced twice. The first time is by Liana Telfer (Lena Olin) who, hoping to recover the Telfer copy of *The Nine Gates*, ambushes him at his apartment, has sex with him, and then flies into a rage when Corso won't hand over the book (which he has left with his friend Bernie). The scene ends with Liana smashing a bottle on Corso's head, rendering him unconscious. The second time he is seduced is by The Girl after he has put Balkan out of his misery. He returns to his car and lights a cigarette, only to be shocked when a hand removes it from his mouth—The Girl has appeared out of nowhere next to him. She removes his glasses, strokes his face, and a close-up shot of her eyes together with the ambient and pulsing soundtrack suggest that she exercises a kind of mesmeric control over Corso. The two embrace and the next sequence depicts the girl gyrating atop Corso with ecstatic joy against a background of flames while Corso lies prostrate on the ground, the more passive partner as the two copulate.

Indeed, conventional gender roles to a certain extent are inverted throughout the film. The Satanist Liana Telfer is depicted as mercenary and cold— she shrieks like a harpy and flies at Corso's face with her fingers extended like claws when he doesn't quickly produce the *Nine Gates* after their sexual encounter. The Girl is represented as mysterious and, although she saves Corso's life, is coded as demonic through her representation as the Whore of Babylon on the ninth engraving. Two more examples of the "unnatural" woman are included within the film: the brusque, imperial, and wheelchair-bound Baroness Kessler and her secretary whose short hair and masculine appearance code her as a lesbian. In contrast to Liana Telfer and The Girl, the baroness is desexualized through her disability, age, and her demeanor. Whether she reciprocates her secretary's desire, which is conveyed to the viewer through her disapproving glare at Corso, or not is uncertain; what is, however, clear is that she has no interest in conforming to stereotypes of femininity—the woman who loves the devil is rendered unnatural.

At the very end of the film, however, the tables are righted, so to speak. Corso, having been used as a pawn and acted upon through the film, asserts himself for the first time. He seeks out the authentic ninth engraving of his own accord, returns to the forbidding castle represented on the ninth engraving, and the final shot of the film has him walking upright and alone without hesitation toward the gates as they swing open of their own accord to facilitate his passage. Having journeyed from ignorance to knowledge, and from unbelief to belief, he now acts with determination and agency, concerned with something other than satisfying his employer and with his percentage. He has become, like Balkan, hungry for the power knowledge permits and is prepared to meet the devil it if allows him to become someone who acts rather than is acted upon. In terms of conventional gender codes, the knowledge gained and the belief restored over the course of his journey have effected a re-masculinization of Corso, who stands on his own two feet in the end, determined to be damned if being damned is what it takes to exercise masculine determination.

Knowledge, Belief, Manhood

Until almost the end of *The Ninth Gate*, there is little in the film that can be characterized as explicitly fantastic. And even when the fantastic does explicitly intrude with The Girl's flying down, Peter Pan–like, to rescue Corso in Paris and then again at the Telfer mansion, it is fleeting and so understated it is easy to miss. The devil himself never appears and, while it is suggested that the Girl is a demonic presence, the Whore of Babylon come to facilitate Corso's damnation, it is never unquestionably confirmed. The film, therefore, is arguably not one about the devil himself but instead about the desire for him and for the existence of the transcendent more generally. In *The Secret Life of Puppets*, Victoria Nelson asserts that the premodern worldview that "holds there is another, invisible world besides this one, that our world of the senses is ruled by this other world through signs and portents, that good and evil are physically embodied in our immediate environment . . . is alive and well today in science fiction and supernatural horror films."[3] This would seem to be borne out by *The Ninth Gate*, which further supports her claim that discredited belief in the supernatural in modern culture can only find expression through the demonic.[4] Curiously enough, true damnation, suggests the film, inheres in confronting not the devil but the void.

The Ninth Gate from this point of view plays on the viewer's desire for precisely the kind of worldview advanced by the film: one in which God and the devil contend for souls and the supernatural is an active force in the world. *The Ninth Gate*'s twist on this desire is to ally it with the pleasure of excessive knowledge and then to suggest that the restoration of such a worldview would also restore conventional gender roles. Access to the transcendent in the film is granted not by way of incantation or spells but rather through attentiveness to baroque detail and the pleasure of knowledge. The devil is in the details of the engravings, not the body of the text, and becomes available only to those who luxuriate in the details of books and who savor knowledge about them. This excessiveness of arcane lore then restores mystery as it leads to confirmation of the existence of the transcendent. Ironically, knowing too much leads to the realization that one does not—and cannot—know everything, except through a kind of Faustian bargain. To truly know, one must believe again, suggests the film—and belief allows access to sources of power closed off to modern, secular citizens.

This reconceptualized universe and access to power finally reinvigorates the enervated modern man who, knowing where he stands, can reassume a conventional gender role and assert himself at last. Dean Corso's triple journey takes us from ignorance to knowledge, unbelief to belief, and from impotence to manhood as the film reasserts a premodern view of the universe and conventional gender roles. The pleasures of the seemingly unimportant detail and of excessive knowledge that exceeds utility in the end are the keys to moving beyond the material plane to reach the transcendent, restoring in the process not only a conventional moral framework with God and the devil contending of human souls but also conventional gender roles correlating masculinity with power and assertiveness. The film's desire for the devil thus reflects a modern nostalgia—perhaps particularly among scholars, intellectuals, and all those who know antique books well but place no faith in the worldview they express—for belief in something other than the material world. Better the devil and damnation, suggests the film, than nothing.

Notes

1. Victoria Nelson, *The Secret Life of Puppets* (Baltimore, MD: Johns Hopkins University Press, 2001), viii.
2. Nelson, 19.
3. Nelson, viii.
4. Nelson, 7.

Agency or Allowance

*The Satanic Complications of Female Autonomy
in* The Witches of Eastwick *and* The Witch

Simon Bacon

This essay looks at constructions of female agency through communion with the devil in *The Witches of Eastwick* (George Miller, 1987) and *The Witch* (Robert Eggers, 2015). Although the tone of the two movies is quite different, with Miller's being something of a dark comedy whereas Eggers's is an out-and-out horror film, they share a similar structure in that Satan is shown to provide a means of female empowerment in a world of stifling patriarchy. The main female characters in both films are trapped or oppressed by the male-controlled societies around them and are forced to negotiate differing forms of personal autonomy through supernatural means and a negotiation with the devil himself. Satan in these films, as a male figure, may or may not represent that very patriarchal system, complicating any kind of deal the female protagonists are able to make with him. Consequently, the women in the two narratives manifest the cultural anxieties in relation to the female body that resists societal control and containment as well as the ongoing struggles in gender politics.

Although separated by almost thirty years, the two films share similar concerns over the acceptable levels of allowance for female autonomy within a patriarchal society, as well as intimating that, over time, this might not have increased in a manner expected in the twenty-first century. Consequently, the present study also considers the specific historical moments that the films were made in, if not the narrative setting, to assess how this might affect the level of female freedom finally achieved as well as how it configures the type of demonic master involved in this cultural negotiation.

Thus, I argue that any feminine liberation gained or granted under the auspices of an excessively masculine, if often transgressive, figure such as Satan

149

is still preferable to a life under the oppressive regime of patriarchy. This is nowhere seen more clearly than in *The Witches of Eastwick* with its self-proclaimed "horny little devil."

New Women in New England

It is no coincidence that both films discussed here are set in New England with its connection to Salem and its infamous witch trials, and perhaps equally unsurprising is that they also feature witches as main protagonists. However, the witches from Eastwick from the late twentieth century are represented as far more acceptable characters than those in Eggers's movie set three hundred years earlier.

Miller's film is based on John Updike's novel of the same name from 1984. Updike's book was seen as something of a reaction to feminism in America and framed the story as "an answer to the women's movement."[1] Indeed, in the novel the women are punished for their dalliance with the devil and for their socially transgressive behavior. The story of the film, however, sees the "wives"—Alexandra "Alex" Medford played by Cher, Jane Spofford played by Susan Sarandon, and Sukie Ridgemont played by Michelle Pfeiffer—more as bored (repressed) housewives turned Wyrd Sisters who somewhat scandalize 1980s rural America with their independence and self-assurance. All three have been abandoned by their respective husbands, which virtually bestows upon them the status of "widow" in the eyes of the very religious local community. Their categorization as being outsiders brings the women closer together and causes them to meet weekly as a form of support group—unknowingly forming their own coven—to discuss the nature of the man who might come and save them. Curiously, at this stage the three women only see their friendship as a way to help them cope with life until they can find a man and effectively reenter the society that has expelled them.

The movie intimates that the women are witches but do not realize it, as though it is a latent "gift" waiting for the right circumstances to express itself. Further, in some respects it can be seen to suggest, at least in terms of the fictional Eastwick, that any woman that exceeds the limits of what Miller calls "the women's sphere" is automatically a witch.[2] Local gossip reaches fever pitch levels when their "wishes," dabbling with the dark arts, bring forth not the "tall, dark, prince traveling under a curse" they had hoped for but a wealthy tycoon from New York, Daryl Van Horne (Jack Nicholson), who buys the local mansion and proceeds to woo the three women in turn. Van Horne immediately appears to be different from all the other men in Eastwick largely because he seems to listen to the women and is attentive and persuasive.

There is a sense that he is almost a different kind of being from the other men they know, which helps to convince the women he might offer a form of "escape from patriarchy" which has entrapped them thus far.[3]

Van Horne is played by well-known Hollywood lothario Jack Nicholson, and it is his physical presence and personality that make his Satan, in his own words in the film, "just your average horny little devil." Van Horne is a character who is very much at home in his own skin, luxuriating in its physicality—he is a being centered totally on his own pleasure. It is not surprising then that the release that he offers is a sexual one, which posits that taking pleasure in one's physical/sensual self increases self-confidence and one's connection to the world. However, his pursuit of the three women, with all its clumsiness and "charm," is solely for his own ends and is meant to bind his sexual conquests to him rather than promote their own sense of individual worth. This denotes him clearly as a fellow misogynist in a patriarchal world that is seemingly created solely for the pleasure of men.

The choice of Nicholson to play Van Horne is interesting as his manner is one that is designed to "glamour" the audience as much as it is the three women. Roger Ebert sees this power as concentrated in the actor's eyebrows, which prominently display his changing emotions throughout the film, but also as they seem to speak directly to the audience, sharing his delight with us and making "us conspirators with Nicholson,"[4] and by extension with the devil. Satan's form in the film is then meant to beguile us; it is a living temptation to follow his actions, to join in and be just like him, which equally entails an affirmation of the kinds of misogyny that he performs.

The film allows a similar engagement to occur with the three female witches as, once they have been wooed by Van Horne, they all suddenly become extremely glamorous and sport typically 1980s large, loose, curly hair—embodying the patriarchal notion of a connection between "looseness" of hair, character, and sexual availability. At this stage of the film witchcraft appears to be highly beneficial to the women, freeing them from the bonds of social expectation and giving them individual agency, even if the narrative implies it is largely due to great sex with Satan. However, the situation still leaves them as outsiders to the local community, which ordinarily would force them into even greater dependence on the devil—something he clearly wants. But what he had not bargained on was the bonds of sisterhood between the women, which are only strengthened by the magic spells they perform together.

The narrative reinforces this positive reading of magic and its relation to feminine agency—unlike a film such as The Craft (Andrew Fleming, 1996), for example, where power dynamics/hierarchies dominate any sisterly ties—and more so the supportive and inclusive nature of the coven. Consequently, the increasing independence they feel makes them tire of Van Horne's attentions and they decide to try to get rid of him. To do this, they make a small wax effigy of him and use it to make him regurgitate cherry stones—something he had earlier made happen to the rather histrionic puritanical wife, Felicia Alden played by Veronica Cartwright, of the local newspaper. This is important as the earlier acts of magic the women performed were quite small scale or "safe," but in trying to get rid of Van Horne, they are attempting something far more dangerous—life threatening even—as well as killing the last vestiges of male control in their lives.

The spell itself involves the three women working closely together—emphasizing their actions as one body—and, as it starts to take effect, Daryl launches into a diatribe about "women," finally revealing his true misogynistic self:

> Do you think God knew what He was doing when He created woman? Huh? No shit. I really wanna know. Or do you think it was another one of His minor mistakes like tidal waves, earthquakes, floods? You think women are like that? S'matter? You don't think God makes mistakes? Of course He does. We all make mistakes. Of course, when we make mistakes, they call it evil. When God makes mistakes, they call it . . . nature. So whaddya think? Women . . . a mistake . . . or did he do it to us on purpose?

This again reinforces the notion of the three witches being women who have exceeded their patriarchally apportioned sphere, and Satan's histrionics imply that he is just a cog in a much larger, systemic, universe of male misogyny. Simultaneously though, it also intimates that these three women in particular, Alex, Jane, and Sukie, are not controlled by anyone and are very much their own creations—in fact, because of the nature of the coven described above, they are each other's creations.

Just as Van Horne reveals his true nature through words, his physical self begins to transform as well. His shape begins to bulk out and become more ursine and his shoes are ripped open by his now bear-like feet. This metamorphosis is accompanied by his increasing bad temper as he hurries to get back to his mansion, where he knows the women are casting the spell. Sensing this, the "wives" hurry to clear away the evidence of what they are doing, and the wax effigy gets thrown around and dropped, causing Van Horne to copy these violent jerks and throws in real life, making him even more agitated. By the time he reaches his mansion, he has grown large tusks from his bottom jaw, seems to have lost his human form, and bounces, half ape-like, half bear-like, through the rooms of the building. Upon reaching the room where the women are, the wax doll is dropped and broken, causing the now-revealed Satan to go through a series of uncontrolled metamorphoses until he disappears. One assumes that this means his invitation has been revoked and he has been sent back to hell. Unlike Updike's book, the women survive intact and are now in charge of their own lives, and they still look extremely glamorous—"beauty" more clearly represented as the result of self-confidence and self-possession rather than the result of demonic conjugation.

Cutting to "one year later," the film shows the three of them each having given birth to a male child, presumably Daryl's. This is confirmed when the three toddlers group around a bank of television sets on which the face of their Satanic father appears, once more in human form. However, the three women quickly appear and switch the television off, intimating the devil has over-stepped the bounds of his paternal visiting rights and that they are still firmly in control.

Miller's film then ends on a positive note, if one with some reservations. The three friends remain outcasts from the local community but, within the confines of the mansion and with what is left of Van Horne's wealth, live an independent life. Witchcraft and their subsequent dealings with the devil, although doing little to change their status as outsiders or some of the more conventional aspects of their identities as women, has strengthened their friendship and mutual support system providing a form of collective agency. Although this can be described as a form of sisterhood, Miriam M. Johnson qualifies this through the notion of "maternal agency" where care and mutual support are paramount. Johnson sees this as a means to avoid the sometimes perceived anti-family aspects of feminism,[5] and this very much echoes what is seen in *Witches of Eastwick*. The idea of feminism as such is never brought to the fore in the narrative and it instead makes the story about three likable female characters being treated badly by the community they live in. The mutual care among them is already there, but magic lifts it to the more than normal, beyond the patriarchally acceptable, to where it provides the strength and confidence to be themselves—even if it is magic, seemingly provided by Satan, that provides the authority to do that.

The effects are also shown to be lasting as the devil is reduced to the role of a divorced father, no longer able to visit his children and seemingly power-less against his former wives who can "switch him off" with the flick of a remote control. Of course, it should not be forgotten that maternal agency can also be read as a positive spin on the more traditional roles or subject positions already attributed to women under patriarchy with their confinement to the mansion expressing something of this. In this sense, much of their continued agency comes through their children and reproduction rather than their own individual identities.[6] Yet one feels that cavorting with the devil has not denied individual choice to Alex, Jane, or Sukie, even if their choices are not necessarily particularly radical. In contrast, such choice is withheld from the young girl who decides to be a bride of Satan in *The Witch*.

The Trials That Make a Witch

The Witch is a very different film from *Witches of Eastwick*—where the latter seemed excessive in its Hollywood gloss and special effects, Eggers's film is stripped back to the dirt and grime of settler life in seventeenth-century New England. Subsequently, the lead character's decision to embrace witchcraft is not one made because of boredom or ennui, but because her very existence depends upon it.

Set in Salem in the 1630s, it predates the infamous witch trials that would take place sixty years later but suggests that there might have been some historical precedent for them. From its beginning, it speaks of religious fundamentalism and shows a family being cast out from a Puritan settlement because the family's patriarch, William (Ralph Ineson), calls the settlers false Christians, while they believe he talks improperly about the word of God. William, along with his wife (Kate Dickie) and five children, is forced to set up his own small farm in the wilderness—the metaphorical land beyond the forest—where the supernatural holds sway. Indeed, unbeknownst to them a witch lives in a small cabin in the woods not far from their farmstead. She is responsible for stealing their youngest child while it is being looked after by their eldest daughter, Thomasin, played by Anya Taylor-Joy. The witch here lives alone and is completely different from those seen earlier in Miller's film. While she is shown as being young and glamourous, not unlike her later Wyrd Sisters from Eastwick, this is only due to grinding up the body of a baby— Thomasin's baby brother—and covering herself in the blood and pulp. Once the effects wear off, she returns to looking like an old hag.

Thomasin herself is also portrayed as a transformative being as she is on the verge of becoming a woman, which creates increasing tensions within the family and appears to be the focus of the escalating evil that befalls the family—the disappearance of baby Sam, mentioned previously; the catatonic state and eventual death of the eldest brother, Caleb (Harvey Scrimshaw), who has been bewitched by the witch; and even the failing crops and the goat's milk turning to blood. Thomasin herself just wants to be good but is constantly forced to leave the places she feels secure in because of her father's extremist views—she is the only child old enough to remember their previous life in England, and also the only one who seems truly upset in being forced to leave the settlement. As a result, she feels constantly as though she is unwanted or an outsider, something which is exacerbated when she overhears her parents wanting to sell her off to another family.

However, the true outsider, the absolute other, is Satan who has been hiding in plain sight but unrecognized in the midst of the family since the narrative's beginning. Here, unlike the human-looking Van Horne, the devil is Black Philip, a large black ram that has been with the family since their time in the settlement.[7] Goats were not uncommon with settlers in the Americas, as the film's director David Eggers observes: "When the settlers came over here, they brought goats with them, and there was a lot of people with goats, because goats could clear the land very efficiently and they were small, to travel with."[8] Yet the black ram is particularly distinctive, even more so as the young twins, Mercy (Ellie Grainger) and Jonas (Lucas Dawson), spend much time playing with him and singing songs about him "eating lions" and ruling the world.[9] There are extenuating, cultural factors as to why none of the adults suspects Black Philip of being Satan, with the main one being that the medieval tradition of representing the devil as a goat, or with goat-like features, is not a particularly English one and was more common in Continental Europe.[10] Satan here is constructed as a very different entity to the silver-tongued millionaire misogynist in *Witches of Eastwick*, although he shares a similar ability to glamour those around him. His nonhuman form would appear to situate him outside of normative gender politics, as does his seeming exclusivity to female associates, though, as seen at the end of the film, this has its complications.

The situation on the farm gets increasingly worse after the death of Caleb, with Thomasin and the twins coming under suspicion of being witches and being shut in the goat barn with Black Philip. Meanwhile, Thomasin's mother is becoming more and more unstable, and while the children are locked in with Philip, she thinks she is caring for and breastfeeding her dead baby Sam, when in fact a raven is seen picking at her breast. During the night, the witch enters the barn and kills all the goats and vanishes with the twins, leaving Thomasin asleep. The next morning, the young woman awakens to find Black Philip killing her father by ramming him into a woodpile that subsequently collapses on him. The girl's mother appears and realizes that her twin children have now also been taken from her and tries to kill Thomasin, who she thinks is responsible. In the struggle that ensues, Thomasin kills her mother, leaving herself and the black goat as the only survivors.

Lost and alone, she goes to the barn where Philip is and offers herself to him. Unlike the God that she has been praying to throughout the film, begging for Christ's love and "for His mercy and His grace to save her soul from fiery torment,"[11] Philip responds to her with a human voice, and briefly assumes human form. It is an important moment in the film as throughout Satan has only been seen in the form of Black Philip, and it opens up the possibility that he has been possessing the animal or using it as a familiar.[12] The human figure the ram transforms into—a man with long black hair and beard and dressed in black period costume (oddly reminiscent of Royalist Cavalier costume although the date predates that slightly)—has cloven hooves and quickly reverts back to Black Philip once Thomasin has given herself to him and signed away her soul.

Thomasin's change of heart is key to the ultimate meaning of the narrative as the film portrays her as very much a conformist who wants to be accepted, even though events seem to constantly conspire against her and result in her feeling increasingly ostracized. Indeed, in many ways she is different from the rest of the family and her fellow siblings in particular; as David Crow notes, unlike the rest of her family, she misses, "the 'luxuries' of both first the Commonwealth and then that of dear departed England, whose charms and beautiful glasswork she recounts to her uncomprehending younger brother Caleb."[13] This creates just another reason for her to feel different from the rest of her family—a family that already finds her problematic. Crow further feels that she suffers from a level of self-loathing due to wanting things that are different from the desires of her family: "This ability to quietly covet worldly things is also why she hates her own weakness and, on a certain level, desires her family to loathe her too, hence 'spinning fantasies' to young sister Mercy about selling her soul to Satan and eating flesh." This last fantasy relates to a scene where one of the twins says Thomasin is a witch and, rather than continually denying it, the teenager replies that, yes, she is one and will eat her younger siblings.

This is the first time the otherness of Thomasin is given a name—that of witch—and it is repeated with increasing conviction through the remainder of the story. As such, by the tale's denouement, it is with a sense of resignation that she decides that if she is going to be accused of being a witch, she might as well be one and gain some form of control over her life, no matter the consequences. In this way, her act of embracing both witchcraft and Satan falls into revisionist readings of witches in which they are women that defy patriarchal containment and the strictures of normative society and are subsequently persecuted for it.

Female agency can also be found in a more metaphorical reading of Thomasin's narrative that sees it more akin to the fairy tale of Red Riding Hood—and the film often feels as though it's taking place in such a fairy-tale world.[14] Wolves abound in the movie from the lone witch stalking her prey through the forest to Thomasin's father and elder brother becoming increasingly aware of her burgeoning womanhood, and of course Black Philip, the proverbial wolf here in goat's clothing. Thomasin's "red cape" is her menstruation beginning, and potentially an indication of her inclination toward sin,[15] and while she never walks through the woods to grandma's house, she lives next to the forest and constantly strays into it. She feels that she does everything she can to stay on the "right" path but, unlike her fellow siblings, she desires more from the world as she has lost more and so is constantly tempted to leave its safety and look for something better. Finally, as in pre-Perrault versions of the tale, rather than seeing the young girl saved and returned to patriarchal society, she strips and dances naked with the wolf—Ziolkowski notes that evangelical Christian interpretations of the tale interpret the wolf as being the devil[16]—to become a woman and act on her own behalf.

If these two readings see a young girl growing up to be her own woman, one can equally read the unfolding events as Thomasin being groomed by Black Philip. One can assume that he is easily able to direct the actions of the witch in the woods and that he has purposely insinuated his way into the religious extremist's family, knowing that they, or their eldest daughter, are ripe for plucking. Their young children can be offered as reward to his servants, the witches, and, of course, there is a girl on the cusp of womanhood who can be turned into a new disciple (wife of Satan). Consequently, each disappearance and death of a family member is orchestrated to separate the young woman from her home and redirect her religious fervor away from Puritanism and unknown heavenly rewards to that of Satanism and an earthly life lived "deliciously." Here any form of agency given to the young girl is that allowed by patriarchy and one that will demand the ultimate price, which Thomasin will be unable to avoid.

Allowance or Agency

The two films, while vastly different, appear to offer the women involved some form of agency both through witchcraft—a not unfamiliar construction post-1970s—and because of their respective dealings with the devil. In *Witches of Eastwick*, the three women find friendship and support through witchcraft. And while they had much of that previous to beginning their own coven, it is the sense of achieving change and influence in the world around them through working together that makes the biggest difference to their lives. This is most dramatically seen in their banishing of Satan back to hell, which is an act of considerable achievement. As such, it makes the somewhat domesticated freedom they decide to live at story's end something of an anticlimax.

Rather than leaving the community that ostracized them, they choose to exile themselves and live holed up in Van Horne's mansion with the only improvement to their earlier situation being that they now have a manservant to do their shopping for them. As Jen Chaney notes, while they seem to have put the devil in his place, "they've also been reduced to little more than traditional caregivers, forced, albeit seemingly happily, to raise his kids."[17] Their freedoms are oddly self-limiting and directly linked to traditionally female roles as imposed by patriarchy. Indeed, the children are all boys and so it can also be read that Satan purposely withdrew once he had inseminated the women knowing that another generation of "little devils" would be released into the world and his direct presence was no longer needed.

If Alex, Jane, and Sukie chose to become witches because of boredom then the reason for Thomasin's turn to the dark arts could not be more different. To be called a witch in New England in the late twentieth century might imply you have a rather nasty side to your personality, but in the early seventeenth century, it could get you killed. Eggers's film very much plays into that view of the world where angels, demons, and witches were very real and physical presences. Thomasin's options at the end of the narrative are very few. Being the only surviving member of her family, none of whom has died from natural causes, would cast a huge amount of suspicion upon her, especially as they were cast out of the nearest settlement because of their unorthodox and sacrilegious beliefs. Consequently, the probability of her being tried and convicted as a witch would have been extremely high, so choosing to be what everyone believes you to be may seem a logical decision—one made even more so by the fact that Satan has actually revealed himself to the impressionable young woman whereas her God has remained unresponsive and unreachable. Her choice in the film would seem to doom her to a life of exile and solitude, except for the sabbaths where all the witches come together to dance naked in invocation to the devil—as shown in the closing sequence of the movie as they are all rapturously lifted into the air. And, as noted previously, this life beyond patriarchal control requires the destruction of young children and babies so that she may remain young and virile. There is a sense in this ending that the female agency or womanhood achieved by Thomasin, through real or metaphorical sex with the devil, is one that is necessarily nonreproductive, and that the maternal and motherly sisterhood of caring and child rearing that typified the 1980s is not possible for women in the 1630s or maybe even the 2010s.

In a 1984 review of Updike's book, Margaret Atwood wrote, "What a culture has to say about witchcraft, whether in jest or in earnest, has a lot to do with its views of sexuality and power, and especially with the apportioning of powers between the sexes."[18] And it is this aspect that is possibly the most dramatic change between the two films—despite the thirty years between them, and the fact that the most recent is set in the past, the outcomes for female agency beyond patriarchy seem even more limited. If one sees the portrayal of witch-craft in each narrative as the attempt to gain control over one's life under patriarchy, then Miller's film sees it in vaguely parochial terms, where Satan—the man of the House—lets his wives do as they will as long as they stay home and bring up the kids. In *The Witch*, Thomasin lives a life of oppression and exclusion under patriarchy and her only chance for release from it is self-exile. However, unlike Alex, Jane, and Sukie, there is little option for sisterhood under her particular Dark Lord who only allows for brief sojourns of commu-nion in an otherwise solitary existence. Both films then suggest that self-exile is an allowable form of female agency with the earlier film quite happy for its community of maternal women to live together on its own, permitted terms. Eggers's film concludes on a slightly edgier note as his exiles are not so passive in their separation from society, with their explosive incursions into civilization a reminder that patriarchy is nowhere near as secure as it would like to think.

Notes

1. Kim A. Loudermilk, *Fictional Feminism: How American Bestsellers Affect the Movement for Women's Equality* (London: Routledge, 2004), 94.

2. In terms of the internal logic to *Witches of Eastwick*, this is true as women who have lost their men are expected to settle for any that will take them and, in the meantime, act, almost literally, like grieving widows.

3. Robert Reece, "Sex as Subversion: The Ethnosexual Protestor and the Ethnosexual Defender," *Routledge International Handbook of Race, Class, and Gender*, ed. Shirley A. Jackson (London: Routledge, 2015), 117.

4. Roger Ebert, "Review: Witches of Eastwick," Roger Ebert.com, June 12, 1987, accessed July 14, 2017, http://www.rogerebert.com/reviews/the-witches-of -eastwick-1987.

5. Miriam M. Johnson, "Maternal Agency vs. the Brotherhood of Males," *Provoking Agents: Gender and Agency in Theory and Practice*, ed. Judith Kegan Gardener (Chicago: University of Illinois Press, 1995), 164.

6. The reproductive imperative here being configured as a patriarchal and heteronormative means of ideological control and reinforcement. See Lee Edelman, *No Future: Queer Theory and the Death Drive* (Durham, NC: Duke University Press, 2004).

7. In the Catholic medieval bestiary, which can be seen to inform much Satanic imagery, the bear and the wolf are both equated to the devil whereas the goat is allied to Christ, both having a love of high mountains. However, Isidore of Seville (seventh century) sees them as hot-tempered, lustful creatures whose blood can

dissolve diamonds. See "Beast Index," Medieval Bestiary, February 1, 2012, accessed July 14, 2017, http://bestiary.ca/beasts/beastalphashort.htm.

8. Forrest Wickman, "All *The Witch's* Most WTF Moments, Explained: A Spoiler-Filled Interview with the Director," Slate, February 23, 2016, accessed July 14, 2017, http://www.slate.com/blogs/browbeat/2017/07/18/george_romero_s_movies_were _about_more_than_zombies.html.

9. The words to the song sung by the twins in the film are as follows:

Black Phillip, Black Phillip/A crown grows out his head,/Black Phillip, Black Phillip/To nanny queen is wed./Jump to the fence post,/Running in the stall./Black Phillip, Black Phillip/King of all.

Black Phillip, Black Phillip/King of sky and land,/Black Phillip, Black Phillip/King of sea and sand./We are ye servants,/We are ye men./Black Phillip eats the lions/From the lions' den.

10. Gary Jensen, *The Path of the Devil: Early Modern Witch Hunts* (Lanham, MD: Rowman and Littlefield, 2007), 155–156.

11. David Crow, "Explaining *The Witch* Ending," *Den of Geek*, October 1, 2016, accessed July 14, 2017 http://www.denofgeek.com/us/movies/the-witch/253108/ explaining-the-witch-ending.

12. The witch in the woods has been seen using a wild rabbit as a familiar earlier in the film.

13. Crow, "Explaining *The Witch* Ending."

14. It can be argued that the "Satanic" interpretation of events all takes place in Thomasin's mind, and one theory of the film's meaning suggests that the mound growing on the family's corn crop produces hallucinogenic effects, though the film's director denied this is what is happening in the movie. See Wickman.

15. Jack Zipes, ed., *The Trials and Tribulations of Little Red Riding Hood* (New York: Routledge, 1993), 382.

16. Jan M. Ziolkowski, *Fairy Tales from Before Fairy Tales: The Medieval Latin Past of Wonderful Lies* (Ann Arbor: University of Michigan Press, 2009), 105.

17. Jen Chaney, "*The Witches of Eastwick* Is a Fascinating Movie to Watch Post-Weinstein," *Vulture*, October 30, 2017, accessed November 28, 2017, http://www .vulture.com/2017/10/the-witches-of-eastwick-30years-later.html.

18. Margaret Atwood, "The Witches of Eastwick," review, *New York Times*, May 13, 1984, accessed November 28, 2017, http://www.nytimes.com/1984/05/13/ books/updike-witches.html.

"Roaming the Earth"

Satan in The Last Temptation of Christ
and The Passion of the Christ

Catherine O'Brien

The battle between Christ and Satan is first announced in the Book of Genesis, when the Lord God says to the serpent: "I will put enmity between you and the woman, and between your offspring and hers; He will strike at your head, while you strike at his heel" (Gen. 3:15).[1] It is a combat between good and evil that is clearly identified in the New Testament: Jesus tells his followers, "I have observed Satan fall like lightning from the sky" (Luke 10:18); the First Letter of St. John states that, "the Son of God was revealed to destroy the works of the devil" (1 John 3:8); and the Letter to the Hebrews maintains that God became man so "that through death he might destroy the one who has the power of death, that is, the devil" (2:14). This essay contrasts the visual representation of the conflict between Christ and the devil in two of cinema's most polemical productions: Martin Scorsese's *The Last Temptation of Christ* (1988), which is based on Nikos Kazantzakis's novel *The Last Temptation* (1955), a reworking of the New Testament narrative; and Mel Gibson's *The Passion of the Christ* (2004), which draws on the Gospels and extra-biblical texts such as *The Dolorous Passion of Our Lord Jesus Christ* by the nineteenth-century mystic Anne Catherine Emmerich. Notably, both Scorsese and Gibson represent Satan as a being rather than an abstraction, and they follow those interpretations of Satan's physiology that reach a "general consensus that he required a proxy body in order to interact with human beings"[2]—the kind of character who is "roaming the earth" in the Book of Job (1:7) and causing a good deal of trouble.

Although it is clear that neither Scorsese nor Gibson are theologians—and, indeed, *The Last Temptation of Christ* opens with the caveat that the film "is not based upon the Gospels"—these biblically inspired narratives raise important theological questions and present the machinations of Satan during the cosmic encounter with the Savior in intriguing celluloid forms. One of the key issues in assessing the warfare between Christ and Satan is the status of the opponents. In his "Dialogues concerning natural religion," David Hume repeats Epicurus's question about God: "Is he willing to prevent evil, but not able? then he is impotent. Is he able, but not willing? then he is malevolent. Is he both able and willing? whence then is evil?"[3] Is Satan "a full-blown adversary, a loose cannon or simply an agent of an omnipotent God?" queries Peter Stanford in his biography of the Prince of Darkness.[4]

Satan has been "transformed from a devouring monster in the late Middle Ages to a more nuanced, and perversely human figure at the beginning of the modern age,"[5] as reflected in the contentious feminization of evil in the two films by Scorsese and Gibson: the dark, hooded figure (Rosalinda Celentano) who tempts Jesus (Jim Caviezel) to relinquish his mission in *The Passion of the Christ*; and the young girl (Juliette Caton) who invites Jesus (Willem Dafoe) down from the cross in the "dream sequence" in *The Last Temptation of Christ*. St. Athanasius saw the devil as "an incorrigible tempter dressed in black and often seemingly as innocent as a child,[6] and the films offer both perspectives.

Scorsese and Gibson have been labeled as directors with a Catholic "sensibility" (whatever their current standing with the Vatican might be[7]). While glimpses of Hell were more common in the Catholic "fire and brimstone" sermons that preceded the modernizing efforts of the Second Vatican Council (1962–65), the significance of Satan as a frightening reality has not ended in the postconciliar Catholic Church. During a General Audience in Rome in November 1972, Pope Paul VI famously informed his listeners: "Evil is not merely an absence of something but an active force, a living, spiritual being that is perverted and that perverts others. It is a terrible reality, mysterious and frightening."[8] Indeed, Satan has been back in the headlines since the election of Pope Francis, who has stated: "I believe that the Devil exists. Maybe his greatest achievement in these times has been to make us believe that he does not exist."[9] The following discussion considers the disparate ways in which Scorsese and Gibson succeed in bringing Satan back to the forefront of the action and, despite their apparently dichotomous approaches to the power struggle, present a confrontation between Christ and Satan that ends with the downfall of evil.

Satan in the Desert

A desert temptation scene is recorded in the Gospels of Matthew, Mark, and Luke. Mark treats the incident very briefly: "At once the Spirit drove [Jesus] out into the desert, and he remained in the desert for forty days, tempted by Satan" (Mark 1:12–13). However, both Matthew (4:1–11) and Luke (4:1–13) relate that there were three devilish invitations that Jesus rejected, despite his physical weakness. In the Gospel accounts, Jesus is tempted to rebel against God, and his clear refusal is expressed in language found in the Book of Deuteronomy (8:3; 6:13; and 6:16).

The Last Temptation of Christ presents a revisioning of the biblical temptation scene with a markedly different dynamic to the scriptural account—an angle that is signaled in the oft-quoted prologue to Kazantzakis's novel *The Last Temptation*: "My principal anguish and the source of all my joys and sorrows from my youth onward has been the incessant, merciless battle between the spirit and the flesh."[10] Vrasidas Karalis argues that "the metaphor employed by Kazantzakis of a reconciliation between God and man is not commensurate with the idea of a battle between flesh and spirit" but rather with "the indivisible unity of both flesh and spirit in an attempt to disavow the highly spiritualized and disembodied image of Jesus projected by established churches."[11] The filmic adaptation by Scorsese embraces this dimension by adopting the opening words from Kazantzakis's novel via a title card and subsequently focusing on the temptation of sexual seduction. *The Last Temptation of Christ* offers a controversial perspective on the New Testament verse in the Letter to the Hebrews that states that Jesus is able to sympathize with human weakness because he "has similarly been tested in every way" (Heb. 4:15).

Adhering to cultural representations that have traditionally imagined Satan in animal form, the desert temptation scene in *The Last Temptation of Christ* produces a snake, a lion, and a jet of flame—with all three choices having the advantage of strong biblical credentials while also creating logistical complications for the filmmaker. A serpent is notably an evil protagonist in the Book of Genesis and is described as "the most cunning of all the animals that the LORD God had made" (Gen. 3:1), but despite its substantial endorsement as a wily foe, there is always the danger of unintentional humor involved with talking cobras.[12] Scorsese explains that the desert temptation scenes could have been done with "just voices and sound effects, but I wanted to take the risk and keep the supernatural on the same level as the natural."[13] As a result, he films the snake very simply with a voice-over—the fact that it is the voice of Barbara Hershey, who plays Magdalene, adding an obvious *frisson* to the proceedings by clearly equating the devil with a specific woman—a childhood friend of Jesus who has turned to a life of prostitution.[14]

Several critics have echoed Scorsese's protestation (in the face of severe criticism from Christian commentators) that the film's central temptation itself is for "an ordinary life—marrying, raising children, and growing old."[15]

"To love and care for a woman, to have a family. This is a trick?" asks the snake. However, the tempter's final utterances clearly bring the topic around to sex, as Scorsese admits when discussing the artistic choices in this scene: "Maybe I should have changed the voice, not used Mary Magdalene's voice for the snake. . . . For me, being a Catholic from before Vatican II, sex has always been portrayed as the most evil sin. . . . And it stayed with me that sexuality is evil."[16] While the original New Testament narrative focuses on hunger when Jesus is encouraged to "command this stone to become bread" (Luke 4:3), the on-screen Jesus in Scorsese's film is lured by bodily pleasures ("Look at my breasts," urges the cobra) that continue an ongoing theme of the screenplay: the equation of Satan with women, sex, and, therefore, sin.

The second temptation is in the form of a lion—a devilish metaphor that St. Peter himself adopts in his writings: "Be sober and vigilant. Your opponent the devil is prowling around like a roaring lion looking for (someone) to devour" (1 Peter 5:8). As the animal is voiced by Harvey Keitel, who plays Judas, the aura of Magdalene's sexuality is now replaced by the atmosphere of betrayal by a friend. In discussing the dialogue, screenwriter Paul Schrader made the point: "You can't do it in King James English and you can't do it in Aramaic, which would be the only way to make it realistic,"[17] so the lion offers the temptation of world domination in a genial New York accent: "You said it was God, but you really wanted power. Now you can have what you want. Any country you want." However, Jesus finds this option easy to reject ("The Kingdom of Heaven is enough") and threatens to pull out the animal's tongue.

While the first two temptations introduce themselves as part of Jesus's essence (the snake identifies itself as Jesus's "spirit," while the lion claims, "I'm you. I'm your heart"), the third visitor is more obviously Satan himself in a pillar of flame. While flames are evidently a traditional dimension of hell, they do not necessarily have evil connotations: The "fire flaming out of a bush" when the angel of the Lord appears to Moses (Exod. 3:2) or the "tongues as of fire" when the Holy Spirit descends upon the apostles in the Book of Acts (2:3) are prominent positive examples. Indeed, Jesus initially makes the mistake of misrecognition in *The Last Temptation of Christ* and pleads, "Archangel, move back. Move back, you're blinding me"; and Satan's utterances (which blend the voices of Scorsese and Leo Marks) strive to sow further confusion by greeting Jesus as "the Son of God" before offering a devilish pact: "You'll sit in judgment, and I'll sit next to you. Imagine how strong we'd be together." It is at this point that Jesus finally recognizes his antagonist: "Satan." When an apple tree appears miraculously, there is an obvious analogy to the biblical scene when Eve follows the serpent's coaxing and brings sin into the world by tasting the forbidden fruit in the Garden of Eden (Gen. 3:1–7). Like Eve, Jesus bites into the attractive fruit but he reveals that the apple is inwardly rotten and filled with blood, thereby confirming that Satan's inducements are the way of corruption.

It is the first enticement (in the voice of a woman), urging Jesus to abandon "the arrogance to think [he] can save the world" and to enter domesticity instead, which is the most potent of the three invitations. While "liberal theologians have recognized the unacceptability of posing sexuality and spirituality as contradictory attractions,"[18] they are at the heart of Scorsese's approach in which the sexual act is equated with sin. The snake explodes in both the novel and the film, but whereas Kazantzakis's protagonist shouts "No! No! No!" on the printed page,[19] the on-screen Jesus does not explicitly express rejection of the reptile's offer, so that the lack of verbal repudiation appears to have left the door open to subsequent danger.

According to the *Catechism of the Catholic Church*, "Jesus' victory over the tempter in the desert anticipates victory at the Passion, the supreme act of obedience of his filial love for the Father."[20] Scorsese admirably wanted to avoid making a film in which Jesus "glowed in the dark," because "if He was like that, we always thought, then when the temptations came to Him, surely it was easy to resist them because He was God."[21] Yet, explaining the concept behind his script, Paul Schrader said, "It's a tortured human struggle about a common man possessed by God and fighting it. God is a demon in that way,"[22] and it is here that the difficulty behind the intention lies. Jesus is evidently not "a common man" for Christians—he is fully divine as well as fully human. The *Catechism of the Catholic Church* reads: "This is why Christ vanquished the Tempter for us: 'For we have not a high priest who is unable to sympathize with our weaknesses, but one who in every respect has been tested as we are, yet without sinning.'"[23] One reason why Scorsese's film caused outrage for some viewers is that the latter distinction ("yet without sinning") that completes the verse in the Letter to the Hebrews (4:15) was not made clear enough in the film, given that the central protagonist's identity crisis is expressed in the blasphemous statement (adapted directly from Kazantzakis) that "Lucifer is inside me." St. Gregory the Great saw Satan as the "master psychologist who tailors his suggestions to his victims' sensibilities,"[24] and, at this point in the proceedings, there is a lack of conviction in Scorsese's protagonist that makes the mission of Salvation appear to be in danger.

Satan in the Garden

In contrast, the audience senses that Satan has met a much tougher opponent in Gibson's *The Passion of the Christ* when different tactics are employed: It is potential despair (rather than desire) which is manipulated in the opening Garden of Gethsemane scene. Although there is no biblical testimony of Satan's materialization at this point of the narrative, Gibson was inspired by Anne Catherine Emmerich's mystical visions in which Jesus asks, "O my Father, can I possibly suffer for so ungrateful a race?" as Satan appears on the night before the Crucifixion, sometimes "under the form of a gigantic black figure."[25] While Gibson does not adhere to Emmerich's sense of scale, he also chooses a character dressed in black. In the film, Satan's traditional cloven hooves and horns are rejected in favor of shaved eyebrows, unblinking eyes, and maggot-infested nostrils to create "an ashen androgynous figure that seems to appear and vanish at will [and] is the film's most otherworldly presence."[26] "It looks almost normal, almost good—but not quite" explained Gibson,[27] thereby manifesting Saint Augustine's view that evil can be understood as "the absence of good."[28]

In *The Passion of the Christ*, there is no backstory to the relationship between Jesus and Satan (as the Gospel temptation episode is not presented in the flashbacks), but the audience senses that Jesus has met this Satanic adversary before, given that there is no introductory exchange of names. Satan speaks in Aramaic in a male voice using a series of negatives: "No one man can carry this burden, I tell you. It is far too heavy. Saving their souls is too costly. No one. Ever. No. Never"—but Jesus does not engage directly with his tempter. While Scorsese's English-speaking protagonist appears confused in his dialogue with Satan in *The Last Temptation of Christ*, Jesus ignores his evil interlocutor and prays in Hebrew in the language of the psalms in *The Passion of the Christ*. In *The Last Temptation of Christ*, Satan addresses Jesus as the "Son of God" (an identity with which Jesus wrestles throughout the film); but Satan's attempt to undermine the certainty of Jesus in *The Passion of the Christ* (by asking "Who is your father? Who are you?") is treated with contempt. When a snake emerges from beneath Satan's robes and slithers across the earth, in an analogy to a new Garden of Eden in which Jesus is the New Adam, Jesus stamps down hard upon the reptile (as prophesied in the Book of Genesis 3:15), and it is evident that this specific contest has been won. There is none of the uncertainty that is witnessed in *The Last Temptation of Christ*.

Roaming the Earth

In both films, the humanized forms of Satan are constantly on the move, initially refusing to admit defeat. One of the most contentious elements in *The Passion of the Christ* is a perceived visual link between Satan and the Jewish protagonists, which appears to draw on "one of the earliest, most enduring and most pernicious examples of the Christian habit of stigmatising as servants of the Prince of Darkness everyone who did not share their beliefs"[29]—the kind of anti-Semitic attitudes in the Catholic Church that the Vatican II document *Nostra Aetate (Declaration on the Relation of the Church to Non-Christian Religions*, 1965) aimed to abolish. Given that Gibson had been inspired by the private revelations of Emmerich, who described the Jewish leaders as "priests of Satan,"[30] he repeatedly had to defend his film against accusations of anti-Semitism.[31]

A particular cause for concern is Satan's physical presence among the Jews, as if he is on their side rather than their enemy. In the scene when a group of children cruelly mock Judas, who is in despair after having betrayed Jesus, Satan appears silently amongst the boys as if endorsing their actions. When the persecution drives Judas to take his own life, Satan's presence may fit the "popular tradition that the bodies of suicides belonged to the Devil."[32]

Having achieved success in the tormenting of Judas, Satan moves on to join the Jewish spectators at the flagellation scene, in a manner that some observers argued "repeats the medieval myth that Jews are his agents."[33] There is no visual interaction between Satan and the Jewish onlookers, and they do not appear to be aware of his presence but, as Susan Thistlethwaite contends, "he seems quite at home, almost indeed like one of them."[34] However, amid the outcry over anti-Semitism in Gibson's film, a number of critics singled out the importance of Mary as a Jewish mother, especially as Maia Morgenstern, who plays the role, is Jewish herself. It is in Mary that Satan meets his strongest human opponent.

One of the most debated moments in *The Passion of the Christ* is when Satan glides through the crowd, apparently holding a baby—until the infant turns around to reveal disfigured, adult features. Gibson himself explains that he "wanted something *really* creepy at that moment,"[35] and he came up with an idea that seems "weird, it is shocking, it's almost too much."[36] There are traditions that have "predicted the coming of Antichrist in an anti-nativity,"[37] and there is no doubt that the distortion of the joyous image of the Madonna and child is particularly startling, especially as Mary is watching her own son being tortured at this moment. Darren Oldridge claims that Satan is the only person in the film, other than Christ, "who understands fully the purpose of the incarnation, and paradoxically he confirms its inestimable value" by manipulating the traditional iconography.[38]

Monica Migliorino Miller suggests, "This satanic mother and her baby are what the Devil wants Mary and Christ to be. If Satan can get Mary to be a clinging mother, then Christ's mission might be thwarted."[39] In other words, Satan in *The Passion of the Christ* has another strategy in mind by directly

confronting the mother of Jesus. As a result, Mary is given a particularly prominent role in comprehending her son's mission in the film, and Gibson succeeds in adding an interesting angle on popular Catholic Marian devotion
when the eyes of Satan and Mary meet across the Via Dolorosa. A translation
in the Latin Vulgate Bible ensured that centuries of Catholics read the verse
in Genesis (3:15) as "She will crush your head, and you will lie in wait for her
heel," and the image has been recreated in religious art in which Mary (rather
than Christ) crushes a serpent beneath her foot. Gibson manages to be faithful to the Bible by having Jesus trample on the snake in the Gethsemane
scene, while also adhering to the view of Catholic exegetes that Mary played
a role in the overthrow of evil by giving birth to the Messiah, so that the Marian statues and paintings in which she tramples on the reptile have validity.[40]
In Gibson's film, Mary stares straight at her devilish opponent and is the first
to turn away to focus on Jesus, illustrating the fact that she is not under Satan's
thrall. Mary, as a Jewish woman, acts as a powerful example of Jewish opposition to the villainous adversary who is here masquerading in feminine form.

While Gibson's "slithery, effeminate Satan" is clearly a representation of
evil[41]—so that both Jesus and Mary are conscious that they are facing a wicked
foe—the devilish figure who appears in the final temptation sequence in
Scorsese's film is a more complex enemy, initially seeming to be closer to "the
Satan" in the Book of Job who is represented as a servant of God. The Hebrew
word *stn* means an "opponent or someone who obstructs,"[42] and Job himself is
tormented "to see if he will stay true to his God."[43]

Anyone unfamiliar with the story by Kazantzakis may not immediately
have read the cinematic signs that indicate the move to a dream-like state in
The Last Temptation of Christ: the tilting of the cross, the change of light, and
the fact that Jesus can no longer hear the taunts from the crowd. At the foot of
the cross appears a new character who was not visible in any of the previous
shots on Golgotha. In Kazantzakis's original novel, this Satanic personality (as
it will ultimately be revealed) is male, and his body is "supple and firm, a blue-
black disquieting fluff enwrapped his legs, from the shins to the rounded
thighs; and his armpits smelt of beloved human sweat";[44] but after the death
of Magdalene he turns himself "into a negro boy" who "runs errands."[45] It is
understandable that the screenwriter Paul Schrader preferred to avoid this
specific representation "to escape charges of prejudice."[46] However, the final
decision to choose a young girl to play the part (rather than Lew Ayres, who
had been selected when the film was first cast in 1983), ensures that the Satan
of the Temptation sequence "masquerades as an angel of light" (2 Cor. 11:14)
and is a more devious antagonist because of her cherubic features. Indeed, she
provides her own misleading identification: "I'm the angel who guards you.

Your father is the God of mercy, not punishment. He saw you and said, 'Aren't you his guardian angel? Well, go down and save him. He's suffered enough.'" Within his dream-like state, Jesus falls into the trap identified by Saint Augustine in *City of God* when a person is "supposing that he is enjoying the friendship of good angels when in fact it is evil demons that he has as his false friends, and when he thus suffers from the enmity of those whose harmfulness is in proportion to their cunning and deceit."[47] Babington and Evans point out that, "given the dualistic distrust of women's sexuality and over-valuation of their purity which Scorsese's films dramatise from the culture at large, the innocent, pre-sexual girl is the most powerful advocate, the most seductive disguise of all."[48] Scorsese has added a further element to Kazantzakis's original idea by creating a female Satan who will lead Jesus into the final temptation.

Nevertheless, the *mise-en-scène* does offer warning signals. When the young girl kisses the feet of Jesus, the blood does not mark her lips (in contrast to an analogous shot in *The Passion of the* Christ when Mary kisses the wounds of her son and is thereby united in his suffering). In Kazantzakis's novel, the "guardian angel" tempts Jesus with the words: "Once upon a time your heart did not want the earth; it went against her will. Now it wants her—and that is the whole secret."[49] As if following an Augustinian line of thought that "in their fallen state, all men and women were inclined to neglect divine and eternal things in favour of earthly and impermanent ones, and were consequently drawn towards falsehood,"[50] the young girl's hair and robe blend with the warm brown tones of the ground, and as she helps Jesus to come down from the cross, it is the downfall of humanity that she seeks. In fact, Peter Gabriel, who wrote the film score, initially wanted to use traditional church music during Satan's appearance so as to increase the level of confusion: "The devil's music, if you like, would have been religious."[51] Notably, this Satan speaks in a British accent—often an indication of piety in traditional biblical epics but also of "the bad guy" in Hollywood action movies. When the young girl states, "There's only one woman in the world. One woman with many faces," her pronunciation should cause warning bells to ring, even if the misogyny in this utterance (which continues the equation of women and sexual sin) is missed.

After the wedding of Jesus and Magdalene within the hallucination, Satan is sitting outside their house as if keeping watch to ensure that nothing prevents their union. Despite Scorsese's efforts to shoot a marital sex scene that was intended to show "great gentleness, mutual tenderness,"[52] some Christian commentators were "deeply disturbed and repulsed by the sheer visual-emotional impact of a close-up depiction of Jesus Christ passionately kissing a woman in bed. . . . That the picture was part of a 'temptation' scene doesn't mend matters at all; the sheer force of the image is greater than its context."[53] The fact that Satan is now sitting inside the room, apparently keeping guard, increased the overall sense of "wrongness" for some spectators.

Saint Augustine wrote of the "flesh's sickness" and "sweet deadliness,"[54] seeing a failure to control human passions as a result of the Fall; and Thomas Aquinas argued that "virginity seeks the soul's good . . . marriage seeks the body's good. . . . Without doubt the state of virginity is preferable."[55] As Scorsese received a Catholic education that "taught that, if you entertained fantasy for a while, it became an occasion of sin,"[56] he has decided to emphasize sex as "a powerful symbol of Jesus' humanity" in *The Last Temptation of Christ*.[57] The danger is that the narrative succumbs to the idea that Scorsese "was using Jesus's struggle with inner demons as a vehicle for uncovering and confronting his own psychological and spiritual conflicts."[58] Consequently, given the over-emphasis on the humanity of Jesus at the expense of his divinity, the Satanic character appears on the verge of success.

Yet, Satan's plans fortunately go awry. When Magdalene dies, Satan struggles to hold the attention of the distraught Jesus and has to shout after him ("Didn't you hear me, Jesus?") as he walks away. Having persuaded Jesus to join Mary and Martha in a *ménage à trois*—a situation that undermines the idea that the "last temptation" is a conventional life with a wife and family—the never-aging Satan (whose confusing status is enhanced by bearing a close resemblance to one of Jesus's supposed daughters) then faces a fresh obstacle with the appearance of Paul. Suffering from a lack of power or friendly persuasion, she fails to prevent the encounter between Paul and Jesus, which troubles the latter's mind. Satan's weak efforts, such as referring to Jesus's bodily concerns ("Aren't you going to eat? . . . You don't have to go there"), are followed by a loss of authority when an attempt to stifle the conversation ("Quiet!") between the two men is also ignored.

Nevertheless, the dream sequence endures until the destruction of the Temple in Jerusalem in 70 CE, so that the last hallucination scene is set against a background of flames, smoke, and screams. As Jesus lies dying, Satan sits beside Jesus in a popular devilish location: "The deathbed was another site of temptation. Here Satan made a final bid to lure men and women in 'their last sickness' to damnation."[59] It is at this point that (a very much alive) Judas arrives with some of the other apostles to save the day.

There is a citation in the Gospel of Luke that records that "Satan entered into Judas" (Luke 22:3) when he decides to betray Jesus, which is reflected in *The Passion of the Christ* via the cross-cutting between the scenes in the Garden of Gethsemane and the palace of Caiaphas, in which Judas receives the thirty pieces of silver. However, in Scorsese's sympathetic approach to Judas (in which he is playing a part in God's plan rather than acting as the traditional traitor), it is the apostle who becomes Satan's antagonist, waking up Jesus in the temptation scene by pointing out the true identity of Jesus's angelic-looking companion. The young girl is transformed into a column of fire that is double framed in the printing, so it is slower and more insidious.[60] In the voice that Jesus last heard in the third temptation episode in the desert, Satan says, "There's nothing you can do. You lived this life. You accepted it. It's over now. Just finish it and die. Die like a man."

However, within the dream, Jesus fights back, crawling his way to Calvary. Robin Riley does not regard the ending of the film as a triumph over evil "because it suggests that waking up from a dream constitutes an act of free will. Common sense tells us that under such contrived conditions, Jesus is neither conscious nor capable of acting on his decision to refuse Satan."[61] Yet, the final scene is a close adaption of Kazantzakis's own ending when Jesus awakens to find himself nailed to the cross: "A wild indomitable joy took possession of him. No, no, he was not a coward, a deserter, a traitor. . . . He had stood his ground honourably to the very end; he had kept his word."[62] Jesus's last words in Scorsese's film present a triumphant—and biblical—conclusion: "It is accomplished!" When the final take of Dafoe on the cross was damaged by exposure (when "leakage spilled ribbons of color onto the final frames of the scene and the rest was consumed by edge fog"), Scorsese was not disheartened and said, "Leave it; that's the resurrection!"[63]

Conclusion

There is no doubt that Scorsese and Gibson expressed sincere motives for their individual decisions to bring a New Testament–themed narrative to the screen. "I made it as a prayer, an act of worship," insisted Scorsese,[64] whereas Gibson claimed that the "Holy Ghost was working through me on this film, and I was just directing traffic."[65] Yet, both *The Last Temptation of Christ* and *The Passion of the Christ* received condemnation by some opponents who thought that evil forces—rather than sincere intentions—were behind the production of the films.

In 1988, there were Christians (whether or not they had seen the film) who accused Scorsese of heresy: "May the weight of debt bring all who were with this act of Satan to total failure, and those who see they have wronged the Savior pray for forgiveness with earnest hearts," was one published response in the *Fort Worth Star-Telegram*;[66] and Mother Angelica, the founder of the Catholic Eternal World Television network, described the film as "the most blasphemous, the most disrespectful, the most Satanic movie ever filmed."[67] Blockbuster video refused to stock the film, a cinema in Paris was firebombed in protest, and Scorsese spent a year with body guards. Sixteen years later, there were some fundamentalist Christian critics who detected a devilish dimension in Gibson's attempt to recreate the Passion narrative using extra-biblical, overtly Catholic symbolism: "This movie was not inspired by God, but rather by Satan, as he blinds us to the truth and causes us to accept unscriptural beliefs as we head into the end times," claimed one reviewer on the Christianity Today website.[68] Both directors were greeted with vilification for their artistic efforts, although there is no doubt that Gibson's film received a much more glowing reception from Christian audiences overall with accompanying box office receipts.[69] Indeed, Middleton argues that, "the Christians who 'lost' in 1988 'won' in 2004 and vice versa."[70]

Yet, what of Satan's balance sheet? Saint Augustine "always believed in the vast power of the devil: God had shown His omnipotence most clearly in restraining this superhuman creature, whose aggressive force was so great that he would obliterate the whole Christian church if released."[71] Consequently, it is heretical to view the Son of God and Satan as equal opponents, and the *Catechism of the Catholic Church* reflects on the traditional victory of light over darkness: "The power of Satan is, nonetheless, not infinite. He is only a creature, powerful from the fact that he is pure spirit, but still a creature. He cannot prevent the building up of God's reign"[72]—a view that the narratives of *The Passion of the Christ* and *The Last Temptation of Christ* conclusively support.

Comparing the two films, Richard Alleva points out that Gibson "elected to make a ritualistic work rather than a dramatic one,"[73] and this decision is evident in the conflict between Christ and Satan. From the opening scene of *The Passion of the Christ* the victory over Satan is assured, in keeping with Jesus's comforting words to his disciples at the Last Supper in the Gospel of John that "the ruler of the world is coming. He has no power over me" (John 14:30). Discussing a potential sequel, Mel Gibson underlined this aspect when he claimed, "I think that often times, I made the ultimate superhero film in *The Passion of the Christ*."[74] The film, which presents Jesus's "superhuman" ability to withstand pain, offers a High Christology that leaves Satan screaming in impotent rage at the end.

However, while Satan has potential success in the dream sequence in *The Last Temptation of Christ*, Paul Schrader also saw the final scene of his screenplay as "a kind of superman triumph—calling yourself back to the Cross by force of will,"[75] while Scorsese regarded it as a victory for good: "At the last second, snatched from the jaws of hell."[76] Scorsese's words evoke the description of Saint Augustine, when he "wrote of Christ's passion, death and resurrection as God offering his son to the Devil as the food in the mousetrap.

Satan made a grab for Jesus but overestimated his own powers, for Christ was not only a man but God incarnate."[77] Satan may have spent his time roaming the earth in *The Last Temptation of Christ* and *The Passion of the Christ* in the hope of foiling God's plan of Salvation, but his efforts end in ignominy. Whatever the obvious differences between the two films, both Scorsese and Gibson adhere to a conviction in Satan's ultimate defeat.

Notes

1. All biblical quotations are taken from *The New American Bible*.

2. Darren Oldridge, *The Devil: A Very Short Introduction* (Oxford: Oxford University Press, 2012), 57.

3. David Hume, *Dialogues and Natural History of Religion* (Oxford: Oxford University Press, 2008), 100.

4. Peter Stanford, *The Devil: A Biography* (London: Arrow Books, 2003), 75.

5. Oldridge, *The Devil*, 36.

6. Stanford, *The Devil*, 106.

7. When Scorsese's film *Silence* premiered to an audience of Jesuits in Rome on November 29, 2016, followed by the director's meeting with Pope Francis at the Vatican on November 30, 2016, the contrast with the reception of *The Last Temptation of Christ* was examined in the press; see, for example, Christopher Hooton, "What Martin Scorsese's New Film *Silence* Premiering at the Vatican Tells Us About It," Independent, November 30, 2016, accessed November 12, 2019, http://www.independent.co.uk/arts-entertainment/films/news/martin-scorsese-new -film-silence-2016-2017-vatican-premiere-adam-driver-andrew-garfield-liam-neeson -a7447271.html.

8. Pope Paul VI, "Confronting the Devil's Power," *General Audience*, November 15, 1972, accessed September 19, 2016, www.ewtn.com/library/papaldoc/p6devil.htm.

9. Jorge Mario Bergoglio and Abraham Skorka, *On Heaven and Earth*, trans. Alejandro Bermudez and Howard Goodman (New York: Image, 2013), 8.

10. Nikos Kazantzakis, *The Last Temptation of Christ*, trans. Peter A. Bien (London: Faber and Faber, 1961), 7.

11. Vrasidas Karalis, "The Unreality of Repressed Desires in *The Last Temptation*," in *Scandalizing Jesus: Kazantzakis's The Last Temptation of Christ Fifty Years On*, ed. Darren J. N. Middleton (New York: Continuum, 2005), 77–78.

12. The DVD commentaries on the films indicate the difficulties. There is the threat of a *Cult of the Cobra* ambiance rather than a genuine sense of torment, as Scorsese points out, in *The Last Temptation of Christ* (New York: Criterion Collection, 2000). The on-screen appearance of a snake in the Gethsemane scene in *The Passion of the Christ* (Los Angeles: 20th Century Fox, 2007) also brought its own headaches: in this case, water was poured onto the ground to encourage the thirsty creature to wend its way in the right direction toward Jim Caviezel.

13. Martin Scorsese, *Scorsese on Scorsese*, ed. Ian Christie and David Thompson (London: Faber and Faber, 2003), 143.

14. Both *The Last Temptation of Christ* and *The Passion of the Christ* equate Magdalene with the "woman who had been caught in adultery" (John 8:3), although the conflation of the two biblical women is unfounded.

15. Peter T. Chattaway, "Battling the Flesh. Sexuality and Spirituality in *The Last Temptation of Christ*," in *Scandalizing Jesus*, 157.

16. Quoted in Mary Pat Kelly, *Martin Scorsese: A Journey* (New York: Thunder's Mouth Press, 1996), 227.

17. Paul Schrader, *Schrader on Schrader and Other Writings*, ed. Kevin Jackson (London: Faber and Faber, 1990), 136. Of course, Gibson himself later countered this argument with his decision to use Aramaic (along with Hebrew and Latin) in *The Passion of the Christ*.

18. Melody D. Knowles and Allison Whitney, "Teaching the *Temptation*," in *Scandalizing Jesus*, 18.

19. Nikos Kazantzakis, *The Last Temptation*, trans. Peter A. Bien (London: Faber and Faber: 1961), 265.

20. *Catechism of the Catholic Church* (West Sedona, AZ: Veritas Publications, 1994), 539. Hereafter abbreviated as *CCC*.

21. Scorsese, *Scorsese on Scorsese*, 124.

22. Schrader, *Schrader on Schrader*, 136.

23. *CCC*, 540.

24. Oldridge, *The Devil*, 28.

25. Anne Catherine Emmerich, *The Dolorous Passion of Our Lord Jesus Christ*, ed. Klemens Maria Brentano (El Sobrante, CA: North Bay Books, 2003), 55.

26. Oldridge, *The Devil*, 87.

27. Quoted in Gaye W. Ortiz, "'Passion'-ate Women': The Female Presence in *The Passion of the Christ*," in *Reviewing the Passion*, ed. S. Brent Plate (New York: Palgrave Macmillan, 2004), 116.

28. Quoted in Vernon J. Bourke, ed., *The Essential Augustine* (Indianapolis, IN: Hackett Publishing Company, 1974), 65.

29. Stanford, *The Devil*, 120.

30. Emmerich, *Dolorous Passion*, 210.

31 The views held by Gibson's father, Hutton Gibson, who rejects the Second Vatican Council, together with the director's own anti-Semitic remarks during a DUI arrest in Malibu in 2006, added fuel to the flames. See Jake Tapper, "Like Father, Like Son?" *ABC News*, July 31, 2006, accessed January 20, 2017, http://abcnews.go.com/Entertainment/story?id=2256719&page=1.

32. Oldridge, *The Devil*, 53.

33. Marvin Perry and Frederick M. Schweitzer, "The Medieval Passion Play Revisited," in *Reviewing the Passion*, 12.

34. Susan Thistlewaite, "Mel Makes a War Movie," in *Perspectives on the Passion of the Christ* (New York: Hyperion Books, 2004), 131. An original idea for the scene, which would have involved "multiple demons, whispering in the ears of the crowd during the trial" would certainly have increased the inflammatory tone. See John

Bartunek, *Inside the Passion* (Milwaukee, WI: Ascension Press, 2005), 94. This would especially be true following the extant episode in which "Jewish children [morph] into demons" to torment Judas. See Paula Fredriksen, "Gospel Truths: Hollywood, History, and Christianity," in *Perspectives on the Passion of the Christ* (New York: Hyperion Books, 2004), 32. Defending Gibson's artistic choice, John Bartunek argues that this particular special effect was "another way to manifest the film's conception of evil as something good gone horribly wrong." See Bartunek, *Inside the Passion*, 40. However, some critics pointed out that it, "knowingly or not, plays upon the age-old trope of Jews as the children of the devil." See Adele Reinhartz, *Jesus of Hollywood* (Oxford: Oxford University Press, 2007), 194. Others suggest it was "a case where poetic licence became reckless and lacking in sensitivity." See Ben Witherington, "Numbstruck: An Evangelical reflects on Mel Gibson's *Passion*," in *Perspectives on the Passion of the Christ*, 84.

35. Quoted in Monica Migliorino Miller, *The Theology of The Passion of the Christ* (New York: Alba House, 2005) xiv.

36. Quoted in Ortiz, "'Passion'-ate Women," 117.

37. Oldridge, *The Devil*, 47.

38. Oldridge, 87.

39. Miller, *Theology*, 7.

40. Catherine O'Brien, *The Celluloid Madonna* (New York: Wallflower Press, 2011), 1.

41. Quoted in Ortiz, "'Passion'-ate Women," 115.

42. Stanford, *The Devil*, 42.

43. Stanford, 43.

44. Kazantzakis, *Last Temptation*, 454.

45. Kazantzakis, 469.

46. Eftychia Papanikolaou, "Identity and Ethnicity in Peter Gabriel's Sound Track for *The Last Temptation of Christ*," in *Scandalizing Jesus*, 224.

47. Saint Augustine, *City of God*, trans. Henry Bettenson (New York: Penguin Books, 2003), 19:9.

48. Bruce Francis Babington and Peter William Evans, *Biblical Epics. Sacred Narrative in the Hollywood Cinema* (Manchester: Manchester University Press, 1993), 166.

49. Kazantzakis, *Last Temptation*, 457.

50. Oldridge, *The Devil*, 55.

51. Quoted in Kelly, *Martin Scorsese*, 235.

52. Quoted in Michael Henry Wilson, *Scorsese on Scorsese* (London: Phaidon Press, 2011), 155).

53. Steven Greydanus, "The Last Temptation of Christ: An Essay in Film Criticism and Faith," *Decent Films*, n.d., accessed September 19, 2016, www.decentfilms.com/articles/lasttemptation.

54. Saint Augustine, *Confessions*, trans. Garry Wills (New York: Penguin Books, 2002), 6.21.

55. Quoted in Stanford, *The Devil*, 142.

56. Quoted in Rhonda Burnette-Bletsch, *"The Last Temptation of Christ*: Scorsese's Jesus among Ordinary Saints," *Scorsese and Religion*, ed. Christopher B. Barnett and Clark J. Elliston (Leiden: Brill, 2019), 116.

57. Elizabeth H. Flowers and Darren J. N. Middleton, "Satan and the Curious," in *Scandalizing Jesus*, 151.

58. David Sterritt, "Images of Religion, Ritual, and the Sacred in Martin Scorsese's Cinema," *A Companion to Martin Scorsese*, ed. Aaron Baker (Hoboken, NJ: Wiley Blackwell, 2015), 95.

59. Oldridge, *The Devil*, 55.

60. According to the DVD commentary, Schrader had the idea that the angel would sprout black wings. Scorsese tried a skull figure but it looked like "Spooks on the Loose."

61. Robin Riley, *Film, Faith, and Cultural Conflict: The Case of Martin Scorsese's The Last Temptation of Christ* (Westport, CT: Prager Publishers, 2003), 52.

62. Kazantzakis, *Last Temptation*, 507.

63. Quoted in Thomas R. Lindlof, *Hollywood under Siege: Martin Scorsese, the Religious Right, and the Culture Wars* (Lexington: University Press of Kentucky, 2008), 121.

64. Quoted in Kelly, *Martin Scorsese*, 6.

65. Quoted in Thistlethwaite, "Mel Makes a War Movie," 140.

66. Quoted in Flowers and Middleton, "Satan and the Curious," 147.

67. Quoted in Kevin Lally, "Resisting *Temptation*," in *Scorsese: A Journey Through The American Psyche*, ed. Paul A. Woods (Medford, NJ: Plexus, 2005),166.

68. Quoted in Miller, *Theology*, 139.

69. See, for example, James Abbott, "Following His True Passion," *Through a Catholic Lens*, ed. Peter Malone (Lanham, MD: Rowman and Littlefield, 2007), 231. Enthusiastic Evangelicals, such as Darrell Bock, reportedly gave Gibson the benefit of the doubt with regard to the extrabiblical elements, accepting that the director had to fill in the gaps, and focusing on "the extent of Jesus' suffering and the idea that he did this 'for me.' That is what most people are connecting to when they see the film." Quoted in Deborah Caldwell, "Selling *Passion*," in *Perspectives on the Passion of the Christ* (New York: Hyperion Books, 2004), 218.

70. Darren J. N. Middleton, "Celluloid Synoptics: Viewing the Gospels of Marty and Mel Together," *Reviewing the Passion*, ed. S. Brent Plate (London: Palgrave Macmillan, 2004), 76.

71. Peter Brown, *Augustine of Hippo: A Biography* (Berkley: University of California Press, 2000), 398.

72. *CCC*, Article 395.

73. Quoted in Miller, *Theology*, xxvi.

74. Quoted in Samuel Smith, "Mel Gibson Tells Greg Laurie 'Passion of the Christ' Sequel 'The Resurrection' May Be His Next Project," CP Entertainment,

August 29, 2016, accessed September 19, 2016, www.christianpost.com/news/mel
-gibson-tells-greg-laurie-passion-of-the-christ-sequel-the-resurrection-may-be-next
-movie-168722/.

75. Schrader, *Schrader on Schrader*, 137.

76. Director's commentary, *Last Temptation of Christ*, DVD.

77. Stanford, *The Devil*, 88.

Lucifer, Gabriel, and the Angelic Will in *The Prophecy* and *Constantine*

Regina M. Hansen

The *Prophecy* (1995) and *Constantine* (2005) posit a narrow distinction between the angelic and the demonic, giving us not just expressly evil "fallen" angels but also supposedly "good" angels who do evil deeds even while seeing themselves as performing God's will. This depiction reflects Christian—and often specifically Roman Catholic—scriptural and theological texts in which angels are seen as beings of pure spirit meant to carry out God's will, even when it leads to destruction. In these films, good angels behave monstrously despite and indeed because of their professed love for God—as well as their entrenched belief in their own unalterable goodness. By contrast, the fallen angel Lucifer, or Satan,[1] is portrayed as the more honest and rational of the angels, as a sometime ally of humans, and as the character most likely to follow God's rules. This filmic Satan's power is still limited in that it always depends on the consent of human beings, again reflecting theological concerns surrounding free will and conscience. In *Constantine* and *The Prophecy*, we see the progenitors of the "Satan as ally" trope now familiar from television shows such as *Lucifer*. These portrayals both reflect and critique Christian—and particularly Catholic—theology regarding both the will and moral culpability of angels. While these theological issues may not have been familiar to all audiences in the 1990s and 2000s, their inclusion in the films to be discussed reflect cultural attitudes that reject blind adherence to religious orthodoxy in favor of human intellect and conscience.

The idea of Satan as a fallen angel remains part of Christian, and especially Roman Catholic, theology.[2] In fact, the notion's importance in Catholic teaching is particularly relevant in *The Prophecy* and *Constantine* since, as Jeffrey M. Tripp notes, both films take place in "a notably Roman Catholic world."[3] Regarding Satan/Lucifer as an angel, the Gospel of Luke describes Satan as falling "like lightning from the sky" (Luke 10:18 NAB),[4] while the Book of Revelation depicts a "war in Heaven" (12:7 KJV/NAB) in which the good angels defeat Satan and his followers, casting them to Earth. The use of the name "Lucifer" to denote Satan or the devil was inspired by a passage in the King James translation of Isaiah 14:12 ("How art thou fallen from heaven, O Lucifer, son of the morning!") and popularized in Milton's *Paradise Lost*. Writing in a discipline called angelology, early Christian and Medieval theologians teach that, after the fall from Heaven, the disobedient angels became what we now know as demons, with Satan as their leader. In his *Summa Theologica*, Thomas asserts, "The fallen angels that beset man on earth carry with them their own dark and punishing atmosphere, and wherever they are, they endure the pains of hell."[5] *The Catechism of the Catholic Church* describes Satan as "a seductive voice, opposed to God." The text continues, "Scripture and the Church's Tradition see in this being a fallen angel, called 'Satan' or the 'devil.' The Church teaches that Satan was at first a good angel, made by God: 'The devil and the other demons were indeed created naturally good by God, but they became evil by their own doing.'"[6] This last phrase "by their own doing" suggests an understanding of the angelic will—and a critique of that understanding—that is at the core of both films to be discussed here.

Thomas Aquinas and others assert that angels have free will, but that their intellect is superior to that of humans.[7] Because of this intellectual superiority, the proper choice for angels is clear—to align themselves with the will of God. The connection between intellect and free will, for better or worse, is why some angels come to be fallen while others remain forever obedient servants of God. In the third century CE, Augustine of Hippo wrote about the angelic intellect in *City of God*: "He created nothing better than those spirits to whom He endowed with intelligence, and made capable of contemplating and enjoying Him, . . . and in which the material of their sustenance and blessedness is God Himself."[8] In his *Summa Theologica*, Thomas Aquinas further explains, "wherever there is intellect, there is free-will. It is therefore manifest that just as there is intellect, so is there free-will in the angels, and in a higher degree of perfection than in man."[9] In other words, as noted by twentieth-century commentator John A. Hardon, SJ, the good angels do God's will "because they want to."[10] With their superior intellects, angels are viewed as more fully aware of the consequences of the choice to remain in Heaven or to rebel, unlike human beings whose understanding is limited.

Because angels are believed to "know better," the choice to rebel becomes for them a deliberate and conscious decision not just to *do* evil but to *be* evil forever after. At the moment of rebellion—as depicted in the Book of

Revelation—if angels chose good, their free will became forever aligned with God's. The same was true if they chose to rebel. This latter situation is summed up, again, in the *Catechism*: "This 'fall' consists in the free choice of these created spirits, who radically and irrevocably *rejected* God and his reign. We find a reflection of that rebellion in the tempter's words to our first parents: 'You will be like God.' The devil 'has sinned from the beginning'; he is 'a liar and the father of lies.'"[11] So, according to Catholic theology at least, because Satan and his angels knowingly chose evil that one time, they can never repent. The *Catechism* continues: "It is the *irrevocable* character of their choice, and not a defect in the infinite divine mercy, that makes the angels' sin unforgivable."[12] Once an angel chooses good, they are good forever; if an angel chooses to rebel, they become forever fallen.[13]

Whether on purpose or merely as an echo of cultural tradition, the films we are looking at engage with issues of the angelic will—and the irrevocable nature of both the fallen and unfallen state—giving us angelic characters, specifically Lucifer and the angel Gabriel, who react in divergent fashion to what they believe to be their unchangeable status as good or evil. The character of Lucifer, while still portrayed as evil, also seems to understand themself more fully as fallen, and to accept their place in Creation. In a limited way, this self-understanding amounts to a somewhat—though not entirely—more sympathetic portrayal of Lucifer, favorably contrasting the fallen angel to Gabriel, who is portrayed as mad with the belief in their own irrevocable goodness. Gabriel's sense of unalterable goodness also recalls the moral self-assurance and hypocrisy of many leaders of the United States Religious Right movement, as well as the extreme conservatism of traditionalist Catholicism, which arose in response to the reforms of the Second Vatican Council. According to journalist Tom Roberts, extreme right-wing Catholicism began "out of 1980s evangelicalism" and its suspicion of secular liberalism; at the same time, "the 35-year traditionalist reign of popes John Paul II and Benedict XVI allowed the [Catholic] Far Right to flourish."[14] Though not all encompassing, this rightward swing within Christian religious practice and representation—coupled with the tragic and ongoing revelations of child sexual abuse in the Catholic Church—invited critiques of Christian religious orthodoxy both in politics and popular culture.[15] The representations of Gabriel and Satan in *The Prophecy* and *Constantine* reflect these critiques.

Jeffrey Tripp writes that "the foundational image of Gabriel in the Western, Christian imagination" is historically "an image that has not been tarnished by extra-biblical expansions."[16] A hero of Christian myth, Gabriel is the compassionate angel of the Annunciation, who in Luke 1:26–38 proclaims to Mary that she will be the mother of God and who "comforts Daniel in exile."[17] In popular post-Biblical tradition, though never mentioned in this role in the Bible, Gabriel is also known as the angel who blows the trumpet to start the Apocalypse.[18] *The Prophecy* subverts that traditionally positive view of Gabriel, instead giving the viewer a character who is leading a second war in Heaven. The origins of this war are detailed in a fictional extra chapter of the Book of Revelation, with details later filled in by Lucifer. We learn that no human souls have entered Heaven since the Fall, because Gabriel and some other "good" unfallen angels are now battling to keep humans out of Heaven and to retain the angels' superior position in God's grace. To break what Lucifer calls "the stalemate" in the war, Christopher Walken's Gabriel needs to find the world's most evil soul, which another "good" angel, Simon (a *good* good angel as opposed to a *bad* good angel like Gabriel), has hidden in the body of a little girl. Tripp notes that the girl's name, Mary, is one of the film's many twists on Gabriel's role in the Annunciation.[19] Out to stop Gabriel is Thomas Dagget, a policeman and smoker who dropped out of Catholic seminary after seeing visions of angelic war during his Mass of Ordination. The film follows Dagget and schoolteacher Katherine, as they attempt to save Mary and ultimately to open Heaven for humanity.

Although they are essentially rebelling against God, just as Lucifer did, Gabriel clings to the notion of their own goodness, which reflects the theology regarding the angels' one-time irrevocable choice for good or evil. Throughout the narrative, Gabriel behaves cruelly while constantly asserting their "goodness"; and the filmmakers imply that this cruelty results not from Gabriel's jealousy of humans but from the destructive acts God has required angels to perform. The film overtly critiques biblical representations of unfallen angels performing God's will in violent ways.[20] In the film, Dagget—who once wrote a thesis on angels—articulates this paradox: "Did you ever notice in the Bible, how whenever God needed to punish someone or make an example or whenever God needed a killing, he sent an angel. Did you ever wonder what a creature like that must be like? A whole existence spent praising God, but always with one wing dipped in blood? Would you ever really want to see an angel?" Gabriel's own words suggest how this state of being might twist the angelic psyche, reminding us of the violence of the angels in the Bible: "I kill firstborns while their mothers watch. I turn cities into salt. I even, when I feel like it, rip the souls from little girls, and from now to kingdom come the only thing you can count on, in your existence, is never understanding why." The speech is both proud and tortured, and it seems possible that Gabriel also does not understand.

Note, however, Gabriel's use of the phrase "when I feel like it," an assertion of free will, which leads us to the film's critique of Christian/Catholic theology regarding good and bad angels. In a warped reflection of the theology, Gabriel believes that their choice to remain obedient during the first war in Heaven makes them irrevocably good, even though in ripping away Mary's soul for their own purposes (because they "feel like it"), not to mention waging this second war, they are clearly no longer following God's will. Gabriel consistently self-represents as a "good" angel, even to the point of admonishing people not to use "profanity."[21] When Katherine shoots Gabriel, telling them to "Go to Hell," Gabriel insists that Heaven is the proper "zip code." Jeffrey Tripp compares this self-delusion to that of a human "religious zealot" who insists on religious and moral "purity."[22] And, in fact, the film expertly portrays fanatical and uncompromising interpretations of Catholic doctrine—specifically of the idea that good angels are always good—as indistinguishable from madness. The insanity inherent in Gabriel's continued assertion of unalterable personal morality is crystalized for the viewer when Katherine suggests that Heaven and Hell are "all the same" to the angel. "No," Gabriel asserts. "In Heaven we believe in love," but he also adds that they love "cracking your skull." This violent adherence to religious orthodoxy would have resonated with mid-nineties' audiences, who would have followed news stories of violence provoked by extreme interpretations of Christian dogma, particularly with regard to abortion, notably the 1994 murders of Shannon Lowney and Leanne Nichols at women's health clinics in Brookline, Massachusetts.[23]

While Gabriel is torn (tortured) by love for God and a deluded belief in their moral superiority in their "unfallen" state, the fallen angel Lucifer is characterized by self-knowledge. This difference is evident in Gabriel's interactions with Lucifer. Gabriel clearly sets themself apart from Lucifer, describing the fallen angel as "sitting in [their] basement, sulking over [their] break-up with the boss." Early in the narrative, Gabriel attempts to get the loyal angel Simon to join the second angelic rebellion, relishing past victories: "We cast out Lucifer's army. You and I. We threw their rebel thrones from the wall." Even as Gabriel implicitly draws a distinction between the "rebel" Lucifer and the current war, Gabriel makes clear that they are no more willing to take second place to humans than Lucifer is said to have been in Christian tradition and scripture. Gabriel tells Simon, "I bow to no human in Heaven," nor will Gabriel cede their perceived rightful place to those they think of as "talking monkeys." Lucifer recognizes Gabriel's pride, and that jealousy of human beings, as exactly comparable to Lucifer's own, and fully intuits the reasons for the second war in Heaven. Lucifer tells Katherine, "Other angels have made it this way, because they hate you. You and all humans. God has put you in His grace and pushed them aside." While Gabriel wants to have their own way, not God's, and still be seen as a good angel—and thus different from and superior to Lucifer—Lucifer is played by Viggo Mortensen as both unrepentantly evil (as we would expect, reflecting the theology) and fully accepting of their fallen state.

In *The Prophecy*, Lucifer displays many of the specific qualities attributed to Satan in the Bible and Christian theology. Lucifer growls and roars like a lion, like the devil depicted in the Gospel of Peter (5:8);[24] speaks in a kind of infernal dialect; and even has a little demonic minion. Moreover, other characters smell sulfur in Lucifer's presence, an allusion to the "infernal atmosphere" that Thomas Aquinas describes as surrounding fallen angels. At the same time, though fallen, Lucifer very much self-describes and is addressed by others as an angel. Lucifer still has the birdlike mannerisms established for the angelic characters in the film—perching on things, sniffing the air, moving their head in a kind of jerking motion. Lucifer also remembers the special place they held in Heaven before the Fall: "I am the first angel, loved once above all others. A perfect love." The allusion to the Gospel's affirmation that "perfect love casteth out fear" (1 John 4:18 KJV) also suggests that Lucifer knows the Bible, however mockingly spoken.

By maintaining that Lucifer remains an angel, the film further obscures the moral distinction Gabriel has drawn between themself and Lucifer; and both angels view themselves as superior to the aforementioned "talking monkeys." At the same time, Lucifer does not try to justify or deny their hatred or evil, as Gabriel does. Instead, Lucifer revels in being the *Catechism's* "seductive voice opposed to God," telling Katherine, "God is love. I don't love you." Lucifer glories in cruelty and loves to make people afraid, giggling while addressing Dagget: "How I loved listening to your sweet prayers every night. And then you'd jump in your bed, so afraid I was under there. And I was." Lucifer also is upfront about the desire to corrupt as many souls as possible: "I am always open, even on Christmas." Still, within the moral universe of the film, Lucifer's self-knowledge and complete unrepentance makes them less monstrous than a character as delusional as Gabriel.

Lucifer becomes allied to the humans not "because I love you or because I care for you but because two Hells is one too many, and I can't have that." While this assertion makes clear their selfish motives in keeping with the fallen state, it also suggests Lucifer's belief that there is a natural order to Heaven, Earth, and Hell; and that Lucifer expects that order to be maintained. In the end, the fallen angel's temporary allegiance with Dagget and Katherine makes it possible for them to save Mary. Lucifer comes to claim Gabriel for Hell, proclaiming moral rules that supersede Gabriel's supposedly irrevocable grace: "Your war is arrogance. That makes it evil. That's mine." Knowing themself to be evil, Lucifer can recognize evil in Gabriel; in claiming Gabriel for Hell, Lucifer helps to open Heaven. When a shaft of light parts the clouds as in a Thomas Cole painting, Lucifer's demonic sidekick drags Gabriel away. The viewer is left with the suggestion that Lucifer has been aligned not only with Dagget and Katherine but with God, more like the Adversary of early Hebrew scripture, than the fallen angel of Christian belief.[25] At any rate, Lucifer as a character has come to appreciate the moral rules of the universe and expects others to follow them, too.

Despite their fallen state, Lucifer benefits from rules and a hierarchy in which they play a specific and definable role. At the same time, while Lucifer expects Gabriel to follow the rules, the fallen angel also remains bound by them, an idea explored in the final interaction between Lucifer and Dagget.[26] Only after the delusional Gabriel is dragged to Hell does the film reveal the weakness of Lucifer's character in relation to humans. A bloody-faced Lucifer begs and coaxes Thomas and Katherine to come with them to Hell, claiming—in an alternately cajoling and hysterical voice—to love these humans "more than Jesus." The fact that both Thomas and Katherine are able to reject Lucifer's advances once again reflects the *Catechism of the Catholic Church*: "The power of Satan is, nonetheless, not infinite. He is only a creature, powerful from the fact that he is pure spirit, but still a creature."[27] While Lucifer can claim Gabriel because of that angel's sin, the fallen angel is unable to claim Thomas or Katherine without their consent. At the same time, Thomas's response to Lucifer's "seductive voice," further undermines the idea that angels have any special moral standing: "I have my soul. And I have my faith. What do you have . . . angel?" In disparaging Lucifer as "angel," Thomas draws no distinction between Lucifer and the so called "good" angels, all of whom—with the possible exception of Simon—are portrayed as inferior to humans. Daggett also asserts the impotence of Lucifer and other angels in the face of human will, which—unlike that of the supposedly irrevocably "good" angels—remains entirely free regardless of past decisions. Of course, Lucifer does not leave fully defeated: The triumph of good is left in doubt at the end of the film, with Lucifer growling at Thomas to "Leave the light on" before disappearing in a flock of crows. The narrative suggests that while Lucifer's self-knowledge allows the fallen angel to get the better of the delusional Gabriel, human beings are in charge of our own destiny.

The 2005 film *Constantine* also depicts a fanatical Gabriel, who insists on their own unchangeable goodness, and explores the angelic obsession with rules and rule-breaking. The film is based loosely on Garth Ennis's "Dangerous Habits" arc of the comic book series "Hellblazer," but is so different that it is necessary to take the movie on its own terms. The hero is John Constantine, another dark-haired smoker whose faith has been tested by visions of what he calls the "world behind the world" in which angelic and demonic beings (called half-breeds) work through others to influence human souls for good or evil, because angels and demons are supposedly not allowed to fully break through to our world. Constantine must stop a new war in Heaven and avert the Apocalypse. The "great détente of the original superpowers"—God and Satan/Lucifer—will be broken if the devil's son Mammon enters our world through the vessel of another possessed female, the detective Angela. All this has been predicted in yet another extra chapter of the Bible, the fictional 17 Corinthians, from the version of the Bible only read in Hell. As in *The Prophecy*, the antagonist orchestrating this Apocalyptic scenario is named Gabriel, who plans to free Mammon using the "spear of destiny," the weapon that pierced the side of the crucified Christ. Although the narrative rules of the film make it clear that Gabriel is a half-breed, not a full angel, the choice of name and the character's self-imposed role as judge of human behavior allows the viewer to understand the character as a version of the biblical Gabriel.

While *The Prophecy* takes place among Catholics and has a protagonist who has lapsed from the faith, *Constantine*'s characterization of Gabriel—and in fact the whole narrative of the film—turn very particularly on the rules of Roman Catholicism, at least as the filmmaker chooses to understand them. Not only are the Catholics in the film subject to the rules of the Church as (mis)represented[28]—so that the Bishop refuses a Catholic funeral to Angela's sister Isabel, who has committed suicide—but the supernatural rules of the film supposedly reflect Catholicism as well, as when Constantine also finds Isabel, the suicide, in Hell. While Angela complains to the Roman Catholic Bishop about the rules of the Catholic Church, in a parallel conversation with Gabriel, Constantine is complaining about those same rules. Only he is referring to the actual rules that were apparently made up in actual Heaven but happen to be the same as the rules of the Church as represented: "Impossible Rules, endless regulations. Who goes up, who goes down. Why?" So, Christianity—and particularly Catholicism—is portrayed to be the religion of Heaven and Hell. Holy water and Latin even have magical properties to fight demons.

More importantly for the purposes of this essay, we find in the film's depiction of demon half-breeds, called "the fallen," an echo of Thomas Aquinas and the other Christian angelologists, especially in the depiction of Gabriel, played by Tilda Swinton as a self-righteous bureaucrat. Like Walken's Gabriel, Swinton's Gabriel does evil while also criticizing the behavior of humans. Gabriel reprimands Constantine for "squandering" his gift of prophecy on "several occasions" and for trying to "buy his way into Heaven," despite his suicide attempt. In direct contradiction of the rules of (Catholic) Heaven, as represented in the film, Gabriel rejects and resents the concept of repentance and absolution, core elements of the Christian worldview: "You just have to repent, and God takes you into his bosom. In all the worlds, in all the universe, no other creature can make such a boast, save Man. It's not fair." In that rejection of the concept of forgiveness, Gabriel rejects God's will and shows jealousy of humans. *Constantine*'s Gabriel also believes in their own irrevocable goodness and characterizes themself as doing God's work. Gabriel tells Constantine that releasing the son of the devil is a way to "inspire mankind" to greatness, another way of just being a good angel: "I'll bring you horror so that you may rise above it, so that those of you who survive this reign of Hell on Earth will be worthy of God's love." As in *The Prophecy*, this insistence is portrayed as a sort of mental illness. In fact, Constantine calls Gabriel "insane." Gabriel's behavior recalls the Christian-centered violence and insanity mentioned in relation to *The Prophecy*. Moreover, it may again reflect the filmmakers' understanding of the dangers of religious orthodoxy, especially since the film was released only a few years after the Boston *Globe* Spotlight Team's 2002 reporting on the cover-up of child sex abuse by priests in the Archdiocese of Boston, revelations that led many to question the Catholic hierarchy and its dogma surrounding celibacy, the role of women, and even the sanctity of confession.

Again, as in *The Prophecy*, Gabriel asserts their moral goodness as a contrast to the fallen angel Satan, whom Constantine addresses as "Lu." Satan's comfortable insanity and evil are brought to life by Peter Stormare in a white suit out of *Saturday Night Fever* and bare feet covered in burning tar, another echo of the "infernal atmosphere" Thomas Aquinas describes.[29] *Constantine*'s Lucifer also growls like the lion in Peter 5:8. As in *The Prophecy*, this Lucifer behaves erratically while evincing a full knowledge and acceptance—even enjoyment—of their fallen state. Like Mortensen's character, Stormare's Satan also understands and mocks Gabriel's self-delusion. In an attempt to distinguish themself from Satan and retain their place as a warrior of God, Gabriel hurls Biblical insults at the fallen angel: "'Son of perdition' (John 17:12 KJV). 'Little horn' (Daniel 7:8 KJV/NAB). Most unclean." Satan responds with humor, as someone who is happy in their position and thus untouchable: "I do miss the old names." As in *The Prophecy*, Satan allies with Constantine to foil Gabriel's plan, though always for avowedly selfish reasons: "You're the one soul I would come up here to collect myself." Satan is a tempter even to the point of helping Constantine to a cigarette. At the same time, Gabriel's self-righteous belief in their own goodness, and the destruction that delusion threatens, also temporarily put Satan and God on the same side (again as in *The Prophecy*). When Gabriel vows to smite Satan "in His honor," God stays

Gabriel's hand. Lu remarks, "Looks like somebody doesn't have your back anymore." God punishes Gabriel by turning them human, and Gabriel ends the film as a ridiculous figure.

At the same time, like Mortensen's Lucifer, Stormare's Satan is portrayed as impotent in the face of human will. As in the *Catechism*, this Satan's power is not infinite. "Lu" is not all knowing; Constantine has to explain the spear of destiny to them, as well as other elements of Gabriel's plan. Satan's limited understanding also does not allow them to recognize Constantine's sacrifice of his own soul to save Angela, landing him on the straight road to Heaven and out of Satan's grasp. As in *The Prophecy*, what undoes Lucifer, at least temporarily, is a human being's refusal to give in to temptation. At the same time, like Mortensen's Lucifer, Lu understands the rules of this religious universe and recognizes themself as bound by them, unlike Gabriel who attempts and fails to transcend the rules. Like Mortensen's character, Lu is also content to bide their time. The fallen angel takes away Constantine's cancer, so he won't die yet and go to Heaven, thus giving him a "chance to prove that [his] soul truly belongs in Hell." Like the Lucifer in *The Prophecy*, Satan/Lu still has a sense that they will eventually win, telling Gabriel: "This world is mine, in time." Yet, while both films leave the fate of the world in doubt, with Satan/Lucifer still very much a threat, both films adhere to the idea that Lucifer's ultimate victory or defeat will depend on the consent and free will of human beings. In so doing, both films elevate human free will over the supposedly superior intellect and inherent goodness of angels.

In both *The Prophecy* and *Constantine*, Gabriel and Satan appear trapped within their choices and the rules that govern them. If, as Thomas Aquinas says above, "where there is intellect, there is free will," the human characters seem to make better use of their free will, perhaps because their supposedly imperfect intellects allow them to acknowledge and regret bad choices. In both films, Gabriel clings to the belief in their own unalterable goodness, becoming shackled to religious orthodoxy and rule-following for its own sake, while Satan insists on strict interpretation of the rules of Heaven in order to maintain their role as ruler of Hell. On the other hand, the human protagonists in these films question both their decisions and their own faith, and this questioning is what ultimately helps them to defeat both Gabriel and Satan.

While able to defeat the deluded "good" angels, through self-knowledge and rationality, both Satan characters also fail in their attempts to enslave the films' human protagonists. This fact leaves the viewer to wonder if Satan/Lucifer's assurance that evil will win in the end is its own form of self-delusion, akin to Gabriel's but masquerading as self-knowledge. While these two films do have more sympathy for the devil, portraying them as more self-aware and rational, in the end, the filmmakers place human beings at the moral heart of both narratives. In *The Prophecy*'s closing narration, Thomas Dagget reflects on the human understanding of our own imperfections and the conscience that informs our free will: "If faith is a choice, then it can be lost for a man, an angel, or the devil himself. And if faith means never completely understanding God's plan, then maybe understanding just a part of it, our part, is what it is to have a soul." Within the moral universe of *The Prophecy* and *Constantine*, while the choice to do evil is clear-eyed and irreversible, the choice to do good—the state of goodness—is constantly under threat. Each film's representation of the fragility of moral goodness directly reflects the historical period in which they were released, when the supposedly unalterable "goodness" of religious doctrine was undermined by religiously motivated violence and tragic scandal. Finally, both narratives suggest that if moral goodness is to be preserved, it will not be because of religious orthodoxy or supernatural intervention, but because of human will and conscience.

Notes

1. In *The Prophecy*, the character is credited as "Lucifer," in *Constantine* as "Satan," although in the latter they are addressed by the main character as "Lu." When discussing specific films, the character will be referred to as credited. In other contexts, the term "Satan" will be used.

2. Scholars of both theology and media remind us that this understanding was also part of late or post-Biblical Jewish tradition, as the figure of Satan moved from being merely an adversarial—but not fully evil—figure to the personage we know from Christianity. See Christopher H. Partirdge and Eric S. Christianson, *The Lure of the Dark Side: Satan and Western Demonology in Popular Culture* (London: Routledge, 2014), 2. See also Jutta Wimmler and Kienzle, Lisa, "I am an angel of the Lord: An Inquiry into the Christian Nature of Supernatural's Heaven Delegates," in *TV Goes to Hell: An Unofficial Road Map of Supernatural*, ed. Stacey Abbott and David Lavery (Toronto: ECW Press, 2011), 180, cited in Erika Engstrom and Joseph M Valenzano III, *Television, Religion, and Supernatural: Hunting Monsters, Finding God* (Lanham, UK: Lexington Books, 2014), 30. The apocryphal text The Life of Adam and Eve portrays a Satan who refuses to bow before humans. See *Vita Adae et Evae*, 14:3, cited in Elaine Pagels, *The Origin of Satan* (New York: Random House, 1995), 49. The concept of fallen angels as corrupters of humankind, is also found in a pseudepigraphical text, *The Book of Enoch* (91, 109, 223).

3. Jeffrey M. Tripp, "Gabriel, Abortion, and Anti-Annunciation in *The Prophecy, Constantine*, and *Legion*," *Journal of Religion and Popular Culture* 27, no. 1 (2015): 62. While writings on angelic theology or angelology predate the start of the Protestant Reformation (1517) and thus may be referred to as generally Christian, the Catholic Church is more likely to take the niceties of angelic theology as matters of faith, and

to maintain angelology as a systematic theological discipline. Moreover, the Christianity portrayed in these films bears all the contextual elements of Roman Catholicism, including Catholic schools and churches and the portrayal of priests and bishops.

4. The quote is taken from the New American Revised Edition (NAB), a Roman Catholic translation of the Bible. In this essay, I will use both the King James (KJV) translation of the Bible, used by many Protestant denominations, and the New American (Catholic) version. When translations differ markedly, they will be noted in the text.

5. Thomas Aquinas, *Summa Theologica*, trans. Fathers of the English Dominican Province, 2nd rev. ed. (1920 [ca. 1265–1273]), I.64:4.

6. *Catechism of the Catholic Church, Revised in Accordance with the Official Latin Text Promulgated by Pope John Paul II*, 2nd ed. (New York: Image Books, 1995), 391. Hereafter abbreviated as CCC. Here the *Catechism* cites John 8:44; Revelation 12:9; and then Lateran Council IV (1215): DS 800.

7. See Bernard of Clairvaux, *The Treatise of St. Bernard, Abbot of Clairvaux, Concerning Grace and Free Will*, trans. Watkin A. Williams (New York: MacMillan, 1920), 55–57; Thomas Gallus, "Prologue to the First Commentary on the Song of Songs," in *Angelic Spirituality: Medieval Perspectives on the Ways of Angels*, trans. Steven Chase (New York: Paulist Press, 2002), 244–245; and Anselm of Canterbury, "On the Fall of the Devil," in *Three Philosophical Dialogues*, trans. Thomas Williams (Indianapolis: Hackett , 2002), 52–100.

8. Augustine of Hippo, *City of God*, trans. Marcus Dods (Peabody, MA: Hendrickson Publishers, 2009), XXXII:1.

9. Thomas Aquinas, I.59:3.

10. Fr. John A. Hardon (SJ), "At the Beginning of Time, God Created the Angels as Individual, Immortal Spirits with Intelligence and Free Will," teleconference transcript, Father John A. Hardon, SJ Archives, The Real Presence Association, Therealpresence.org.

11. CCC, 392. Here the *Catechism* cites Genesis 3:5, and then 1 John 3:8; John 8:44.

12. CCC, 393.

13. Although angels are most often represented in art as male and carry male names, in Catholic/Christian theology, angels are beings of pure spirit, without bodies and without gender (see Aquinas, *Summa* I, 51:1). Moreover, in the films discussed here, while the angelic characters are portrayed with physicality—with bodies to which physical harm can be done—they are also portrayed as either physically genderless (the angels in *The Prophecy*) or androgynous (Gabriel in *Constantine*). So, although they are played respectively by Christopher Walken and Tilda Swinton, in this essay, angels will be referred to by the gender neutral *they*.

14. Thomas Roberts, "The Rise of the Catholic Right," *Sojourners*, March 2019, accessed June 10, 2020, https://sojo.net/magazine/march-2019/rise-catholic-right.

15. A competing strain in Catholicism centers on what may be considered a more left-leaning perspective as part of its teachings on social justice. See articles

collected under "Catholic Social Justice" on *Commonweal*, October 27, 2017), accessed June 10, 2020, https://www.commonwealmagazine.org/catholic-social -justice.

16. Tripp, "Gabriel, Abortion, and Anti-Annunciation," 58.

17. Tripp, 58. See also Daniel 9:12.

18. See Vernon McAsland, "Gabriel's Trumpet," *Journal of Bible and Religion* 9, no. 3 (August 1941): 159.

19. Tripp, "Gabriel, Abortion, and Anti-Annunciation," 57.

20. For instance, 2 Kings depicts the "angel of the Lord" (19:35; NAB) that slays 185,000 Assyrians, while in 1 Corinthians 10:10 (NAB), God's angel is called the "destroyer." See also the entry "Angel," in *The Ashgate Encyclopedia of Literary and Filmic Monsters*, ed. Jeffrey Andrew Weinstock (Surrey, UK: Ashgate Publishing, 2014).

21. See also Tripp, "Gabriel, Abortion, and Anti-Annunciation," 60.

22. Tripp, 60.

23. Throughout the nineties, there were other killings, including that of Dr. David Gunn of Pensacola, Florida; Dr. Bayard Britton; and clinic volunteer James Barrett, all in 1994; and Dr. Barnett Slepian in 1998. See Liam Stack, "A Brief History of Deadly Attacks on Abortion Providers," *New York Times*, November 29, 2015, accessed June 10, 2020, https://www.nytimes.com/interactive/2015/11/29/us/30abortion-clinic -violence.html.

24. See the verse as translated in NAB: "Your opponent the devil is prowling around like a roaring lion looking for [someone] to devour." See also KJV, "your adversary the devil, as a roaring lion, walketh about, seeking whom he may devour."

25. For an explanation of Satan as "Adversary," see Pagels, *Origin of Satan*, 39.

26. Interestingly, while the film's narrative makes clear that Gabriel is not "irrevocably" good, the character of Lucifer remains as irrevocably fallen as portrayed in the *Catechism*.

27. CCC, 395.

28. The film misinterprets current Catholic theology and practice regarding suicide. According to the *Catechism*: "We should not despair of the eternal salvation of persons who have taken their own lives. By ways known to him alone, God can provide the opportunity for salutary repentance. The Church prays for persons who have taken their own lives" (2283).

29. Mary Ann Beavis has suggested that this is not the first time Stormare has played Satan. Referring to his character in the movie *Fargo*, she writes, "Gaear Grimsrud [Peter Stormare], the sociopathic serial killer, is the most obvious personification of pure evil—a Satan figure. He has virtually no personality; he is voraciously hungry, like 'the devil' who 'prowls around like a roaring lion, seeking someone to devour' (1 Pet. 5–8)." See Beavis, "*Fargo*: A Biblical Morality Play," *Journal of Religion and Film* 4, no. 4 (2016): 11–12.

Advocating for Satan

The Parousia-Inspired Horror Genre

David Hauka

In America, Satan abides. From the Puritan colonies of the seventeenth century to the biblically illiterate America of the twenty-first, Satan is fused into the historical foundations of the nation. Indeed, Satan is part of America's DNA. Satan is sometimes regressive, difficult to see, and easy to deny. But Satan is such a powerful force in American history, culture, and myth, it finds ways of expressing itself, especially in American movies.

Focusing on two films, Taylor Hackford's *The Devil's Advocate* (1997) and Francis Lawrence's *Constantine* (2005), I examine what is perhaps the most potent representation of an American cinematic Satan—that which is inspired by the Christian Parousia and, in so doing, describe the narrative formula specific to American films of the Parousia-inspired horror genre. While each film represents different versions of Satan, they originate from the same source—they are America's Satan. What also unites the two films most directly, as I will address toward the end of this essay, is their shared emphasis on control over women's bodies and reproductive systems as Satan's objective.

Unlike most biblical narratives adapted for American cinema, the Parousia is largely confined to the genre of supernatural horror, and for good reason: It is the story of the Second Coming of Christ and the End of Days as described in the Bible's Book of Revelation, a book that is as deeply embedded in American history and culture as Satan is. The Book of Revelation lays out a specific cause-and-effect narrative formula that must unfold precisely for Jesus to return and, with Him, the reward of eternal life for the faithful and eternal damnation for unbelievers. Satan is a critical element of that cause-and-effect narrative, along with a figure that has frequently been referred to as his son,

the Antichrist. In Parousia-inspired horror, the birth of the Antichrist is frequently the main subject.

   Constantine and *The Devil's Advocate* have much in common; both films
are closely aligned with the beliefs of American Christian fundamentalists
and End Time fundamentalists, the most important of which are the iner-
rancy, frequently meaning a literal reading, of the Bible; the return of Jesus
heralding the End of the World; and a suspicion and misunderstanding of
Roman Catholicism. Both films use of the most prevalent narrative formula
found in Parousia-inspired horror: the impending birth of a child of Satan (a
"naziresis" of evil according to Cowan[1]) or of a holy child who may be Jesus.
The narrative usually centers on a rational nonbeliever who discovers and
must act to prevent the birth of the naziresis or protect and facilitate the birth
of the holy child. Various forces—both natural and supernatural—are deployed
against the hero, but he will only triumph once he rejects rationality in favor
of belief.

Constantine

Angela Dodson (Rachel Weisz) has been transformed: Formerly a beautiful
young woman and gifted police detective, she writhes in agony on the floor,
belly swollen in a grotesque parody of pregnancy. Angela is being assaulted
from within; Mammon, Son of Lucifer, is seen screaming in frustration as he
attempts to chew his way out. He extends his clawed hands and tries to rip
open her already too-taut flesh, but to no avail.

   Standing astride Angela is Archangel Gabriel (Tilda Swinton), who, seeing
Mammon's face distorting the woman's belly, smiles and raises his right arm.
Gabriel holds the one ancient relic that can cut open the flesh that holds back
Lucifer's son: The Spear of Destiny—the blade that pierced the body of God's
son Jesus, ending his suffering on the cross. Gabriel's smile widens and he
plunges the spear toward the woman's belly. Time stops: The Spear of Destiny's plunge is arrested centimeters from its target.

   In the next room, Lucifer (Peter Stormare) has arrived, and he's in a good
mood. Unaware of Gabriel's ritual, Lucifer, using his supernatural powers to
suspend time, has inadvertently prevented the crossing of one threshold to be
present for another: John Constantine (Keanu Reeves) has died, and as promised, Lucifer has come to personally collect his soul.

   This violent scene illustrates multiple narrative elements typical of
Parousia-inspired horror. Among them are cause and effect, the interruption
of a "religious" ritual meant to bring about the Apocalypse, woman as vessel
for Cowan's "unseen order" and the monstrous transformation of her body, and

Peter Stormare's Lucifer dressed in white in Francis Lawrence's *Constantine.*

the self-sacrifice of the skeptical hero.[2] The scene also neatly summarizes the bizarre interpretation of Roman Catholicism central to the genre; the story of Christ's death on the cross is changed so that the Spear of Destiny took his life, not crucifixion; the Archangel Gabriel, the angel at "the left hand of God," is now a "half-breed"—placed on earth as part of a wager between God and Lucifer where human souls are the winnings. Central to this wager is a "rule" that the balance between good and evil must be maintained, as Constantine explains to Angela early in the film:

When I came back [from Hell after his suicide], I knew all the things I could see were real: heaven and hell, right here, behind every wall every window, the world behind the world, and we're smack in the middle.

Angels and demons cannot cross over into our plane, so we get what I call "half-breeds," the influence peddlers. They can only whisper in our ears, and a single word can give you either courage, or make your favorite pleasure into your greatest nightmare. Those who the demons touch, like those part angel, living alongside us, they call it "The Balance." I call it hypocritical bullshit. So, when a half-breed breaks the rules, I deport their sorry ass straight-back to hell.

Constantine also holds another element intrinsic to Parousia-inspired horror: the stability required by the system until the arrival of the Apocalypse. During his confrontation with Gabriel, Lucifer says, "This world is mine—in time. You, best of all of us, Gabriel, should understand this." Or perhaps not, for Lucifer can grant the damned entry to heaven; God is seemingly absent, and the supernatural creatures representing Him are passive or traitorous, while those of Lucifer are active and dedicated to their Satanic cause. What is established firmly is that *Constantine*'s universe is structured dualistically, with "good" and "evil" in balance, demons and angels working for their cause in the quest for souls.

The (mis)representation of Roman Catholicism in Parousia-inspired horror is one of its most clearly establish elements. Almost all aspects of Catholic belief and practice are open for use, in large part because of a radical anti-Catholicism practiced by early Protestant denominations. This historic foundation, combined with the "radical certainty" associated with American Christian fundamentalism, "with its dualistic division of believers and nonbelievers," reinforces the otherness of Roman Catholicism, aligning it in the most extreme cases with the Satanic.[3] Paradoxically, this othering can also increase the attractiveness of Catholicism, mostly because of ornate and mysterious rituals, and exploiting the transformative nature of ritual is central to Parousia-inspired horror. By appropriating Catholic ritual, Parousia-inspired horror takes advantage of American Christianity's suspicion of the faith and religious illiteracy.

Constantine is of interest for several reasons. First is the film's use of the most common Parousia-inspired horror narrative formulas (preventing the birth of the naziresis and an artifact possessing Holy Power). In addition, the film's depiction of Roman Catholic rituals and iconography are derived from the screenplay's origin in the alt-narratives created for supernatural and occult-inspired graphic novels and other popular media: *Constantine* is an adaptation of the graphic novel series *Hellblazer* (Vertigo and DC Comics).

Constantine also takes advantage of elements identified as being central to Pamela Grace's "hagiopic"[4]—starting with a short, authoritative text that situates the viewer in the film's "imaginary" Catholicism: "He who possesses the Spear of Destiny holds the fate of the world in his hands. The Spear of Destiny has been missing since the end of World War II."

This title fades and is replaced by the film's first image: the ruins of a Christian Church in a desolate landscape. Inside the ruin, beneath giant, concrete crosses, two men are looking for anything of value. One man, Scavenger (Jesse Ramirez), breaks through the floor and discovers the Spear of Destiny, wrapped in a Nazi flag. Grasping the Spear, Scavenger runs but is hit by a speeding car, his body cutting a deep hole into the vehicle. But he is not dead! Possessed by demonic power, Scavenger, clutching the spear, runs toward Los Angeles. He has an appointment to keep: the birth of the Son of Satan.

While this opening sequence and the description of the possessed man's journey that follows contain narrative elements common to the hagiopic's representations of Christian eschatology, as this is Parousia-inspired horror, these elements are in most cases inverted, acting against the narrative commonly associated with them. The authoritative text that seems vaguely biblical is a construct based on extra-biblical sources; the possession of the Spear of Destiny (an object of controversy in the church) by the Nazis and its disappearance after World War II has more to do with conspiracy theory than biblical prophecy. Yet their pervasiveness in popular culture has made the imagery and story familiar to most viewers. That the narrative is a collage of conflicting sources is secondary to what agrees with the genre's popular narrative—in this case the culturally charged Spear of Destiny has been discovered, the destroyed church signals its inability to keep it safe, and that evil is loose in the world.

Shifting the action to Los Angeles, we meet the film's hero, Constantine, who, with the aid of Catholic Father Hennessy (Pruitt Taylor Vince), attempts to exorcise a demon from a possessed little girl. Constantine, using a variety of Christian-themed symbols and objects, forces the demon, which is attempting to burst out of her tortured body in a parody of birth, into a mirror. During the exorcism, Constantine recites (in Latin) portions of the Catholic ritual of Extreme Unction. The demon leaves the child's body and enters the mirror, which Constantine throws out the window. The demon-carrying mirror crashes to the street, destroying both mirror and demon.

Later, his doctor informs Constantine, a chain-smoker, that he has terminal lung cancer, which merely reinforces his negative view of the world. Constantine can see what "normal" people cannot—that the earth is inhabited with divine and Satanic creatures who vie to win the souls of the living as part of a "wager" (an obvious parody of Job) between God and Lucifer. Constantine has a lot riding on this wager: He attempted suicide as a youth to escape the visions of demons and angels but was revived, which damned him to Hell in this narrative's interpretation of Catholicism. To win favor with God, and perhaps admission to Heaven, Constantine has become an exorcist—a very good, albeit skeptical, one. So good in fact, that Lucifer himself said he would personally come to collect Constantine's soul.

Angela's character is introduced during a confession, which reveals Angela to be a police detective with an uncanny ability to "know" where the bad guys are and kill them. The confession occurs on the same night that her twin sister Isabel, incarcerated since childhood, classified as insane for claiming to see the same angels and demons as Constantine, commits suicide. We discover that Angela's policing talent is due to her possessing the same psychic gift as her "insane" twin. Angela, wanting to be accepted as "normal," suppresses and eventually forgot her ability, betraying her twin in the process. When she convinces Constantine to prove to her that Isabel is in Hell, he reawakens her psychic abilities through a sexualized ritual that confirms masculine control over her body and soul. For all her "special" abilities, Angela is defined by the established order, and only when that order is renewed—through Constantine's "real" act of self-sacrifice—can she be freed from her monstrous transformation.

The fact that God is absent from the action deserves special comment. There are plenty of angels and demons—and the ultimate Fallen Angel, Lucifer—but God and Jesus are missing. It is left to the human players to act on God's behalf, especially the skeptical hero: Constantine slashes his wrists to die and summon Lucifer in the hope of saving Angela and preventing Mammon's entry into the world, but even that sacrifice is insufficient to gain entry to Heaven; Constantine is simply bargaining with Lucifer, which seems to be more about his growing affection for Angela than saving the world.

Constantine's problem centers on the difference between faith, which is based on "a spiritual apprehension rather than proof," and "knowing," which involves acts done in full awareness or consciousness.[5] Constantine seems incapable of salvation because he is aware of the existence and power of the unseen order—an imaginary Catholic expression of it—trapping him in a strange double-bind from which there would seem to be no escape.

In an early scene, set in the library of the Basilica for the Bishop of Los Angeles, Parousia-inspired horror's inaccurate Roman Catholic "rules" of salvation are starkly laid out by the Archangel Gabriel:

CONSTANTINE: Haven't I served him enough? What does he want from me?
GABRIEL: Only the usual: self-sacrifice. Belief.
CONSTANTINE: Oh, I believe, for Christ's sake!
GABRIEL: No. No—you know, and there's a difference. You've seen!
CONSTANTINE: I never asked to see . . . I was born with this curse.
GABRIEL: A gift, John, one that you have squandered on selfish endeavors.

CONSTANTINE: Like pulling demons out of little girls? Who's that for?

GABRIEL: Everything you've ever done you've only done for yourself, to earn your way back into His good graces.

CONSTANTINE: Impossible rules, endless regulations! Who goes up, who goes down! . . . Why me, Gabriel? It's personal, isn't it? I didn't go to church enough, I didn't pray enough, I fell short in the collection plate. Why?

GABRIEL: You're going to die young because, you've smoked thirty cigarettes a day since you were fifteen, and you are going to go to Hell, because of the life you took. You're fucked.

Also in the library, Angela is negotiating with Father Garret (Francis Guinan), an assistant priest to the bishop, concerning her sister who has committed suicide. The "rules" are echoed, but as they are applied to people who "don't know":

ANGELA: She has to have a Catholic funeral, Father. She has to . . .

GARRET: Angela, it's still considered a mortal sin.

ANGELA: She didn't commit suicide.

GARRET: The bishop believes otherwise. You know the rules, Angela . . .

ANGELA: Oh, rules! Father . . . David; this is Isabel—God is the only person she ever believed loved her. Please?

GARRET: I'm sorry, Angela.

Seemingly occupying two very different positions, Angela and Constantine share a common problem: access to Heaven instead of a confirmed reservation in Hell.

This commonality between the film's protagonists leads to another crucial Parousia-inspired horror narrative element: Woman as "vessel" for the supernatural. In a disturbing scene, Angela is confronted by Scavenger, who we now understand to be possessed by Mammon, in the same pool her twin sister died in. Angela, half submerged, fires her pistol at Scavenger, who holds the Spear of Destiny in his outstretched hands. Angela's bullets have no effect, and she screams in terror as Scavenger forces her under the water. While rape is in progress the film cuts to another scene, the violence of which substitutes the violence against Angela.

The speed with which the action moves from Angela's rape camouflages the act, permitting the viewer to forget what's happening and enjoy watching Constantine dispatch an army of Mammon's demons. Angela's rape is the penultimate act of the ritual that will bring Mammon into the living world. That we do not see the demonic insemination suggests, in conformity with the majority of female characters in Parousia-inspired horror, Angela's passive position: She is reduced to a vessel to be "occupied" or worn by the masculine antagonist, and in the process transforms into a monstrous female.

During the film's climax, and in keeping with the inversion of how religion is portrayed in Parousia-inspired horror, we discover that the force behind the death and mayhem on-screen is Archangel Gabriel. Gabriel's plans are thwarted when Lucifer appears to collect Constantine's soul. It is Lucifer who releases Isabel from damnation, granting Constantine life while sending Mammon back to Hell where he can keep an eye on him. Lucifer also dispatches Gabriel, reducing the former archangel to "human" status.

With Mammon safely home—freeing Angela's body from its monstrous form—and with Gabriel neutralized, Lucifer turns his attention to the man whose soul he's come to collect: Constantine. Time reestablished, Lucifer has only a few moments to ask what the dying Constantine wants in exchange for revealing Mammon and Gabriel's plot—part of maintaining the balance. Constantine remains silent, prompting Lucifer to offer to extend his life. Instead of taking the offer, Constantine requests that Angela's damned twin Isabel be "allowed to go home." Lucifer grants the request, freeing Isabel from eternal damnation in exchange for Constantine. What Lucifer doesn't realize is that he has unintentionally set into motion the critical ritual of Parousia-inspired horror: the skeptical hero's sacrifice. Lucifer watches, seemingly helpless, as the soul of now heaven-bound Constantine flips him "the bird" as he ascends toward a distant and beautiful celestial city. Constantine is transformed into a new state of being through ritual, leaving behind what he was: He is to be among what are called in American Christian eschatology "the Elect." Lucifer interrupts the ritual and drags Constantine back to earth. Lucifer plunges his hands into Constantine's chest, ripping the cancer from his lungs. Lucifer then departs, whispering to Constantine, "you will live," if only to prove he belongs in Hell.

"The balance" reestablished—and along with it the social order Angela craves to be a part of—*Constantine*'s Parousia-inspired horror narrative draws to a close. Constantine gets close to Angela and hands her the very phallic Spear of Destiny, entrusting her to conceal it from evil and from him. This action, which neutralizes the possibility of a relationship between the male and female protagonists, allows Constantine to return to his former outsider/skeptical status and for Angela to return to her policing duties. This end also seals this example of Parousia-inspired horror particular narrative, with its imaginary version of Roman Catholicism and its endlessly arcane rules firmly in place.

The *Devil's Advocate* and *Constantine*:
Literary Sources and Satanic Representation

The Devil's Advocate, based on best-selling author Andrew Neiderman's 1990 novel of the same title, occurs in a "realistic" setting. As part of the Parousia-supernatural horror genre, *The Devil's Advocate* is unusual in that an American Protestant denomination is in the narrative's foreground, rather than Catholicism. This departure from the genre's "norm" may stem from the American Evangelical belief that Satan is always present in the life of Christians as a spiritual/demonic force, tempting the believer to sin and damnation. As noted by Poole, this ever-present Satan is an expression of America's complicated cultural history, and even today, "Tens of millions of evangelicals and Pentecostals in America believe they are engaged in . . . a struggle with Satan every day of their lives."[6]

The individual struggle with Satan, and the Protestant evangelical belief in a "corporate"—meaning community—eschatology, are other significant differences between the Satanic representations in *The Devil's Advocate* and *Constantine*: In the former, John Milton and his project to bring about the birth of the Antichrist, and with it the Apocalypse, aligns with the centrality of the evangelical beliefs that End Time is imminent and desired, and only members of their community of true believers will be saved from the fires of Hell at the Last Judgment. In the latter, Lucifer, and his actions to *prevent* the "premature" birth of his Satanic offspring so he can inherit the world "in time," resonates with the Catholic faith's "individual" eschatology, wherein the Apocalypse takes place at an undetermined future date, and entry to heaven is granted to the individual believer by the grace of God.

Comic book series versus "stand-alone" novel, appropriation and (mis)representations of Catholicism as opposed to Protestant religious traditions and practice, always present or requiring to be summoned: The difference in source materials, religious practice, and "presence" are of great importance to the two representations of Satan. What unites these seemingly different cinema constructs of Satan, however, are the cultural and historic sources from which they evolved, which are most clearly articulated in the Bible's New Testament and Book of Revelation. Their portrayals also are subject to the "rules" followed by the majority of American Parousia-inspired horror films that make use of these sources, specifically those in which demonically inspired forces attempt to conjure Christian eschatology's main antagonists, Satan and his "son," the Antichrist, to bring about the events described in the Book of Revelation.

A Premillennial Satan: John Milton

The film opens during a trial, where attorney Kevin Lomax (Keanu Reeves) is defending a teacher accused of molesting a girl. After hearing her testimony, and witnessing his client touch himself under the table as she spoke, Kevin requests a recess and retreats to the men's room to decide what to do. He is interrupted by Larry, a local news reporter, who reminds Kevin of his unbroken record of wins as a lawyer. Conscience forgotten, Kevin returns to the courtroom to win the case. Later, a representative of Milton's New York law firm offers Kevin a short-term contract. He accepts, and soon Kevin and his wife Mary Ann (Charlize Theron) leave for New York. John Milton's human manifestation of Satan in *The Devil's Advocate* appears as he watches Kevin leave the city courthouse. Milton then turns away and walks down the subway station stairs, melting into the crowd.

Al Pacino's portrayal of Milton/Satan is rooted in the mundane—at least at first. Milton has huge appetites for sex, food, drink, and money; he revels in rubbing shoulders with people of all types and social classes, but strives not to

"You'd never think I was a Master of the Universe, would you?" Al Pacino's Satan in Taylor Hackford's *The Devil's Advocate*.

draw attention to himself, as he explains to Kevin: "Don't ever let them see you coming, that's the gaffe, my friend. You've got to keep yourself small and be the little guy . . . Look at me. Underestimated from day one. You'd never think I was a Master of the Universe, would you?"

Milton interrogates Kevin about his record as a lawyer (never lost a case), as a son (dead father, unmarried mother), and as a Christian ("on parole for time served"). During the exchange, Milton pauses frequently, dark eyes within his weathered face not so much as assessing Kevin, as drinking him in. Milton's tongue moves about his mouth before and after speaking, as if tasting the young man. The film's editing enhances Milton's disquietingly sensual assessment of Kevin; close-ups on Milton's face often last far longer than "feels" right for the visual rhythm of the scene, holding on him until the image feels awkward, as is the silence that extends between their dialogue.

Milton's "interview" of Kevin is carefully structured, as is the entire film. After a point-of-view shot of the skyscrapers of Manhattan, Milton offers Kevin the world (of criminal clients) if he can take the pressure, summon his talents at will, and still sleep at night. Milton takes Kevin through a narrative that parallels that of Jesus, who after his baptism by John is transported to the wilderness to be tested by Satan. When offered dominion over all the kingdoms of the world in exchange for worshiping Satan, Jesus rebukes the fallen angel, driving him away. Kevin, however, is not the Son of God. Taking only a moment to consider Milton's "offer," he asks when they will talk about money. With this, Kevin enters a world of unlimited material wealth and pleasures of the flesh.

Satan as represented through the character of Milton fits in the world of wealth and excess that was a product of the economic boom experienced in America during the 1990s—the period within which The Devil's Advocate was produced and distributed. Ten years of unprecedented growth that would end with the collapse of the "dot com" bubble in early 2001 had produced a generation of financially ambitious young men, each a self-identified "Master of the Universe." Milton appears to be a man cut from this cloth: one whose behavior might be appalling, but he has never broken the law. Milton is a very human Satan.

The Satan of The Devil's Advocate is also planning for the future, and the turning of the millennium is an important event in his late 1990s date book. The drive and urgency of Christian eschatology is tied directly to the concept of the millennium, a temporal framework that seems to add structure and justify urgency for the believer, as it allows for the arrival of the apocalypse in their lifetimes. Millennialism also accounts for the frequency of millennial cults over the history of Christianity, for, "if the End Time is likely to occur in one's lifetime, then it makes sense to prepare by becoming a member of the faithful remnant."[7] How millennialism relates to the "humanized" representation of Satan in *The Devil's Advocate* is of interest, for its development as a part of Christian eschatology's narrative is tied directly to Satan's evolution from the Old Testament's angel of the Lord to the fallen angel of the New Testament. In keeping with Poole's 2009 analysis, John Milton of *The Devil's Advocate* represents a physical form of Satan with which contemporary evangelicals and fundamentalists in America struggle every day.

That Kevin cannot recognize Milton for who and what he is makes his seduction and fall all the more likely. However, Kevin is not the only one who is deceived by Milton; his own family is, too. Late in the film, Kevin loses his wife Mary Ann, who has been driven mad by demonic visions, to suicide. Still wearing clothes soaked in Mary Ann's blood, he forces his deeply religious mother, Alice (Judith Ivey), to confess that, thirty years ago, she had met a young John Milton. Using words that echo Mary Ann's when she tried to convince an unbelieving Kevin that Milton had viciously raped her, his mother reveals that Milton had seduced her.

Instances of Milton's ability to seduce escalate as the film progresses, but he is careful to keep on the edge of plausible social behavior—Satan remains "human" in the eyes of others. In the end, however, Milton must go too far—his appetite to consume the world requires it. Kevin walks out of the hospital and into the supernatural where time has stopped. As in *Constantine*, Satan has arrived to collect what is his: a skeptical son and through him, the future. But one final seduction remains to be completed, and it must take place during a Satanic ritual meant to bring forth the Antichrist—and Kevin needs convincing.

Milton's office transforms into a Satanic temple as Milton taunts Kevin. Recounting his rape of Mary Ann, Milton infers it was consensual, and Kevin, gun in hand, shoots but the bullets have no effect. Milton forces Kevin to admit he cares only for himself and "winning," using the rules of the law to do so no matter the cost. These rules mirror the ones set by God for man and, as it is in *Constantine*, they seem rigged.

The scene transformed into Satanic ritual, Milton offers Christabella (Connie Nielsen), now revealed to be his daughter, to Kevin, demanding that his son perform an act of incest to bring about the birth of the Antichrist. However, Milton's Satanic appetite drives Kevin to exercise "free will" by shooting himself in the head rather than succumb to his father's apocalyptic plans. All self-control forgotten, his anger and dismay at Kevin's choice unleashes the very flames of Hell, turning the office into a furnace, destroying everything. Caught up in the inferno is Christabella, whose beautiful body is transformed into a hideous desiccated mummy as she dies.

Seeing what he has done, Milton's anger subsides, but not before the flames have exposed what he is. Milton transforms—he has become Lucifer, the most beautiful servant of the Lord, now fallen. Unable to contain his sorrow, Lucifer looks up toward the Heaven he has lost forever and howls an unending "no!" The scene closes with the camera plunging into Lucifer's open mouth, revealing an endless swirling whirlpool of hellfire tormenting the souls of the damned. Abruptly, the flames collapse, and we return to the film's beginning.

Given a second chance, Kevin decides to make things right. Instead of defending a man he knows to be guilty, Kevin resigns from the case. Embracing his restored wife, Mary Ann, Kevin dodges all those pursuing him as he leaves the courthouse, save for Larry (Neil Jones), the reporter from the film's opening. Larry convinces Kevin that his act of conscience will actually *save* his career. An "exclusive" deal in place with Larry for his story, Kevin exits, Mary Ann in tow. As he watches the young couple depart, "Larry" transforms into Milton. Smiling widely at the camera, Milton breaks the "fourth wall" and addresses the audience: "Vanity," he chuckles, "definitely my favorite sin!" Milton starts to laugh, and flames engulf the screen.

Milton's taking on the guise of Larry, a person known to both Kevin and Mary Ann, to "offer" suggestions for what the young couple should do makes clear who this particular representation of Satan is. To paraphrase Pagels in *The Origins of Satan*: He is the intimate enemy, a trusted colleague, God's own angel turned into his adversary—he is also a protestant Satan, one who tests those who are "born again" every day with temptation.

Monstrous Women and Satanic Representation

Control over women's bodies and their reproductive systems is often the objective of Satan in the Parousia-inspired horror genre. Women characters, regardless—perhaps *especially* because—of their authority or abilities (police detective Angela in *Constantine*, corporate lawyer Christabella, and "lawfully wedded wife" Mary Ann in *The Devil's Advocate*), are reduced to "vessels" for Satan's child, or some other demonic male entity. Women's bodies are monstrously transformed in this process, and their identities erased until a man sacrifices himself for her. Lucifer and Milton interact differently with the women in their respective films because of their representations' relationship with the men they must contend with. Constantine and Kevin are the "sacrificial male heroes" in the films, but what they sacrifice themselves for differs according to the Satan they confront. In contrast, Angela, Christabella, and Mary Ann, their identities reduced or erased, are simply used.

In *The Devil's Advocate*, women not destined to be a vessel for Milton's children or grandchildren are consumed as a function of Milton's insatiable carnal appetites—Milton suggests as much when he boasts of a sexual conquest during what amounts to a "locker room" exchange with Kevin. The women chosen to bear his offspring—or his grandchild—are destined to be seduced and raped or destroyed, as happens to Kevin's mother, wife, and intended "infernal mate," Christabella, who is also his half-sister through Milton. Frequently, women in the genre are shown to be complicit in their relationship with Satan. Mary Ann (the use of the name "Mary," the Mother of God, could not be accidental), though suffering terrifying trauma to her body and mind from being raped by Milton, thinks she wanted to have sex with him. Kevin's mother, Alice, confesses that she slept with Milton after he seduced her so he could father a son, but only after Kevin, revealing his own potential for abusing women, relentlessly questions her about the act. Finally, Christabella, Kevin's half-sister, may have been a victim of incest with Milton. Having sex with her half-brother to produce the Antichrist remains Christabella's focus throughout the climactic scene until it is too late. Christabella's attempts to seduce Kevin while he is engaged in a battle of wits with Milton underscores her passivity. With Kevin's act of "free will" complete, Christabella has no purpose and is destroyed.

Contrary to Milton's violent sexuality in *The Devil's Advocate*, Lucifer in *Constantine* is not violent to women. He protects one (Angela) from death, healing her monstrous transformation in the process, and then "releases" another (Isabel, Angela's twin sister) from suffering in Hell at the behest of the dying Constantine. This does not mean that this Satan departs from how women are represented and abused in the genre; Lucifer, and the narrative that created him, are intrinsically violent toward women.

Conclusion

The Satan represented in *Constantine* seemingly conforms to one aligned with Roman Catholicism's promotion of individual eschatology and its perpetually deferred Apocalypse. Lucifer, while appearing human, is anything but, displaying his supernatural abilities at all times, along with an unchecked glee at the prospect of making Constantine suffer in Hell. He is also still connected to God and is keenly aware of his part in Christian eschatology. While other demonic or angelic forces may attempt to "hurry along" the Apocalypse,

Lucifer is patient, perhaps because he understands the importance of time, a thing that does not exist for those suffering punishment in Hell. Disinterested in participating in the messy details of the mundane world unless it directly impacts him, Lucifer keeps humanity at a distance, allowing his demons to do the dirty work.

In striking contrast, the "protestant" Satan of *The Devil's Advocate* engages with the Christians of the world as directly as he can. The perfect internal enemy, Milton knows their appetites better than they do, displaying his consumption of Earthy delights for all to see, inviting them to partake, but never forcing them. Corporate eschatology, with its focus on a community of believers, suits his purpose, for he knows their sacred book better than they do, having lived every moment in it and more. Milton has seduced whole families, it seems, from such communities of believers. "They never see him coming," because he fits into the community seamlessly.

Where the films two representations of Satan converge is their point of origin and association with violence: *Constantine's* "Lu" is hardly a Catholic Satan; rather, he, and the entire pseudo-Catholic framework of the film's narrative, is firmly rooted in the long-established anti-Catholic fantasies of some forms of American Protestant Christianity. Milton/Satan, the always present adversary, tempting the righteous to sin, springs fully formed from American evangelical belief and practice. In both *Constantine* and *The Devil's Advocate*, violent acts of increasing severity are presented to the viewer as a function of the Christian eschatology from which they derive; a reading of the Book of Revelation that illustrates brutally what lies in store for those who are not part of the "faithful remnant" who embraces the "pure form" of the religion without question. Finally, Milton and Lucifer are central players in the perpetuation of violence against women and their identities, rendering their bodies monstrous and their place in the social order as being totally subservient to the will of God and men—a chilling coda resulting from the narrative rules of the Parousia-inspired horror genre.

Notes

1. Douglas E. Cowan, *Sacred Terror: Religion and Horror on the Silver Screen* (Waco, TX: Baylor University Press, 2008), 27.

2. Cowan, 6 and *passim*.

3. Robert Glenn Howard, *Digital Jesus: The Making of a New Fundamentalist Community on the Internet* (New York: New York University Press, 2011), 35 and *passim*.

4. Pamela, Grace, *The Religious Film: Christianity and Hagiopic* (Oxford: Blackwell Publishing, 2009), 1.

5. *Oxford Concise Dictionary of World Religions* (Oxford: Oxford University Press, 2000).

6. W. Scott Poole, *Satan in America: The Devil We Know* (Plymouth: Rowman and Littlefield, 2009), 185.

7. Frederic J. Baumgartner, *Longing for the End: A History of Millennialism in Western Civilization* (New York: St. Martins Press, 1999), 3.

Contributors

Simon Bacon is an independent scholar based in Poznan, Poland. He is the coeditor, with Katarzyna Bronk, of *Undead Memory: Vampires and Human Memory in Popular Culture* (2014) and *Growing Up with Vampires: Essays on the Undead in Children's Media* (2018), and the editor of *Gothic: A Reader* (2018) and *Horror: A Companion* (2019). He has published three monographs, *Becoming Vampire: Difference and the Vampire in Popular Culture* (2016), *Dracula as Absolute Other: The Troubling and Distracting Specter of Stoker's Vampire on Screen* (2019), *Eco-Vampires: The Vampire as Environmentalist and Undead Eco-Activist* (2021).

Katherine A. Fowkes is Emeritus professor of popular culture and media production at Highpoint University. She is the author of *The Fantasy Film* (2010) and *Giving Up the Ghost: Spirits, Ghosts, and Angels in Mainstream Comedy Films* (1998).

Regina M. Hansen teaches at Boston University. She publishes and presents on horror, religion in film, neo-Victorianism, and the fantastic. Her works include the edited volumes *Supernatural, Humanity and the Soul* (with Susan George; 2014) and *Roman Catholicism in Fantastic Film*, and a special Stephen King issue of *Science Fiction Film and Television* (with Simon Brown; 2017), along with the novel *The Coming Storm* (Atheneum 2021). Her writing on film, folklore, and the supernatural has appeared in the *Wall Street Journal Review* and the children's magazine *Dig Into History*.

David Hauka teaches film directing and aesthetics at Capilano University's School of Motion Picture Arts and screen writing, scene study, and 3D/virtual environment technique for actors in the Department of Theatre and Film at the University of British Columbia. His academic research focuses primarily on the influence of religion in American horror cinema.

Russ Hunter is a senior lecturer in film and television at the University of Northumbria. He is the coeditor of a forthcoming collection on the cinema of Dario Argento and is currently working on a monograph on the history of European horror cinema and an article exploring environmental discourses within Italian horror cinema.

Barry C. Knowlton teaches history, literature, and classics at Assumption College and has published on a wide range of subjects in the humanities.

Eloise R. Knowlton currently serves as Dean of Undergraduate Studies at Assumption College and is the author of *Joyce, Joyceans, and the Rhetoric of Citation* (1998).

Murray Leeder is an adjunct assistant professor at the University of Calgary. He is the author of *Horror Film: A Critical Introduction* (2018), *The Modern Supernatural and the Beginnings of Cinema* (2017), and *Halloween* (2014), as well as the editor of *Cinematic Ghosts: Haunting and Spectrality from Silent Cinema to the Digital Era* (2015) and *Re-Focus: The Films of William Castle* (2018).

Catherine O'Brien is director of the Centre for Marian Studies at the University of Roehampton, London. She has published widely on the intersections between film and theology, including *The Celluloid Madonna* (2011) and *Martin Scorsese's Divine Comedy: Movies and Religion* (2018).

R. Barton Palmer is Calhoun Lemon Professor of Literature emeritus at Clemson University, where he is the founding director of the World Cinema program. Palmer is the author or editor of more than fifty books on different subjects. He is also the editor of *South Atlantic Review* and *Tennessee Williams Annual Review*. His recent film books include (with Murray Pomerance), *The Many Cinemas of Michael Curtiz* (2018), and (with Homer Pettey) *French Literature on Screen* (2019).

Carl H. Sederholm is professor of Interdisciplinary Humanities at Brigham Young University and chair of the Department of Comparative Arts and Letters. He is the editor of the *Journal of American Culture* and is the author of multiple essays on authors such as Edgar Allan Poe, H. P. Lovecraft, Stephen King, Jonathan Edwards, Lydia Maria Child, and Nathaniel Hawthorne. He is also coeditor (with Jeffrey Weinstock) of *The Age of Lovecraft* (2016), coeditor (with Dennis Perry) of *Adapting Poe: Re-Imaginings in Popular Culture* (2012) and the coauthor (also with Dennis Perry) of *Poe, the "House of Usher," and the American Gothic* (2009).

David Sterritt is editor-in-chief of *Quarterly Review of Film and Video*, contributing writer at *Cineaste*, and film professor at the Maryland Institute College of Art. He is author or editor of fifteen books and his writing has appeared in *Cahiers du cinéma*, the *New York Times, Hitchcock Annual*, the *Chronicle of Higher Education*, the *Journal of Aesthetics and Art History*, and many other publications as well as numerous edited collections. He was film critic of the *Christian Science Monitor* for almost forty years, serving two terms as chair of the New York Film Critics Circle, ten years as chair of the National Society of Film Critics, and ten years as cochair of the Columbia University Seminar on Cinema and Interdisciplinary Interpretation.

J. P. Telotte is a professor of film studies at Georgia Tech's School of Literature, Media, and Communication. He is the coeditor of the journal *Post Script* and has published widely on film history, Disney, animation, and film genres, especially science fiction. His most recent books are *Robot Ecology and the Science Fiction Film* (2016), *Animating the Science Fiction Imagination* (2018), and *Movies, Modernism, and the Science Fiction Pulps* (2019).

Jeffrey Andrew Weinstock is professor of English at Central Michigan University and an associate editor of the *Journal for the Fantastic in the Arts*. He has authored or edited twenty-four books, the most recent of which are *The Monster Theory Reader* (2019), *Critical Approaches to* Welcome to Night Vale: *Podcasting Between Weather and the Void* (2018), *The Cambridge Companion to American Gothic* (2018), and *The Age of Lovecraft* (2016). Visit him at JeffreyAndrewWeinstock.com.

Index

CPSIA information can be obtained
at www.ICGtesting.com
Printed in the USA
JSHW021353101221
21195JS00001B/97